The Last Shot

ALSO BY LYNN SCHOOLER

The Blue Bear

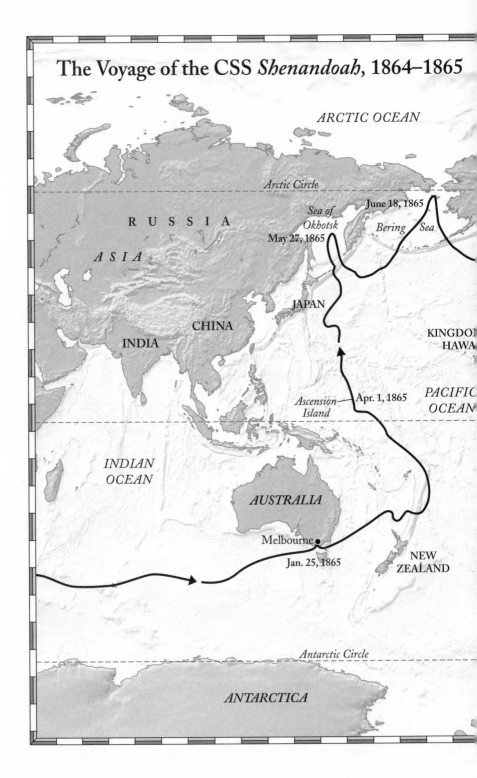

The Voyage of the CSS *Shenandoah*, 1864–1865

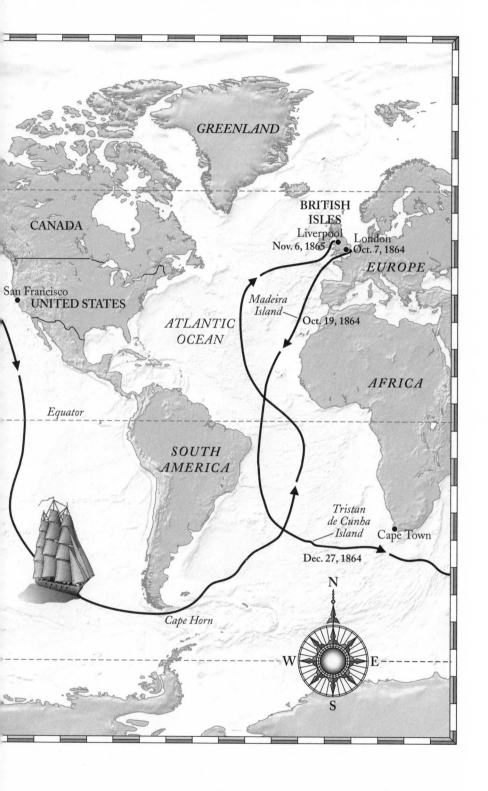

The Last Shot

THE INCREDIBLE STORY OF

THE CSS *SHENANDOAH* AND

THE TRUE CONCLUSION OF

THE AMERICAN CIVIL WAR

Lynn Schooler

ecco

An Imprint of HarperCollins *Publishers*

973.
7
S

HarperCollins books may be purchased for educational,
business, or sales promotional use. For information, please write:
Special Markets Department, HarperCollins Publishers Inc.,
10 East 53rd Street, New York, NY 10022.

FIRST EDITION

Designed by Kate Nichols

Map by Paul J. Pugliese

Library of Congress Cataloging-in-Publication Data

ISBN 0-06-052333-6

04 05 06 07 BVG/RRD 10 9 8 7 6 5 4 3 2 1

CONTENTS

THE LAST SHOT

PROLOGUE

ALASKA'S LITTLE DIOMEDE ISLAND is as far as you can go and still be in North America. The stump of crumbling black rock rises out of the sea a few degrees south of the Arctic Circle and a little over a mile from the International Date Line. Go any farther and you slip into Asia, where west becomes east, and today is tomorrow. Until the cold war ended, Russian soldiers hunkered into concrete bunkers two miles away on Big Diomede Island kept powerful binoculars trained on the handful of Ingalikmiut Eskimos who make their home on Little Diomede, lest any member of one of the Western world's last surviving hunter-gatherer cultures suddenly turn capitalist saboteur.

Today, Little Diomede seems an unlikely place for war to rear its monstrous head. The island lacks oil, minerals, or much of anything else of strategic value, its 142 residents rely almost entirely on fish, crab, and walrus for their livelihoods, much as they have done for centuries, and the isolated outpost remains one of the most difficult-to-reach places in the world. Villagers remain dependent on umiaks, or walrus-skin boats, to cross the twenty-eight miles of open, ice-studded water that separates their island from the mainland for supplies. Every spring, when the winter ice pack begins to crumble and leads of open water reappear, the Ingalikmiut man these same frail craft and launch themselves into the heaving sea in pursuit of one of the few resources that have stood between their families and starvation for more than a thousand years: the bowhead whale.

Up to forty-five feet long and weighing as much as fifty tons, the bowhead constitutes the spiritual and physical foundation of the western Eskimo culture. Harpooned and heaved ashore at the end of a hunt that may last several weeks, a single animal provides enough food for several hundred people, with piles of the rich, dark meat being distributed to relatives and friends in small villages up and down the coast, allotted according to a system based not on social status or finances, but on need. In the distant reaches of the Arctic the bowhead is, and always has been, the only measure of true wealth.

It was the bowhead that brought war to Little Diomede a hundred years before the cold war. In the autumn of 1864, at the height of the American Civil War, the Confederate raider *Shenandoah* received orders to "seek out and utterly destroy" the whaling fleets of New England as part of an effort to bleed the Union of its economic strength—an undertaking that met its greatest success when the raider fell upon a fleet of whalers working the waters near Little Diomede and sank more than two dozen ships in a frenzy of destruction one rebel crewmen described thus: "The red glare from [burning vessels] shone far and wide [and] the crackling of the fire as it made its devouring way through each doomed ship fell on the ear like upbraiding voices."

Before the *Shenandoah*'s voyage ended, the raider had captured or sunk thirty-eight ships. She also took more than a thousand prisoners and led the best warships of the Federal navy on a twenty-seven-thousand mile chase that ended with her escape to England, making her the only Confederate vessel to circumnavigate the globe and the last Southern military force to lay down its arms. And at the end of that journey (which was truly one of the most remarkable in naval history) the effects of the raider's actions reached far beyond the glow of the flames marking the sky above the Arctic ice. The inferno signaled not only the near demise of the New England whaling industry, but also the end of America's growing hegemony over worldwide shipping for the next eighty years and, in the end, the establishment of a body of international law that remains in effect today.

But more important than the tally of damage was the date the final conflagration began: June 22, 1865, the longest day of the year, and more than two months after General Lee laid down his sword at Appomattox. Contrary to contemporary belief, it was not on the battlefield in Virginia, but high in the Arctic, where the last shot of the American Civil War was fired.

I FIRST CROSSED THE WAKE of the *Shenandoah* in 1970, as a teenager, browsing through crumbling back issues of regional magazines in the tiny one-room public library not far from my family's home in Anchorage. Tucked in among the frontier-era ads for mail-order rifles and "flying dress salesmen" scattered through the pages of the April 1937 issue of the *Alaska Sportsman* magazine was a brief article describing the raider's saga. For the next thirty years the story remained nothing more to me than one of those nuggets of obscure information that come in handy when dinner conversations run dry, until an abiding interest in the Aleutian Islands occasioned by a single glimpse of a smoking, fog-wreathed volcano from the deck of a fishing boat began to bloom. South of this necklace of rocky islands is a world that is, as the name implies, relatively pacific, with a variety of personalities ranging from the misty face of coastal Washington to the sensuous bliss of Hawaii. Above is the dominion of fog and wind, icebergs and polar bears. In between is the archipelago itself, home to what meteorologists refer to as a "disturbance regime." In winter, frigid air flowing down from the Arctic collides with the warm, moist air of the Pacific to generate cyclone-force winds one day out of three, earning the region the title "cradle of the storms."

The day I saw the volcano was an unusually calm one, with a flat sea beneath a smoke-colored sky. Curtains of fog had opened and closed around us since daybreak, first wiping out the world or limiting it to a patch of mist and a monotonous silence enlivened only by the chug of the boat's diesel and the cries of invisible gulls, then opening to an expanse of sea and sky so identical in color as to present no horizon. We steamed, throttle set at cruising speed, through a sunless world, with only a compass to indicate east or west, north or south; sometimes it was hard to tell up from down. Only the wake unzipping behind the boat created a sense of motion.

I was on deck, splicing small lines tipped with hooks into a larger line, when I glanced off to starboard (the right side of the boat) and saw a curving blue line in the fog assume the shape of something conical. Like a Japanese painting, the mountain hovered behind a screen of enshrouding fog, its mammoth solidity hidden by a filmy gauze. The curtain parted as I watched, revealing the mountain's sloping snow-covered shoulders, then a broken, crenulated top. At the summit, a plume of smoke or steam escaped from fissured rock, rising like a stream of bubbles trickling upward from a diver's lips. Suddenly the mountain seemed to swell, its shoulders bulging incrementally outward under the pressure of subterranean chambers filled with molten rock. In the space of a heartbeat the utter calm of the day filled with tension. The crust of the earth seemed to strain with hidden forces, lava swarming through veins and passages, eager to find a way out and demonstrate its cataclysmic power.

The live volcano took my breath away. I stared at its fan of rising smoke, wondering at the magnitude of the things we cannot see. A slight roll of the boat and a change in the pitch of the throttle took my attention and I turned away. When I looked back the volcano was gone, erased by the fog.

I never saw the island again, but when the fishing season ended the memory was enough to nudge me into the library, into a stack of books and articles about the archipelago. The Aleutian story was an interesting one, replete with invasions and upheavals, earthquakes and tidal waves, wars and abandonment that left the chain largely uninhabited and one of the wildest and most inaccessible regions in the world. But here and there amid the literature of the region (as sparse and difficult to glean as the region itself, which at its westernmost point lies only a short distance from Japan) glimmered a few cryptic allusions to another, even more fascinating story: a reference in a catalog of historic Alaska shipwrecks to twenty-three ships lost in a single week, a brief newspaper clipping from 1964 about a new U.S. Navy ship, the USS *Waddell,* being christened in honor of a Confederate commander. (How odd, I thought. How many countries name warships after a defeated enemy?)

After a bit of digging it surfaced that these and several other obscure references all led back to the CSS *Shenandoah,* a Confederate ship. Shortly thereafter, I found myself at the Alaska State Historical Library, slipping on a pair of light cotton gloves meant to protect antique paper from the oil of my fingers as a librarian handed me a small leather-bound volume with the warning that I should "be careful, it's brittle."

Published in 1867, the memoirs of Petty Officer Cornelius Hunt of the *Shenandoah* were archaic in style and in places blatantly self-serving, but nonetheless had a quality that carried some appeal. And when the librarian also dug out and brought to me a copy of the same 1937 *Alaska Sportsman* magazine that had piqued my interest three decades before, I felt a sense of history click into place when I realized that the author was a fellow named Robert N. DeArmond. Although quite elderly and confined to a home, Bob is an acquaintance of mine. Furthermore, the sixty-something years that had passed since he wrote the article was the same measure of time that had passed between the date on the magazine and the day Petty Officer Hunt stepped off the *Shenandoah* to take up his pen. Only one small step removed me from Hunt and the other participants in the saga. It was as if Bob—a lively ninety-four-year-old with an inquisitive nature—was standing by my side, and just to his right was another fellow, dressed in a Confederate uniform, who had seen and done all the things in the book. Hunt and I could have leaned out and introduced ourselves, shaken hands.

Suddenly history had a *size*, a dimension that filled space in a way it never had before, leaping up from the horizontal into something living. And if Cornelius Hunt had come alive, then so had the others; for a moment it felt as if every man aboard the ship was nearby.

Bob's article was short, just a handful of column inches, the equivalent of no more than two or three typed pages, but it spoke of storms at sea, collisions with icebergs, and sailing shorthanded through every ocean between the tropics and the Arctic. There was also a passage around Cape Horn and skullduggery with secret agents, mixed with a months-long chase by Union warships. The Confederate raider also captured more enemy shipping in a single day than any other wooden ship in history, and did it with a ragtag, polyglot, multiracial international crew of reluctant volunteers.

It was quite a story. But the thing that floored me was a single line in the next-to-last paragraph saying the *Shenandoah* had ended its voyage by sailing from the Aleutians halfway around the world to England without ever sighting land. It took 122 days to make the trip—over twenty-three thousand miles of thick weather, blazing tropics, freezing latitudes, and hot pursuit. Like the plume of the volcano, that single sentence was a sign of something larger going on.

As Cornelius Hunt wrote at the start of the voyage,

No one, unless he has stood in a similar place can appreciate the crowd of emotions that whirled through my mind. I was about to join, clandestinely, a vessel commissioned by a Government still in embryo, but which I had sworn to support, to cruise against the commerce of another Government which still claimed me as its liege subject. If the cause I upheld was successful, there was wealth, fame, and glory, to be earned; if it failed, a felon's doom impended over me and my associates; but I was too young and hopeful to long contemplate the dark side of the case; the ship I was to join was afloat; the ocean was before us, and sailor-like, I was content to put my trust in Providence, Neptune, and the Southern Confederacy.

Cornelius wrote this as he was standing on a dock in England about to join the ship, at the beginning of what was to be, indeed, a flirtation with glory and doom. And while he may have owned nothing but purple pens, he really would need all the providential aid he could muster.

ONE

THE AMERICAN CIVIL WAR began on April 12, 1861, when forces of the newly declared Confederacy fired on the Union garrison at Fort Sumter. At the time, the South had only one fighting ship, four small cutters, and a limited number of commercial vessels. Building facilities were limited to a few small yards in Florida and Virginia, and none had the capacity to build in the dimensions and materials needed for fighting ships. A few days after Fort Sumter surrendered, President Lincoln ordered the Union navy to initiate a blockade of all Southern ports, adding a proviso that any privateers caught sailing under Confederate colors would be jailed and hung.*

Blockading more than three thousand miles of coastline was a colossal task, but the effort was

---

*A privateer is a privately owned and operated vessel operating against an enemy's shipping under the authority of one of the governments engaged in a war.

largely successful and quickly began to have effects far beyond America's borders. In England, where 80 percent of the cotton consumed in that country's massive textile industry came from the Southern states, thousands of unemployed mill workers were thrown onto the streets. France, where the populace was laboring under the rule of Napoleon III, was in much the same boat. Within months the looms of England and Europe slowed nearly to a halt. Exports of cotton goods, which had reached a value of approximately a billion dollars in 1860, were almost choked off, and with the market so disrupted, the leaders of the Confederacy quickly realized that the war could not be won without a supply of ready cash.

Britain's prime minister, Lord Palmerston, firmly believed that a dissolution of the burgeoning, juvenile America was inevitable (and indeed, like many European heads of state, would probably have preferred such a thing) but nonetheless felt it would be unwise to interfere in the conflict. As a result, two weeks after the blockade began, England officially recognized the Confederacy as a belligerent and issued a proclamation outlining the principles of Britain's neutrality: Her Majesty's subjects were not to enlist in the armed forces of either side, break the blockade, or allow their ships to transport soldiers, military supplies, or dispatches for either side. They were further enjoined from building, arming, or outfitting any vessel that might be used as a ship of war.

Politically, Palmerston's desire for a hands-off policy was sound, but the forces of international trade quickly drove cracks into his country's presumed neutrality. Sniffing enormous profits, British ships began running the blockade with regularity, smuggling goods into the South which could be traded at extortionate rates for cotton that in turn would be nearly priceless in Europe. So great were the margins that captains of "moon chasers" operating out of Nassau in the Bahamas were often paid as much as $10,000 in gold for a single voyage, equal to nearly $160,000 today.

Lucrative as it was, however, the amount of cotton the blockade runners could get through the Union stranglehold was insufficient to supply Europe's needs. In June Lord Palmerston wrote to England's foreign minister, John Russell:

> This cotton question will most certainly assume a serious character by the beginning of next year; and if the American civil war has not by that time come to an end, I suspect that we shall be obliged either singly or conjointly with France to tell the northerners that we cannot allow millions of our people to perish to please the Northern States.

In return the foreign minister proposed that England team up with France early in the coming year to act "on a grand scale" to force terms on the Americans. Ever cautious about antagonizing a nation as strong as the muscular young America, Palmerston rejected the notion of overtly threatening war and replied that "the only thing to do seems to be to lie on our oars, and give no pretext to the Washingtonians to quarrel with us."

Large and powerful as the Federal navy was, it did not have enough ships to both maintain the blockade and protect the Union's own trade routes.* To exploit this weakness, Confederate leaders developed a plan to obtain and arm a number of raiders, voracious, fast-moving predators meant to swoop down on slow-moving Yankee merchant vessels and sink them. In addition to disrupting the Northern economy, the tactic would also force the Union navy to withdraw critical fighting ships from blockade duty to pursue the raiders, leaving the coastline more porous for smugglers. Because the Confederacy was hampered by the lack of shipyards, obtaining foreign-built vessels was the key to the plan. And doing so was the work of one man.

---

*The terms "Federal," "Union," and "U.S." or "United States" are used interchangeably to indicate Northern forces, as are "American" and "Yankee." Today, with the United States so clearly a single cohesive entity, it requires a moment's thought to understand how after secession, the people of the Southern states did not generally consider themselves "American."

COMMANDER JAMES DUNWOODY BULLOCH arrived in England in
June of 1861. He was a glaring, muttonchopped zealot praised by the
Confederate secretary of the navy as an "intelligent and reliable officer." According to one prominent Northwest historian, Bulloch was
also "reactionary to the point of fanaticism . . . competent, hard-
headed, and capable of transforming the surging flood of his emotions
into applied energy"—traits that made the archconservative Georgian
ideal for the demanding job of masterminding the Confederacy's secret service in Europe. His orders were to assemble an entire navy
from scratch.

Armed with no more than some stunningly bureaucratic guidance
from the Confederate secretary of the navy that "the type of ship desired . . . is that which offers the greatest chance of success" and the
promise of a supply of cotton in lieu of adequate currency, Bulloch had
not done too badly. Since landing in London shortly after the blockade
was established, he had built two ships—the *Florida* and the
Alabama—and purchased another, the *Fingal,* which he loaded with
supplies and sailed to Savannah himself. The *Alabama,* launched in July
of 1862, was a tremendously successful raider, burning and sinking
more than five dozen ships. She wreaked so much havoc on America's
commercial shipping that the Union was forced to assign twenty-five
warships to her pursuit, which in turn made it much easier for Southern
moon chasers to penetrate the blockade.*

The *Florida* would go on to capture sixty American vessels before
being taken captive two years later by the USS *Wachusett,* which
steamed into the neutral Brazilian port of Bahia and rammed her while
she lay at anchor. After shooting several of the *Florida*'s crewmen as
they floundered in the water, the *Wachusett*'s master ordered a towing

---

*Bulloch's first two raiders were notable not only for their success at destruction; the *Florida*
was the first iron-hulled ship to make a transatlantic crossing, and the *Alabama* was equipped
with a flush toilet.

line rigged and pulled the *Florida* out of the harbor and all the way north to Chesapeake Bay. Outraged by this invasion of its sovereign territory, the Brazilian government threatened to spread the war to South America. Only a concentrated flurry of Union diplomacy defused the crisis.

For all of their success, however, neither the *Florida* nor the *Alabama* was a match for any of the Union's fighting ships. For that, Bulloch's next step was to pursue the construction of a number of 220-foot "rams," state-of-the-art fighting machines, armed with twelve-and-a-half-ton guns mounted in rotating turrets, framed in steel and sheathed in a foot-thick layer of teak and railroad iron stout enough to allow them to sink an enemy ship by slamming into it and cutting it in half.

Bulloch's success with the *Florida*, *Alabama*, and *Fingal* was giving fits to at least one Yankee; Charles Francis Adams, America's minister to Great Britain, had arrived in England on the very day Palmerston's government recognized the South as a belligerent and had seen no pause in the incessant, not-always-subtle swordplay of diplomacy since. Time after time, Adams's efforts to have Bulloch's rebel cruisers seized for violating Britain's neutrality act had been frustrated by foot-dragging on the part of the officials charged with enforcing it, and on at least one occasion by what could be seen as the interference of a capricious God: the *Alabama* had managed to slip down the river Mersey and out to sea on the same day that Adams filed documents with the British authorities sufficient to order her detained. The queen's advocate who was to have acted on the matter was, and had been for several days, going quietly insane. No one but his wife had noticed, and she, for the sake of appearances, had covered up her husband's frailty, in a burst of misplaced pride that led to the raider escaping and thoroughly disrupting the American dominance of world shipping.

Adams, the son and grandson of presidents, was pointedly brilliant and rational, with little tolerance for human weakness. A graduate of

Harvard at eighteen, he had studied law under Daniel Webster and gone on to a life of public service that in any family but his own would have qualified him as the flower of his lineage. He was absolutely principled and incorruptible, as adamant about the rights of man as he was opposed to slavery; it would be hard to name an American more passionate about doing what was moral and right. For good or ill, however, his giant intellect appears also to have been accompanied by a disdain for bumpkins, backwoodsmen, and Southerners in general that bordered on snobbery, and in the mountain of histories and biographies penned about the man one of the most descriptive adjectives used is "cold." Even his own secretary once called him a "cod." But when he received information that iron rams were being built for the Confederates by British manufacturers, he proved himself capable of great heat by penning a letter to Prime Minister Palmerston threatening bluntly that if the rebels were allowed to obtain the fighting ships, "It would be superfluous in me to point out to your Lordship that this is war."

Faced with the reality that England's behind-the-scenes brinksmanship in pursuit of cotton was dragging their country closer to war, Lord Palmerston and John Russell agreed that it would be suicidal to allow the rebels to take possession of the rams.

Palmerston was teetering on a high wire. Even with the war poised to spiral out of control into a worldwide fray involving Britain, France, Brazil, and perhaps even Russia, preventing the transfer of the ships would not be easy.* Without solid proof that they were meant for the

---

*Early in the war, when a series of stunning victories made it seem as if Confederate forces might roll over Washington and continue north, Russia spent five million dollars to send critical elements of its navy to guard New York Harbor and support the Union flag in San Francisco. The czar was also rumored to have supplied Admiral Farragut with five hundred men for an attack on the port at Mobile, Alabama. The gesture may not have been completely altruistic, however: at the time, Russia was edging toward war with Britain over fur poaching in the North Pacific, which Russia considered its own. Removing the fleet from its ports ensured the czar's ships would not be bottled up in the event of a blockade by the far superior British navy.

rebels, British jurisprudence simply would not allow it. And Bulloch, as a subterfuge, had laid a trail of false but impressively unimpeachable papers: the contract for the ironclads' construction had been let by a French firm, Bravay's of Paris, which supplied documents showing that the vessels—christened *El Mounassir* and *El Tousson*—were destined for the viceroy of Egypt.

Palmerston's solution to the impasse was elegant. There is no record of the leverage applied, but somehow he succeeded in pressuring Bravay's into breaking its arrangement with Bulloch and selling the nearly completed rams to the British navy, where they were promptly rechristened the HMS *Wivern* and the HMS *Scorpion*. They would, suggested Palmerston (who clearly believed that the possibility of going head-to-head with America had not been entirely defused), "be greatly useful for Channel service in the event of war."

Unwilling to give up entirely on the attempt to acquire rams, Bulloch turned to another builder in France. Again a contract was arranged through a willing blind, plans were drawn up, and funds were deposited. But as with the wife of the loony queen's advocate, this effort too was stymied by human foible: a secretary to the Calais shipbuilder simply walked into the office of the American minister to France and offered to sell him proof of Bulloch's involvement. John Bigelow, in true tightfisted Yankee style, "ah-yupped" and allowed as to how he might be interested in such a thing, but requested that the young Frenchman return to the builder's office, burglarize it, and steal the proof of Bulloch's involvement before being paid. Pleased with the results of this felony, Bigelow crossed the secretary's palm with silver, and Bulloch—his months of work down the drain—was forced to return to England without his rams.

Once back in Britain, he found the news from the home front cautiously encouraging: in the bloodiest two days of the war a rebel army had won a fierce battle at Chickamauga. It was a Pyrrhic victory, with combined casualties exceeding thirty-six thousand, of which the South suffered more than half. Nonetheless, the event was exemplary of the

Confederates' fighting spirit, as was the "Battle above the Clouds" at Lookout Mountain, where a mere twelve hundred men had held off twelve thousand advancing Yankees and even launched a counterattack.*

Buoyed by the news, Bulloch abandoned his efforts to acquire rams and focused instead on buying existing ships.

*In what seems a rather revisionist comment, Union general Ulysses S. Grant would later write of the battle that "Lookout Mountain is one of the romances of the war. There was no such battle and no action even worthy to be called a battle. . . . It is all poetry." Then again, perhaps when measured against the horrible carnage that was the standard of the Civil War, the nearly seven hundred causalities suffered by Union forces did qualify the event as a nothing more than a minor skirmish.

TWO

A YEAR LATER, in October of 1864, a young
Virginian checked into the Wood's Hotel in
London's High Holborn district following a fast
passage from the European continent. After signing the register, the tall, athletically built young
man went immediately to his room and stayed
there until eleven the next morning, when he came
down to the coffee shop carrying a copy of the
Times and wearing a handkerchief tucked into a
buttonhole of his jacket. Nowadays these props
seem like clichés out of a spy novel, but this was a
hundred years before Ian Flemming gave us James
Bond, and the mission the Southerner was on
was real.*

A few minutes later a gentleman dressed in the
business garb of the day entered the coffee shop

*Nor is the scene fantasy; a letter from the young covert's superior
officer instructing him to dress, act, and speak in the manner
described remains on file at the National Archives in Washington, D.C.

and scanned the room, settling on the young man where he sat reading the newspaper, fiddling nervously with his improvised boutonniere. The headlines were dramatic: General Sherman's army was burning its way toward Atlanta, and the press was still rehashing how a few months earlier the Confederate raider *Alabama* had been sunk after nearly two years of what Winston Churchill would later call "a grand and glorious career." She had been caught up in the harbor in Cherbourg, France, by the Union sloop of war *Kearsarge* during a vital overhaul. With no way to escape, Rafael Semmes, the Confederate master, had sent a chivalrous note out to the Yankee captain "begging that the *Kearsarge* not depart [until the *Alabama*'s refit was finished], as he intended to fight her . . . and would not delay her but a day or two." Upon sally, the combatants had waltzed far enough offshore to relieve France of any responsibility for the battle and begun a pas de deux that saw the *Alabama* smashed and sunk. With her powder and shot degraded from two years at sea, she had been no match for the *Kearsarge*'s armor of wrought-iron chain.* Fortunately, a British yacht, the *Deerhound*, had swooped in and plucked Semmes and forty of the Confederate sailors from the water and spirited them away to England before they could be taken prisoner. But most of the news was bad. All across the length and breadth of America, the secessionists were being bloodied. The young Virginian folded the newspaper and eyed the approaching stranger.

"Are you waiting for someone?" asked the businessman.

"Are you Wright?" came the reply.

"I am."

The young man rose and introduced himself as George Brown. He was lying. His real name was William Conway Whittle Jr., and he was a lieutenant in the Confederate navy. He was one of a number of rebel officers secreted around Europe who had received instructions to report to England to await assignment to a new ship. Wright was a prosper-

---

*During the battle, Providence was clearly working against the *Alabama;* one of her first shots lodged in the *Kearsarge*'s sternpost just forward of the rudder but failed to explode. If the shell had gone off, the *Yankee* would have been disabled, and Semmes the victor.

ous Liverpool businessman with substantial investments in cotton. His daughter was married to an American, a partner in the firm that acted as the Confederacy's overseas bank. By nature a cautious man, he had been forced by the threat to his fortune and the obligations of family to edge outside of his normal workaday world into one of more clandestine pursuits: for the past month he had been acting as an agent for James Dunwoody Bulloch, organizing the purchase of a large, fast ship and arranging its transfer into Confederate hands.

The plot was a simple one. Britain's Foreign Enlistment Act of 1819 forbade any of Her Majesty's subjects from participating in a conflict in which the British were neutral or supplying either of the belligerents in such a conflict with the materials of war—a category for which the *Sea King*, at 220 feet long and 1,160 tons, probably qualified. Built as a troop carrier and merchantman for the India trade, she was one of the fastest ships afloat, capable of making sixteen knots under sail or nine when thrust along by her 220-horsepower engine. She was only a little more than a year old, her boilers were still in good shape, and the log of her single voyage to New Zealand, Australia, then on to China and back showed a remarkable twenty-four-hour cruise of 320 miles.

Using funds supplied by his son-in-law's bank in return for the promise of a future supply of cheap cotton, Wright had purchased the ship and set about fabricating papers and spreading rumors to indicate that the next voyage of the *Sea King* would be a simple coal run to India. In reality, the plan called for the vessel to sail for the coast of Africa, where she would be "sold" to the waiting Confederates, meet another ship loaded with guns and supplies, and be converted into an armed raider, thus avoiding the letter of the law by having the transaction take place beyond the limits of Britain's jurisdiction.*

---

*A similar subterfuge is still in use today, particularly in states where high sales taxes constitute a substantial portion of vessel prices. Sellers, buyers, and brokers sail offshore until beyond the limits of the state's jurisdiction to enact the transaction, thus legally avoiding collecting or paying the taxes required of a sale taking place on shore.

The subterfuge was necessitated—and complicated—by the political and social atmosphere of the time: many of England's five million textile workers—their looms standing idle because the blockade had cut off the supply of cotton—were roaming the streets hungry, in a state of agitation. Curiously, even with the difficulties caused by the depression, the sympathies of the working class remained firmly behind the Union, whose cause was seen as antislavery. But with stock prices plummeting and the whiff of revolution in the air, it had not been difficult to persuade elements of Britain's aristocracy and business class to participate in Wright and the Confederacy's machinations. (A year earlier, Charles Francis Adams had observed that "the aristocracy are decidedly against the continuance of the Union . . . but the Crown and the people favour it. The commercial classes are in the meantime putting in for the profits at any risk. The danger of a collision [between America and Britain] springs mainly from the action of these last.")

Palmerston, who had worked tirelessly during the early decades of his political career to see slavery abolished in England, was meanwhile stuck between the push-and-pull of his country's divided sentiments, maneuvering madly to prevent the outbreak of war over the tangled issue of cotton, the embargo, and Bulloch's British-built raiders.* He may also have had other, equally pressing matters on his mind: A woman named O'Kane was claiming to have committed adultery with him during a visit to the House of Commons. He had been named as co-respondent in the divorce suit, and her husband was suing him for twenty thousand pounds. Far from scandalizing the public, the affair

---

*Lord Palmerston's humanitarian impulses evidently did not extend to the Irish. During the Irish Famine of the 1840s, a thousand people were removed from Palmerston's estate in Ireland and shipped to Canada in order to allow subsequent "land improvements" to be carried out. Palmerston's agents promised each family from two to five pounds sterling and suitable clothing for the journey, but reneged on the bargain. On their arrival at Quebec, a member of the Legislative Council of Canada reported that the deportees were "in a state of fearful destitution . . . 87 were almost in a state of nudity; the food provided on board the ship was of the worst description; and the ship was excessively overcrowded." The mortality rate aboard the immigrant ship was "upwards of twenty-five percent"—a statistic equal in horror to that of the slave ships operating out of Africa.

was doing wonders for Palmerston's popularity: he was nearly eighty years old at the time.*

Queen Victoria was in seclusion, grieving over the death of her husband, Prince Albert, from typhoid in 1861, but her government was firmly in the grip of Lord Palmerston's roaming hands, which were as adept at juggling his country's two-handed realpolitik as they were at fondling his visitors—a skill reflected in the diplomatic letters of Foreign Minister John Russell, whose instructions to Britain's overseas consuls were that they were not "to *seem* to favor [either] party rather than the other," and those of Russia's ambassador to London, Baron de Brunow, who acknowledged in a letter to St. Petersburg that "the English Government, at the bottom of his heart, desires the separation of North America into two separate republics, which will watch each other jealously and counterbalance one the other."

LIEUTENANT WHITTLE, on the other hand, had little time or patience for such machinations. At twenty-three, he had already been a naval officer for several years, and of the Southerners involved in the transformation of the *Sea King* into a raider, he seems the most likely to be cast as the dashing young action hero if a movie of the ship's voyage is ever made. In 1861 he had been aboard the first Confederate vessel to run the Union blockade, and he was still aboard when the *Nashville* made its return run from England, outrunning several Federal cruisers on the way. The ship tied up at the dock in Beaufort, North Carolina, just in time to be caught between a Yankee army driving on the city and a squadron of gunboats arriving to seal off the port. Arguing against a senior officer's instructions to burn the ship rather than see it captured, the twenty-year-old Whittle had instead gotten

---

*Palmerston, whose nickname of "Lord Cupid" was well deserved, had always been a ladies' man. At one point he was conducting simultaneous affairs with Princess Dorothy de Lieven, Lady Jersey, and Emily Cowper, the wife of Lord Melbourne. During this ménage à quatre, he also proposed marriage to Lady Jersey's sister. After Lord Melbourne dropped dead, he married Emily instead.

permission to rally a handful of like-minded volunteers and steam out
of the harbor in complete darkness, fully expecting to be wrecked and
drowned at any moment as they crossed a shallow bar across the entrance at full speed. Clearing the hazard just as the sun rose, Whittle
had sailed the blockade runner through a line of Union gunboats and
scurried over the horizon.

Twenty-four hours later, exhausted from sailing the 216-foot
Nashville with only a quarter of her normal crew, Whittle had run the
ship aground on a spit while trying to enter Georgetown Harbor after
dark. When a boatload of armed men approached in the darkness, he
had ordered the crew to stand by to repel boarders. With daylight, the
strangers proved to be Confederates, and Whittle, barely out of his
teens, was a hero.*

For someone of Whittle's lineage this was almost to be expected.
His father was a well-respected naval officer. One uncle was a bishop
in the Episcopal church. Another uncle was a many-times-wounded
Confederate hero. A third had been chief surgeon aboard the flagship
of the Wilkes expedition, which explored the world from 1838 to 1842
and among other accomplishments first defined Antarctica as a continent. He was also a direct descendant of the Algonquin Indian leader
Powhatan, whose daughter Matoaka was better known as Pocahontas.

That Whittle was a man of action is inarguable, but whether those
actions were heroic or not is a point about which other accounts of the
Nashville's escapades are at odds. On the first leg of her maiden voyage,
the *Nashville* had run down, captured, and burned the *Harvey Birch,* an
unarmed American schooner. Later, the *Harvey Birch*'s captain told a
reporter from the *London Times* that "the [*Nashville*] was all out of repair; her officers were boys, who wanted courage as much as experience. . . . the crew was a mixture of Irish and other foreigners, who
were shipped at first on false pretenses, and then were compelled to sign

---

*Shortly after the *Nashville* episode, Whittle was captured by Union forces in New Orleans.
A roll of Confederates being held as prisoners of war at Fort Warren, Boston Harbor, dated
June 4, 1862, lists him as an inmate. He was later freed in a prisoner exchange.

other articles at the point of the bayonet." And, he added, he "did not believe they would have fought. Both officers and crew were in great fear lest they should meet some American war-ship on the ocean, and their armament was so poor that they could have made no resistance to speak of."

According to Captain Nelson, the *Nashville* was also "badly fitted out, badly armed, poorly officered and badly manned, and [if] she was a specimen of the southern privateer, it must be either incapacity or treachery that prevents [Union] vessels from catching them."

Poorly equipped and inexperienced or not, by the time Whittle arrived in London he had three more years of war under his belt, and his only concern was getting the latest addition to the Confederacy's meager navy safely down the Thames and out to sea. Doing so without being noticed would not be easy. In 1864, the London waterfront was crawling with Union spies. Bulloch, for his part, had seen the *Sea King* only once before sending Wright out to buy her. Nor during the hurried refit of the vessel in Liverpool had he dared set foot on her, for fear of being spotted by one of the dozens of informers lurking about under the direction of a tall, lean-faced Quaker named Thomas Dudley, the Union's chief spy.

Dudley had arrived in England to take up his cover as the United States consul to England almost simultaneously with Bulloch's departure to run the blockade on the *Fingal*. While the Confederate agent was delivering his load of contraband to Savannah, the Northern agent used his absence to set up a network of pro-Union sympathizers among the dockworkers and laborers of Liverpool. Nineteenth-century Liverpool—a sprawling, rough-and-tumble city blanketed in a fog of coal smoke and subjected to the constant din of forges turning mounds of steel into ships—was hardly ideal hunting grounds for the somber, almost prissy Dudley, whose background as a New Jersey lawyer did nothing to suit him for rubbing shoulders with the working class, who to his mind were not, as he noted in a letter to Washington, "as a general thing very estimable men."

Nonetheless, he was able to overcome his disdain for the sweaty masses and build an effective network of spies. One spook, a retired police detective named Matthew Maguire, spotted the *Sea King* almost as soon as Bulloch did, and his report to Dudley prompted the consul to inform Charles Francis Adams that the vessel was "a likely steamer for the purposes of a privateer." With a cordon of informers thrown up around the ship and others insinuated into the workers reinforcing her, Bulloch and Wright had been forced to move the *Sea King* from Liverpool to London by slipping her in and out of a number of ports along the way, loading and unloading fake cargo to give her the appearance of a common merchantman.

The tactic may have fooled some (and befuddled others, like the stevedores ordered to move stacks of crates off the ship only to be told to reload them), but Dudley and Adams were not among them. Adams fired off a barrage of correspondence to Foreign Minister Russell demanding that the *Sea King* be seized for violating the Foreign Enlistment Act. But as he had done with the *Florida* and *Alabama,* the minister claimed that since the vessel was still owned by a British citizen—Wright—and carried no arms, no evidence was available to support a claim that the law was being broken. In the end, Dudley could only order his spies to keep watch on the *Sea King* when she arrived in London. Knowing this, Wright and Whittle could risk nothing more than strolling by for a quick look on their way to an anonymous pub, where they were to meet with a heavyset man wearing the dark suit of a merchant captain. Peter Suther Corbett was master of the *Sea King,* and once seated, the three men had plotted out the details of how Wright was to come aboard the *Sea King* with Corbett and stay until the ship, gleaming under a new coat of black paint, headed downstream to a coaling station. After the ship was fully loaded, Whittle would wait nearby until the wee hours of the morning, then slip aboard, dressed like a common sailor and reeling as if navigating his way home from the local saloons.

Meanwhile, 175 miles away in fogbound Liverpool, Bulloch was putting his next move into play. He sent a messenger scuttling through the streets of the city, from boardinghouse to boardinghouse and to a series of small hotels. At each establishment the messenger handed a waiting man a ticket for passage to Nassau or Havana aboard the steamship *Laurel*. In accordance with a prearranged plan, each recipient then put on his coat and left his quarters without saying good-bye. Some had been aboard the *Alabama* when she sank off Cherbourg; others had landed in England after running the blockade. All were Confederate officers or carefully selected men. None carried anything in their hands. Nor did any know the purpose of their mission or their ultimate destination. They knew only that before coming to England they had received instructions to pack enough personal gear for a two-year voyage into a wooden crate, label it with a "peculiar mark," and give it to a waiting porter to be taken away. Soon a small but steady stream of men were walking casually toward the Mersey River, where a tug named the *Black Hawk* lay waiting at a pier.

The *Black Hawk* was to shuttle them out to the *Laurel*, a small, fast freighter Bulloch had purchased for $14,750 through a series of blinds and double-blinds, then filled to the gunwales with small arms, munitions, powder, and stores. In her hold, buried beneath barrels of shot and shell, were enough cannons to arm a cruiser, packed in crates marked "machinery." When a telegram informed Bulloch that the *Sea King* had thrown off her mooring lines and was on her way down the Thames, he signaled the *Laurel* to get under way—the first step in a plan that called for the *Laurel*, which had filed the necessary paperwork with the authorities for a voyage to Havana via Matomoros, Mexico, to divert and sail instead for a group of islands off the shoulder of Africa. Once at the Madeiras, she would rendezvous with the *Sea King* and divest herself of her cargo. The *Sea King* would undergo a hurried at-sea conversion from a simple merchant vessel into an armed cruiser, after which she was to be renamed the *Shenandoah*. To give the subterfuge a veneer of legality, Captain Corbett carried a signed power of attorney authorizing him to sell the *Sea King* "at any time . . . for the sum of not less than forty-five thousand pounds sterling." The sale, of course, was to the Confederate government, and to avoid the Foreign Enlistment Act's injunction against selling an armed vessel to a belligerent, would take place before any arms were sent on board.

Dudley and Adams's spies had enough information to be certain of the *Sea King*'s purpose, but the trail of rumors and false papers Bulloch and Wright had laid to indicate the ship's load of coal was bound for India gave Palmerston's government all the excuse it needed to not stop her. Her crew, from the top down, were British seamen, and none, with the exception of Corbett, knew the real purpose of the voyage. Whittle was on the passenger list as "Mr. Brown," an agent for the owner of the cargo.

Rumors of the Confederates' interest in the *Sea King* had been circulating throughout the waterfronts of the world for months. Weeks earlier and thousands of miles away, the USS *Wachusett* (perhaps still reveling in the glow of having captured the *Florida*) had been on patrol in the South Atlantic, where in the days before telegraph or radio it was common practice for ships crossing paths to "speak" each other, or stop for a brief gossip about what other ships they had seen during their travels and where they were going. Heaving to (which is shipspeak for stopping) also provided an opportunity for an outbound ship to hand off mail to a ship heading home, where upon arrival the mail could be handed over to the first person or vessel heading for the home port of the original ship. Once there, it either entered the somewhat sporadic, often ineffectual postal system or was passed hand to hand until with luck a letter might eventually reach the person for whom it was intended. After stopping an American whaler for a gab, Captain Napolean Collins of the *Wachusett* had chitchatted with its officers for a while, then written the following note and asked them to send it on to the Navy Department:

> *Captain Babcock, of the American whaler* Lydia, *was informed by an English merchant at Hobart Town, a man of good standing and reliable, whom he feels sure would not attempt to deceive him (although it is possible that the merchant himself might have been deceived) that*

there was a steam ship fitting out in England called the Sea King. *She was to be ready to sail from England by the middle of January. She was to proceed to Australia, calling en route at some place on Van Diemen's Land for coal. Her object was to prey on the whalers in that sea. The merchant received his information from a person who had it from the agent of the vessel.*

With the mysterious efficiency of rumor in a small town, waterfront gossip seems to have been spreading news of the *Sea King* around the globe much faster than was possible for any official means of communication. Once Captain Collins's note reached the navy in Washington, the news still had to travel by sailing ship from there back to Adams and Dudley in London, after which a decision was made to station the USS *Niagara*, under the command of one Commodore Craven, and a second warship, the USS *Sacramento*, in the English Channel to keep a lookout. On the night the *Sea King* began taking on coal, the *Niagara* was cruising off the mouth of the Thames, only a few hours away. Craven had just made the decision to alter course and head for London when a lookout came running up with the news that a large black-hulled steamer flying the Spanish flag was coming. While Craven studied the steamer through a telescope, his executive officer repeated a bit of scuttlebutt from the ship's acting master—namely, that during a drinking bout in a Dutch tavern a few nights earlier, the master had overheard a Belgian remark that a Spanish freighter had been seen taking on steel plating and a gun turret for delivery to the rebels. It was a thin, thirdhand snippet of rumor vaguely remembered from a rummy night in a bar, but the consequences of allowing parts for an ironclad ship to fall into Confederate hands were too important to let pass. Two years before, in March of 1862, the first Confederate ironclad had steamed into Hampton Roads, Virginia, and attacked the Union fleet blockading the port, ramming the sloop *Cumberland* and sinking it before turning her guns on the fifty-gun frigate *Congress*. The next day the *Merrimac* returned to finish dispersing the fleet, but the United States' own ironclad, the *Monitor*, had arrived during the night, and the two hammered ineffectively at each other until withdrawing. The match was a draw, but it was apparent to everyone watching that a new age in naval power had dawned.* Two months later the *Merrimac* had been blown up to prevent its falling into Union hands, but ever since, it had been the North's worst nightmare that the South might get its hands on another ironclad ship. As Secretary of the Navy Gideon Welles noted, "We have no protection against them." A Confederate ironclad could steam up the Potomac and shell Washington with impunity.

Craven issued the order to give chase.

The *Niagara* pursued the *Cicerone* for eight hours, but just as the U.S. ship overtook her, the Spaniard crossed into British waters. Craven decided to keep following. All that day, and into the night, the *Niagara* stayed behind her quarry. When dawn came the *Cicerone* crossed once again into neutral waters and Craven ordered her stopped and searched. For the next three days, a boarding party from the *Niagara* dug through the Spaniard's holds but found nothing. When Craven went ashore at Dover to report to Adams, a message from the American minister's secretary was waiting:

"I [write to you] about the *Laurel*," said Benjamin Moran's letter.

The rebels bought her at Liverpool last Tuesday. Captain Semmes [former master of the *Alabama*] sailed in her on Sunday with eight officers and about a hundred men. Forty of them were the crew of [the *Alabama*]. She cleared for Matamoras, via Havana and Nassau,

---

*In an almost eerie foreshadowing of the cold war and its nuclear arms race, Charles Francis Adams's son wrote that the invention of seemingly invulnerable all-iron ships like the *Monitor* and *Merrimac* "must someday lead to the development of engines of destruction capable of killing us all." Prescience seems to have run in the family; his brother Henry wrote: "You may think this is all nonsense but I tell you these are great times. Man has mounted science, and is now run away with. I firmly believe that before many centuries more, science will be the master of man. The engines he will have invented will be beyond his strength to control. Some day science may have the existence of mankind in its power, and the human race commit suicide by blowing up the world. Not only shall we be able to cruise in space, but I see no reason why some future generation shouldn't walk off like a beetle with the world on its back, or give it another rotary motion so that every zone should receive in turn its due portion of heat and light."

which means that she will go anywhere. She took on board in cases six sixty-eight-pounders, with the requisite gun carriages, and also small arms. It is doubtless Semmes's purpose to meet and arm some other vessel, as the *Laurel* is not large enough for all the guns, her tonnage being not more than 350. . . . She has one funnel, two masts, is fore-and-aft rigged, has a plain stem, round stern and black hull.

THE INFORMATION in the message was critical, but tardy; Bulloch's ships had already outfoxed Adams's hounds. Sometime during the night of the chase, the *Sea King* had cleared the mouth of the Thames and slipped quietly past the *Niagara*'s stern on a course for the open sea. Moran also made several mistakes in his letter to Captain Craven. His estimate of the Confederate manpower aboard the *Laurel* was way off; there were, according to one passenger involved in the getaway, only twenty-odd officers and a dozen or so handpicked men. And Rafael Semmes was not among them.

After nearly two years of whacking Yankee shipping left and right, the commander of the *Alabama* seems to have taken on the dimensions of a bogeyman. Unaware that the strain of losing the battle with the *Kearsarge* had left Semmes exhausted and huddling under a blanket, Charles Francis Adams and Secretary of the Navy Welles were seeing him everywhere, terrified that he might get his hands on another ship. They seem never to have considered that someone else might be given command of the *Sea King*. They had probably never even heard of James I. Waddell.

A big man, standing over six feet tall and weighing two hundred pounds, Waddell walked with a limp as the result of a pistol ball that remained lodged in his hip from a duel fought when he was a midshipman, at the age of seventeen.* When the *Laurel* was well offshore and

---

*During the sixty-five years before the Civil War, when the notion of personal honor in America was at its height, the navy lost two-thirds as many officers to dueling as it did to combat. Like Waddell, many of the dead were teenage midshipmen, driven by the petty irritations of living in close quarters to taking up pistols or swords against each other at the slightest provocation.

the Confederate officers gathered to celebrate their escape, he sat back and watched. While the others roistered, as Cornelius Hunt put it, "with a well-appointed table and other creature comforts unnecessary to specify more particularly," he was quiet.

Waddell's reserve may have been due to a difference in ages—the commander of the Confederate raider-to-be was forty-two; the majority of his officers, in their teens and early twenties—or it may have been the reticence of untried authority. Lieutenant Commander Waddell had been a mariner for over twenty years, but the *Sea King*, once it became the *Shenandoah*, was to be his first command.

In *The Memoirs of Lieutenant Commanding James I. Waddell*, the commander's autobiography, he adopts a patrician tone throughout the half dozen brief, elliptical paragraphs that describe his childhood in Pittsboro, North Carolina, revealing only that he was, for reasons unexplained, adopted by his own grandfather while still "a little fellow." By his own admission incorrigible, with "all the deviltry committed in and out of that hamlet . . . laid at my door," young James was given the rudiments of an education by "a very estimable young lady who did not believe in moral suasion"—an oblique, perhaps tongue-in-cheek reference to the corporal punishment that was likely a regular element in the little hellion's education, indicative of an obstinacy that was to be a hallmark of his personality all his life.

As a teenager, while he was serving as second lieutenant aboard a supply ship stationed off the Isthmus of Panama, malaria swept through the officers and crew of the *Release*, leaving only young James, one seaman, and a single cabin boy standing. Waddell, though relatively inexperienced, took command of the vessel, close-reefed the topsails, and sailed to the port of Matanzas. After a local pilot refused to come aboard the fever-racked ship, he continued shorthanded into the inner harbor and brought the ship safely to anchor.

Five days later, with the crew only partially recovered, the captain of the *Release* polled his officers for their opinions as to whether they should continue on to Boston, as they had been ordered to do before the star-crossed voyage began, or take the justifiable liberty of truncating their journey by sailing for the closer safety of New York Harbor. Only Waddell insisted that his captain follow orders, but he presented his opinion with such force that he prevailed. The *Release* was delivered to the naval yard at Boston as instructed. Shortly thereafter, the entire crew, including young Waddell, was declared invalid with exhaustion and sent home.

It was stubborness, perhaps apparent in the way a daguerreotype from the period shows him slouching petulantly beneath a bristling mustache, and an obsession with following orders that was to serve him in good stead during the voyage. But for now he was still a passenger, so he sat back and watched Petty Officer Cornelius Hunt, Midshipman John T. Mason, Surgeon Charles Lining, and the rest of his soon-to-be subordinates gather around the table to admire each other in their freshly unpacked uniforms and toast the success of their escape from England and the hope of their voyage to the Madeiras.

Commander James Iredell Waddell, CSN.

Photographed in Confederate Navy uniform, circa 1864–1865.

(U.S. NAVAL HISTORICAL CENTER PHOTOGRAPH.)

Pencil sketch of the CSS Shenandoah,
from the inside cover of a notebook kept by her commanding officer,
James I. Waddell.

THREE

"MADEIRA," wrote Surgeon Charles Lining in a diary he maintained throughout the voyage, "is one of the garden spots of the Earth, one of the most delightful climates perhaps in the world."*

Deep in the wrinkles of their subconscious minds, people who have never even heard of the Madeiras pine for a place like the cluster of Portuguese-speaking islands four hundred miles off the coast of Africa. Even those who think Funchal is a city in China know that somewhere on the planet there is a place where people move slowly and speak in musical tones while harvesting baskets of silver fish from the sea; where, as the diarists aboard the *Laurel* noted, the climate is per-

---

*Although Lining's official rank in the Confederate navy was that of "passed assistant surgeon," he served as the ranking medical officer aboard the ship, or ship's surgeon. Thus, in most records and acccounts of the voyage, he is referred to as Surgeon or Dr. Lining.

fect, neither too hot nor too cold, but just right for tending acres and acres of spreading vineyards.

Today Funchal is still the Madeiras' major port of call. Glistening blue-and-white cruise ships disgorge streams of camera-laden tourists onto the islands on a frequent basis, but this is nothing new; tourism began in the islands in the late 1700s, was in full swing when the *Laurel* dropped anchor in October 1864, and has puttered along very nicely ever since, with the exception of a few periods during World War I and World War II when German submarines made traveling anywhere within the approaches to the Straits of Gibraltar a dicey proposition. Ever since João Gonçalves Zarco blew off course in 1419 and discovered the archipelago by accident, a sort of stolid consistency seems to have been a hallmark of the place: the weather never varies; there is no history of significant social upheaval or violent changes in government; even the famous Madeira wines are the most stable in the world, with vintages fifty to a hundred years old on the market.

"The city has several buildings of considerable architectural pretensions," wrote Cornelius Hunt shortly after the *Laurel*'s arrival.

One in particular, of which we had a fine view from the harbor, is known as Mount Church [and] occupies the summit of a bold bluff several thousand feet above the sea . . . reached by a road that zigzags up the bluff a distance of nearly four miles—a by no means easy pedestrian excursion, and generally performed on horseback, but the return trip is usually made upon sleds. To a native of the Northern States this would be refreshingly reminiscent of the boyish pastime of coasting and some idea of the steepness of the declivity may be gathered by the rate of speed at which . . . the Madeira sleds glide down the rocky pathway, which is paved in smooth, round stones.

"Most tantalizing," sighed Surgeon Lining in his journal. The doctor's wistfulness was deepened by the second night of their stay. It was the queen of Portugal's birthday, and Funchal was celebrating in grand style. Unfortunately, Waddell had ordered that no one, with the exception of the *Laurel*'s Captain Ramsey, be allowed to go on shore, for fear of giving away the true nature of the ship and its passengers. Unable to participate, Lining could only watch the fireworks and dancing through binoculars.

Waddell's caution in not allowing shore leave was justified, but his prudence was in danger of backfiring. After two days of waiting, there was still no sign of the *Sea King*. And for the *Laurel* to continue to sit in the harbor without allowing liberty was odd; people were starting to talk. Bumboats rowing out to sell vegetables or trinkets, or just "have a gam," reported back to those waiting on shore that many of those on board had Southern accents. Only a year before, word of the *Alabama*'s depredations had been emblazoned on the front page of every newspaper in the Madeiras, and the captain of the port was growing meddlesome: Their papers said they had cleared Liverpool for Matomoros. A favorable wind was blowing. When did they plan to leave?

Captain Ramsey deflected the harbormaster's curiosity by digging out and presenting two large broken cogs, which with some foresight he had thought to bring along. "The steering engine," he said with a shrug. "We'll need an ironworker who can weld."

The subterfuge worked well enough to dispel some but not all of Funchal's curiosity, and Hunt noted in his journal that "after remaining at anchor for two days we began to feel some uneasiness in regard to the *Sea King*, as sufficient time had elapsed to enable her to make the run."

Neither Hunt nor the waterfront gossips had long to wait. That night a large black-hulled ship steamed slowly across the entrance to the harbor, signaled with its lights, and coasted away. At dawn it was back, waving coded flags to indicate it was the ship they were waiting for.

Now it was the port captain's turn to dawdle, refusing to come on board and give them clearance until he had performed a customs inspection on a mail steamer arriving from Lisbon. It was nine o'clock before the *Laurel* got under way.

October 20, 1864: Having received everything from steamer *Laurel,* put ship in commission as C.S.S. *Shenandoah* and shipped twenty-three men as petty officers, seamen, firemen, etc. Weighed anchor at 2 p.m. and at 6 parted company with the *Laurel;* 6:15, stood under steam to southwestward.

TAKEN FROM AN EXTRACT of the *Shenandoah*'s journey contained in the *Official Records of the Union and Confederate Navies in the War of Rebellion,* these forty-five words do little to describe the enormity of introducing the raider to the world. Nor does the opening entry in the log, which adds only that the weather was pleasant, with a heavy swell from the north. Both omit some fairly staggering complications.

Once clear of the harbor at Funchal, the *Laurel'*s engine labored to overtake the *Sea King* and follow her to Las Desertas, a trio of scrubby islands a few miles to the south. At Porto Santo, a sandy cove in the sheltered lee of the largest island, the ships dropped anchor in twenty fathoms of water and rafted alongside each other with fenders between them to prevent chaffing. Tackles were strung from the *Sea King*'s yardarm for lifting, and preventers were rigged to act as braces. Leaping across to the deck of the *Laurel,* Whittle discarded his identity as "Mr. Brown" and began giving orders. As executive officer, he had beneath him Lieutenants John Grimball, Francis Chew, Sidney Smith-Lee (Robert E. Lee's nephew), and Dabney Scales. Surgeon Charles Lining would oversee Assistant Surgeon Fred J. McNulty from Connecticut— a Yankee, as was the ship's carpenter, John Lynch of New York.* Acting Master Irvine Bulloch, the nephew of James Dunwoody Bulloch, was in charge of Master's Mates Cornelius Hunt, Lodge Colton, and Joshua T. Minor. At the bottom of the pile were the midshipmen, O. A. Brown and John Thompson Mason.†

---

*The memoirs of the ship's officers differ on the carpenter's name. Lining gives his name as O'Shea but Waddell remembered him as a New York Yankee named Lynch.

†John Thomson Mason was the adopted son of James M. Mason, a Confederate diplomat whose abduction from the British steamer *Trent* by Captain Charles Wilkes of the USS

From the beginning Waddell had known that the *Shenandoah* must begin her cruise shorthanded. A vessel of her size would require a crew of nearly 150 men to be properly sailed and fought, but there had been no way to recruit so many Southerners; the Confederacy had no naval academy, nor was its navy sufficiently large to serve as a training fleet. In addition, it would have been impossible to keep so many men hidden around England while the plot to obtain the *Sea King* and *Laurel* was organized. Instead, there were only ten survivors from the *Alabama* available.

Waddell had convinced himself he would be able to induce a large number of the British seamen aboard the *Sea King* and *Laurel* to join. A romantic, he believed that other men, like himself, hungered for the "glory and honor" of war. Failing that, he felt sure they could be induced by offers of higher than normal pay and a share in any "prizes."

He was wrong.

It took nearly thirty-six hours of "wild excitement and unremitting turmoil" to swing the cargo of cannons, powder, shot, small arms, and supplies from the *Laurel* to the *Sea King*, with officers and men alike working through the night, fueled by shots of rum distributed at regular intervals by trotting cabin boys. While the men were transferring the gunpowder, all lights and fires were dowsed; the moon was bright enough to oversee the task. A three-ton cannon slipped in its sling, crushing a length of bulwark, and when a case of twenty-four-pound

---

San Jacinto on November 8, 1861, sparked the "Trent Affair." Along with John Slidell, the elder Mason was on his way to Europe to rally support for the Confederacy, but their capture aroused so much international resentment, especially among the British, who claimed that their abduction from a neutral vessel was a violation of international law, that British troops were sent to Canada in preparation for war with the United States. To avoid bringing England into the conflict, Secretary of State William H. Seward apologized and ordered the diplomats released. In one of the ironic weavings of history, Captain Wilkes had once been the commanding officer of Lieutenant Whittle's uncle, who accompanied him on his exploratory voyage around the world from 1838 to 1842. And during their captivity, Mason and Slidell were held at Fort Warren in Boston Harbor, where Lieutenant Whittle was imprisoned a few months later after being captured by the Yankees at New Orleans. Wilkes was later court-martialed for conduct unbecoming an officer, but after being found guilty was recommissioned as a rear admiral and retired.

shot broke loose and crashed to the deck, everyone was too tired and harried to corral the loose cannonballs.

In the middle of it all a cry of "Sail ho" fueled a moment of panic; a vessel with "topsails set and very much the appearance of a man-of-war" was bearing right down on them. Swords and pistols were distributed to the officers, but with the heavy armament not yet in place, resisting a Union cruiser would have been futile. Instead, the *Laurel* sailed out toward the invader in hopes of drawing it away and was relieved to discover she was flying British colors.

Returning to the *Sea King*, all hands fell to, shifting enough of the scattered cargo into the hold to allow the work to continue. Finally, at ten o'clock in the morning the job was done, and the officers summoned the men of both vessels to the quarterdeck.

Waddell appeared, dressed in his Confederate uniform, wearing a sword and two gold rings round his cuffs to denote his rank. Corbett, wearing a dapper derby, stood by his side.

"I've sold the ship to the Confederates," he told his assembled crew. "She is to belong to their navy as a cruiser, destroying merchant vessels and whalers. As you are all young men, I advise you to join her, as you will make a fine thing of it. Step forward those who will."

Promising a severance of two months' wages, he added that Waddell was paying a bounty of ten pounds to those signing. The men—exhausted, no doubt coming down slowly from the adrenaline of the man-of-war scare, and, given the amount of grog served over the last day and a half, probably drunk—were not impressed.

"I've contracted for a trip to Bombay [and] you have broken your agreement," argued one of the *Sea King*'s petty officers. "Have you never heard of the Foreign Enlistment Act?"

Of the scene that followed, Midshipman Mason wrote in his personal journal that "[Corbett] was about as much use as a fifth wheel to a carriage. He let his men abuse him like a pickpocket; his first mate was also a useless sort of hand and his second a rough plug-ugly." There were no volunteers.

Waddell raised the ante for signing to twelve pounds, then fifteen, appalled by the English crew's weak lust for adventure. As a last inducement, he had one of his officers bring up a bucket of gold sovereigns from the safe and stood pouring them through his hands as he promised the assembled sailors "a brilliant, dashing cruise" and good wages in the service of "an oppressed and brave people in their resistance to a powerful and arrogant northern government."

The argument did not carry much weight with the British seamen. Not even a chance at "prize money," a bonus paid out as a share of the value of all enemy shipping captured, sunk, or burned, was enough to induce them to come along. Only one engineer, a fireman, a steward, and two cabin boys stepped forward. From the crew of the *Laurel* came five more. Corbett buttoned his coat and declared, "I'm leaving."

Fifty of the fifty-five Englishmen aboard the *Sea King* followed him. Of the 150 men Waddell needed to handle his sails, he had 42—9 English volunteers, 10 veterans from the *Alabama,* and 23 officers of all grades.

He was screwed.

"[YOU] DO NOT HAVE the most remote idea of what confusion is on a vessel if you were not on board the *Shenandoah* when she began her first cruise," wrote Midshipman Mason. "No officer or man on board the ship knew where anything was stowed and there was nothing done properly, . . . all the provisions and stores of every sort seemed to have been thrown on board at random, with everything on top, or rather on the bottom and the least little thing that was wanted required a half hour's search at the smallest calculation. Then no one knew the lead of the ropes, all the men being new and the ropes having a most remarkable lead. Consequently, whenever a brace or a sheet was to be hauled on, ten minutes was required to find it."

Standing amid the chaos of barrels, crates, coal, and cordage heaped about the deck, Waddell read aloud the commission converting the *Sea King* into the CSS *Shenandoah.* The men continued working. There was no time for formality. The British ensign was brought down and the Stars and Bars went aloft while Lieutenant Chew hung over the stern with a paintbrush obliterating the English name. The *Laurel* cleared away, setting a course for Tenerife, then on to her new life as a blockade runner. As the little freighter sailed away, those aboard her saluted the new raider with a halfhearted cheer.

Waddell gave the order to raise the anchor and watched as his feeble crew rushed to the winch. With fifty fathoms of chain out, it would not budge; there were too few men to raise it. Throwing off their coats, the officers, "few, if any of whom had ever performed a day's manual labor," pitched in, working until they thought their arms would break.

"I thought it would never come," said John Mason, "but at last the old anchor made its appearance & we got our old packet under way."

Waddell was not quite as chipper. Surveying the littered deck and undersized crew, he felt dismayed.

"I was truly afloat and, as I had never been before," he wrote, "in command of a vessel constructed for peaceful pursuits . . . to be under my directions metamorphosed into not only a cruiser, [but one] capable of carrying a battery for which she was not constructed. The deck was to be cleared of the stores before the battery could be mounted on the carriages, and gun ports were to be cut, fighting bolts driven, and gun tackles prepared before the guns could be used. All this service, which is ordinarily done at a navy yard before a vessel is commissioned, devolved upon us out in mid ocean, without even a hope of successful defense if attacked or a friendly port to take shelter in if I should desire protection."

The bulwarks were discovered to be too weak to resist close-quarters gunfire, and a place had to be found in the vessel's hold for the construction of a gunpowder magazine. In the interim, the hold being full of coal, the barrels of gunpowder were stored next to Waddell's cabin.

"Was it not a warm companion?" he asked rhetorically. "If we had fallen in with the enemy's cruiser at this time we might, in attempting to escape, have received a missile which, taking effect in the stern of the vessel, would have exploded or otherwise put an end to all our hopes by blowing up the magazine."

Outside the small cove the sea was rough. Pitching and rolling, the crew struggled to move the gun carriages into place and raise the top-sail spars. There was only one person aboard with any shipwright skills, and with no one to assist him, the work proceeded slowly. Shifting the heavy cannons was dangerous; letting three tons of cast iron get out of control on the wildly heaving deck could be fatal.

Deflated, overwhelmed by the endless universe of labor spread out before him and the vulnerable condition of his ship, Waddell summoned his officers aft and laid out their position: with less than half the minimum number of men necessary to sail the ship in a storm—much less fight her—he did not feel equal to the task. As he saw it, they had two options: make a run for Tenerife in the Canary Islands and, once there, hope to recruit more seamen from passing ships; or head for the open sea, where they must work like Trojans to prepare for the chase or battle, all the while praying that inclement weather did not overwhelm them or a chance encounter with a Union cruiser lead to their capture.

Lieutenant Whittle argued that Tenerife was not safe either. What if there were no more men to be had? How long could they wait before word of their presence spread and a Union warship appeared? Remembering what had happened to the CSS *Florida*—rammed, shot, and dragged out of a Brazilian harbor, then taken north, where her men were still rotting in Yankee prisons—he was dead set against it. Of the chase, he added, if successful, there was a chance of recruiting more sailors from whatever merchant ships or whalers they might take.

Waddell hemmed and hawed. As commander, his responsibility for the safety and welfare of the ship wrestled with the importance of the mission. Under the circumstances, success seemed impossible. And what of his men's lives? In their present condition, encountering even a small Union cruiser would guarantee their slaughter. And they were all so young: Lieutenant Whittle was twenty-four; Chew, Lee, Grimbal, and Scales, even younger. The two midshipmen, Mason and Browne, were only twenty.*

A further complication was the nature of his orders. The letter of instructions Bulloch had furnished him with began: "You are about to proceed upon a cruise in the far-distant Pacific into the seas and among the islands frequented by the great American whaling fleet." And through six grindingly explicit pages, the Confederate agent informed Waddell that "the ultimate aim of your cruise must be the utter destruction of the New England whaling fleet." (In spite of its excruciating detail, the letter also included Bulloch's wonderfully bureaucratic injunction that "all details regarding . . . the general conduct of the cruise . . . must be left to your judgment and discretion.")

In other words, Waddell was being told to target civilian ships. And like many military men of his day, he was ambivalent about the ethics of doing so. Throughout the war, newspaper headlines around the world had screamed that the depredations of Confederate cruisers like the *Alabama* and *Florida* were acts of piracy, committed by privateers. Naturally, the *Shenandoah*'s officers disagreed.

"Piracy," wrote Surgeon Lining, "makes one an enemy of the human race." And privateering was little better, being "nothing short of licensed robbery" engaged in for personal enrichment, without influence of patriotism or national obligation. But, Lining argued, vessels of the *Shenandoah*'s class—"a public vessel, owned, armed, equipped, and commissioned by the government whose flag she bore, and whose officers were of regular standing in the Navy of that country"—were no more privateers than John Paul Jones's *Bon Homme Richard* had been during the Revolutionary War.

The fiduciary nature of "prize money" seems to have escaped him. Calculated as a percentage of the value of all ships and cargoes captured or sunk by a raider, prize money was shared out among the officers and

---

*Mason was not completely inexperienced; before becoming a midshipman he fought in the Battle of Manassas (or Bull Run, as it was known by the Yankees). The bloody event claimed nearly five thousand lives. Mason was sixteen years old at the time.

crew as a bonus to their wages. A successful voyage could set a man up for life. But Lining gives no indication he had any problem accepting this.

Not so with Waddell. The distinction between pirates, privateers, and legitimate raiders was a definition that would ultimately be decided by the victors, but in the interim, one of which he (to state it oxymoronically) was decidedly uncertain: "The novel character of my position embarrassed me more than the feeble condition of my command," he later wrote. "I had the compass to guide us as seamen but my instructions made me a magistrate in a new field of duty where the law was not very clear, even to lawyers. To manage a vessel in stormy weather and exposure to the danger of the sea was a thing for which every good sailor was competent. Fighting was a profession we had prepared ourselves for. But now I was to sail, fight, *and* decide questions of international law that lawyers had quarreled about with all their books."

His hesitation was understandable. At the outbreak of hostilities the economy of the industrial North was thirteen times the size of the agrarian South's. After years of blockade the imbalance was even greater. And as the South slowly choked into submission, many like Waddell who had argued for adhering to an old-style chivalry in military matters were beginning to change their tune. Then in August, while the *Sea King* was still in Liverpool being fitted out, Ulysses S. Grant had sent General Philip Sheridan and his troops into the Shenandoah Valley to clear it of rebel belligerents. Recognizing the fertile valley as the "Breadbasket of the Confederacy," Sheridan had ordered it razed during one of the most bountiful harvests on record. According to the official reports, in the two weeks prior to the commissioning of the rebel raider, Sheridan's troops destroyed "2,000 barns filled with grain and implements, not to mention other outbuildings, 70 mills filled with wheat and flour," and "numerous head of livestock [were] driven off and killed." By spring many of the Shenandoah Valley's residents would be starving, and it was falling to the valley's namesake raider to balance the score. Attacking the Yankee whalers was the best way to do it.

The New England whaling industry had hit a peak a decade earlier, in 1853, when 238 ships carried 103,000 barrels of sperm oil and 260,000 barrels of whale oil back to the East Coast to feed the flames of America's lamps. From that same harvest more than 5.5 million pounds of whale bone flowed into the factories of New England, where it was turned into corset stays, hairbrushes, buggy whips, skirt hoops, and chair cane.* After that atrocious slaughter, the herds of sperm whales, right whales, and bowheads that had produced the bulk of the gold in New Bedford and Nantucket's purses diminished rapidly. By 1860, economic factors had cut the fleet in half.† With the advent of war and the blockade, the Federal government bought 40 of the oldest whalers, filled them with stones, and scuttled them off the mouth of Charleston Harbor to block the entrance to the South's primary port. Rebel raiders caught and sank more than a dozen whalers in the South Atlantic as revenge.

By 1863 the formerly bustling ports of New England could muster only forty-two ships, which led to a shortage of whale products and drove the price for what little was available sky-high. In the decade between 1854 and 1864, the price of sperm oil rose by half, from $124 to $178 a barrel, and whale oil more than doubled, reaching $128 a barrel. The value of whale bone increased 500 percent.

Flogged into action by the potential for such immense profits, owners decided it was once again worth risking their vessels to the dangers of Confederate raiders and polar seas. By the time the *Sea King* sailed down the Thames en route to the Madeiras, greasy black smoke was rising from the try pots of fifty-eight American whaling ships in the northern ocean and the water was once again littered with rotting remains. The fleet was, as Bulloch stated in his letter of instructions to

*The "whale bone" refered to was not bone at all, but baleen—a tough, springy material located in the roof of a whale's mouth through which the animal strains enormous gulps of seawater to concentrate krill, the tiny shrimplike creatures on which it feeds.
†Along with the decimation of its primary resource, the whaling industry also faced the threat of a new technology. In 1862 a Canadian geologist named Abraham Gisner devised a method to extract kerosene from petroleum and suddenly the oil wells of western Pennsylvania became the source of something other than than a crude lubricant. After kerosene's introduction in 1863, whale oil rapidly lost its place as the preferred fuel for the nation's lamps.

Waddell, "a source of abundant wealth for our enemies and a nursery for its seamen." And the only way to close the tap on that flow of wealth was to hunt down the Yankee whalers and destroy them.

As commander of a grossly understaffed ship that could be neither properly sailed nor fought, Waddell did not think it could be done, and in counseling with the junior officers he let it be known that he thought the wisest course would be to run for shelter. His officers argued otherwise; some began to grow suspicious of their commander's backbone. "Now it was that the officers came out in their true colors," wrote Lining, hinting at what he suspected was Waddell's lack of courage, "and some, that should have been the last to be disheartened, flunked, and were only kept up to their work, or rather duty, by the influence of some of the officers."

As the debate rolled, the quartermaster interrupted with even more disturbing news. The fighting bolts and gun tackles—washtub-sized blocks riven with large diameter lines that functioned as crude shock absorbers and also allowed a gun crew to maneuver the heavy cannons—were nowhere to be found. Without them, even when the cannons had been winched and pried into position, they could not be fired; the recoil of a sixty-eight-pound gun could throw the three-ton battery backward through the opposite side of the ship.* Without gun tackles, the *Shenandoah* was declawed.

Waddell again polled his officers. To a man, they voted to carry on. Perhaps through sheer bluff they could take a whaler that would supply them with blocks large enough to improvise fighting tackles. Reluctantly, Waddell gave the order to set a course for the open sea. "It [is] my first command," he scrawled in his journal that night, exhibiting an almost Hornblower-like sense of self-doubt. "And upon the accuracy of all the calculations of my judgment in directing a cruise of so vast a scale depends success or failure. Success will be shared by every individual under my command, but who will share failure with me?"

---

*Guns were designated by the weight of their shells.

FOUR

THE NEXT WEEK was a mad, around-the-clock rush of labor and misery. Cargo and stores were heaved about, coal bunkers were built, a powder magazine was finished (critical, since proper storage of the gunpowder was necessary before the men could be allowed to smoke), and the Gordian tangle of lines was sorted out.

It took four days to fake the six guns into position. The dark mouths protruding from the sides of the ship gave the *Shenandoah* a grim and threatening appearance but no bite. Without gun tackles, the only weapons that could be fired other than the pistols and rifles issued to the officers were a pair of twelve-pounders in the stern. Used primarily for signaling, the small cannon were common armament aboard merchantmen but nearly worthless for a raider. All but one of the guns' puny shells were blanks.

"To be sure," wrote Waddell, "[our] appearance would go a long way towards intimidating an un-

armed vessel but very little examination showed clearly our utter incapacity for contending with any show of success against a regularly appointed man-of-war steamer."

And there were other reasons to be concerned. Besides being tooth-
less, the ship was constructed in a way that made it extremely vulnerable. The boiler was above the waterline, unprotected by plating, and
there was nothing to prevent a lucky shot by the enemy from cooking
everyone belowdecks in steam. Nor was anyone sure that the shock of
the heavy battery being fired would not cause the unreinforced decks
to collapse.

Waddell blustered, "I determined to take the offensive immediately.
It is the only way for the feeble to act." Then he fell to worrying that
the weight of his responsibilities was making him appear "unsociable
and peculiar" to his subordinates, of whom his own opinion was high.

"Never was there better officer material than I had associated with
me," he commented—an opinion that did not include the ordinary seamen and sailors who did the ship's work. "Work is not congenial to
Jack's nature," he complained. "He is essentially a loafer. . . . I know of
no character so unreliable." ("Jack," of course, was slang for an ordinary
sailor, shortened from the British "Jack Tar," for the seaman's use of tar
to restrain hair grown long over the course of an extended voyage.)

Nowhere was the schism between the working seamen and the officers more visible than in the ship's articles, a large sheet of paper stock
nearly three feet square upon which the name of each man was written
alongside a notation verifying his pay and position. At the top of the
sheet, a well-penned statement of the ship's purpose and the willingness of the men to serve acted as a combination oath of allegiance and
employment contract. The handwriting in the signature of almost every
seaman who served aboard the *Shenandoah* is identical, having been
written by one of the officers; the illiterate sailors verified their enlistment with an X.

The officers, on the other hand, were to a large degree the cream of
Southern aristocracy, beginning with Waddell, who was the grandson
of Francis Nash, a colonial legislator who became one of George

Washington's favorite generals during the American Revolution and died battling the British at Germantown (and for whom Nashville, Tennessee, is named). Lieutenant Grimball was the great-grandson of Lewis Morris, a signer of the Declaration of Independence from New York. Lieutenant Sidney Smith-Lee's uncle was none other than General Robert E. Lee, and "Smith" lived up to his lineage by being thoroughly dependable, "never idle," and "everywhere lending a hand at once." Acting Master Irvine Bulloch was the nephew of Waddell's own superior officer, the spymaster James Dunwoody Bulloch, who in time would become uncle to another famous American: his sister married a New Yorker named Roosevelt, had a son, and named him Teddy.*

John T. Mason and most of the other junior officers were also of the gentry, elite European-educated cosmopolitans whose writings and mess conversations were as likely to be sprinkled with phrases in French and Latin as with drawling Southern homilies. Quarter Master Peter Wiggins (originally Weigand) also spoke five languages, including his native Russian. Though only a petty officer, Wiggins had proven his allegiance to the Confederacy early in the war by sinking two steamboats he owned in the Savannah River to obstruct the advance of Federal gunboats. Afterward he served aboard blockade runners until he was captured and thrown in chains. After being held for six months aboard the Yankee vessel that sank his "moonlighter," Wiggins was transferred to prison in Pennsylvania. There, he escaped with the aid of a sympathetic guard, decked himself out in a stolen Yankee uniform, and walked 275 winter miles to Boston. There he wrapped his bleeding, frostbitten feet in burlap and talked his way aboard a British ship bound for Liverpool, where he joined the *Shenandoah*. Back in Georgia, his family still thought him dead.

Whether uniformed in homespun or brass, however, all aboard the raider shared a common discomfort. A large swell washing aboard at regular intervals kept dripping down through the poorly caulked berth deck, soaking the hammocks of the men as they tried to grab a few

---

*Some accounts give Irvine as James Dunwoody Bulloch's brother rather than his nephew.

winks of sleep. Even the captain's cabin, which would normally have been outfitted to some degree of luxury, was spartan and uncomfortable, with "one broken plush-velvet bottom armchair, no berth, no bureau, no lockers for stowing my clothing, no washstand, pitcher or basin, [and] a half-worn carpet that smelled of dogs or something worse." It was, said the *Shenandoah's* commander, "the most cheerless and offensive spot I ever occupied." Midshipmen Brown and Mason's quarters were so uncomfortable that they were forced to decamp down into the steerage, which was full of rope and "all sorts of things that smelled bad."

Nonetheless, by the end of the week a semblance of order had been imposed. Bulloch's instructions to Waddell had recommended taking no action against the enemy for a month in order to give Corbett time to return to England and transfer title to the ship, so on Sunday he issued an order that no work was to be done. Leisure brought its own set of problems; idle men grow bored, and restive men complain. Waddell, knowing that a spark of discontent allowed to light among the tinder of overworked men might later burst into flames, canceled the day off and ordered steam raised. As a result, wrote Lining, "the poor engineers and firemen got very little rest."

On Monday, Lining added, all hands started to work again and went hard at it. At sunset they encountered their first squall. On Tuesday the engine broke down but was easily repaired. That evening they encountered a large group of dolphins. On Wednesday it was a school of flying fish—a good sign, the doctor hoped. But when a sail with "very much the appearance of a Yankee" was sighted, it outran them, and that night he ended his journal with a succinct "disgusted."

His chagrin was premature. That night the wind stiffened and backed to the north. The clouds parted to reveal a swath of stars. At daylight on October twenty-seventh, with the increased visibility, extra lookouts were sent aloft. At 11 a.m. came a cry of "Sail!"

"Where away?" bawled an officer.

"Two points on the lee bow, sir."

It was a barque, with the long mastheads characteristic of a Yankee ship.*

"Give chase," Waddell ordered. Bulloch's instructions be damned. He desperately needed tackle to make the battery operational, even worse than he needed more recruits and supplies. And he needed action to divert the grumbling of his men.

"Let me know when she shows her colors," he added. The first chase was on.

"IT WOULD BE DIFFICULT to convey an idea of the interest this colloquy occasioned," Cornelius Hunt wrote. "From every part of the ship swarmed up the little company that composed her crew, and ensconced themselves in the rigging, and wherever there was a favorable point for observation, while spy-glasses were passed hand to hand, and opinions were anxiously exchanged as to what the stranger might prove to be."

It took an hour to draw close enough to make out the British ensign flying at the stranger's peak, but "she looked so thoroughly American that we decided to board her." Waddell ordered an English flag raised to allay the stranger's suspicions—just one of several foreign ensigns the raider carried to disguise its belligerent identity.

An hour later the chase had grown close enough to read the name on the barque's stern—the *Mogul* of London—but suspicious of a Yankee trick, Waddell ordered a blank cartridge fired to bring her round. A boat was launched. Irvine Bulloch and Breedlove Smith— both survivors of the *Alabama* and experienced in boarding potentially hostile vessels—went aboard with six men.

When Bulloch returned, he reported that the ship's papers proved

---

*The use of the terms "barque" and "bark" to indicate a vessel's rig can be confusing. Some references use the spellings interchangeably, while others indicate different rigging and sail arrangements. The difference, or lack of, also appears to be a matter of nationality and geography, i.e., the French barque is completely different from the American, which at times may also be referred to as a "bark." Throughout this story, the spelling used is generally the same as that found in the original source material.

it to be British owned, as claimed, but its lines and rig had not lied. Forty-six days out of Liverpool with a cargo for Ceylon, the *Mogul* had originally been Yankee built, but was one of dozens of American ships sold or transferred into British ownership to protect them from the *Florida* and *Alabama*. Even though the natural hazards of storms, reefs, ice, and human error continued to take a far greater percentage of the Federal merchant fleet every year than the war, the insurance industry—centered entirely in the Northern cities—had seized on the presence of the raiders as all the excuse it needed to start jacking up rates. Within months, coverage for a voyage through the South Atlantic had increased by fifteen times. Prudent businessmen were beginning to sell their ships overseas.

"Such was their greed," rumbled Waddell of the depraved Yankee race, that they would always put commerce above even their own people's needs.

Waddell's view of Northern commercialism was jaundiced by personal experience. At the outset of the war he had been serving in the Federal navy for nearly twenty years, including a stint aboard a warship supporting General Winfield Scott's assault on the Mexican army and a tour in the China Sea, during which he witnessed an attack by British and French forces on the imperial fortifications at Piho (now Bo Hai, the innermost gulf of the Yellow Sea). He was still in Hong Kong when word came of the South's secession, and for the return voyage home he was transferred to the USS *John Adams* (named, ironically, named for the father of Charles Francis Adams, the nemesis of all Confederate raiders in the conflict). When the *John Adams* touched at St. Helena Island, those aboard received their first intelligence of the war, an account of the Battle of Bull Run. With it clear that there was no longer any hope for a peaceful settlement, Waddell had immediately written to Secretary of the Navy Gideon Welles.

Sir:

The people of the State of North Carolina, having withdrawn their allegiance to the Government, and the State from the Confederacy of the

United States; and owing to these circumstances, and for reasons to be hereafter mentioned, I return to his Excellency the President of the United States, the commission which appointed me a Lieutenant in the Navy, with other public documents, asking acceptance thereof.

In thus separating myself from associations which I have cherished for twenty years, I wish it to be understood that no doctrine of the right of secession, no wish for disunion of the States impel me, but simply because my home is the home of my people in the South, and I cannot bear arms against them.

I am, Sir, respectfully,
James I Waddell*

When Waddell asked for the pay due him for his China Sea service after arriving in Maryland, Welles responded with a letter saying that he would be paid only if he was willing to take an oath "engaging upon [his] word of honor to take no part in the war now being waged against the Government."

"It was an attempt on the part of the Hon. Gideon Welles to bribe me," fumed Waddell, "and to confine his bribe to what was not his. . . . It was my money [and] is my money yet; and I hope whenever it is paid to me or mine, the Government will consider the honorable thing and pay interest."

Deeply offended by what he saw as Yankee duplicity, Waddell had "neglected to make any promise to that debased official" and arranged to have himself smuggled south, paying a butcher one hundred dollars to orchestrate a schooner to sneak him and his wife's brother across the Potomac and up the Wicomico River to Dixie. The skipper of the schooner, "a Yankee who was for making money, his love of the Union notwithstanding," demanded an extortionate payment too.

Now, as the *Shenandoah* began a cruise of unknown duration, he

---

*Nearly one-third of all Federal navy officers resigned to join the Confederacy. The Union army fared much better. Only a tenth of its enlisted men deserted to the South.

worried that he had left his wife in financial straits. Anne Iglehart came from a well-to-do family, but four years of war had left the Southern economy in an utter shambles, and the Confederate navy did not always have the money to pay its officers. By October of 1864 many rebel areas were starving, with some of the more unfortunate Confederates reduced to picking through horse manure for kernels of undigested corn. With communication intermittent or nonexistent, Waddell had no way of knowing how his wife was faring. On top of everything else, his concerns for "petite, gentle Anne," who had accompanied him to England but since returned home, weighed heavily on his mind.

The *Mogul,* now legitimately neutral in spite of her Yankee origins, was released, to the frustration of some and the pleasure of others. Hunt, even though he had not been among the boarding party, felt free to gush in his memoir that "the captain and his wife . . . seemed so cozy and contented in their little home on the sea, that I was half glad to find they were really entitled to the protection of the flag they flew, and safe from capture."

He does not mention that immediately after releasing the *Mogul* the rebels spotted and overhauled another ship—again British—but the chase, though unproductive, energized the crew by proving the *Shenandoah* was a fast ship. "I felt assured that it would be difficult to find her superior under canvas in a strong working breeze," said Waddell. "Give her the wind and steam need not be raised."

With the hunt working slowly westward toward the line where wind, currents, and trade routes formed a natural choke point, funneling merchant shipping into the relatively narrow gap between the bulging continents of South America and Africa, there was hope that the promise inherent in the rebel's speed would soon prove true. The crew's blood was up from the tantalizing prospect of future prize money, and their grumbling abated.

On Friday, October 28, the *Shenandoah* was stalking "the line" at a point due south of the Azores and west of Dakar when another sail was sighted. At sunset the ship was still too distant to be identified. During the night Waddell ordered course altered to put the raider in what he hoped would be a better position in the morning. Daylight proved the maneuver to have been mistaken; the stranger was nearly out of sight. The winds being light, he ordered steam raised. It took until 3 p.m. to catch the ship.

"Finally we overhauled her sufficiently for her to see our colors, so we hoisted the English ensign to the peak," wrote Lining. "After a time, she hoisted, to our immense delight, the American flag. We immediately clewed down our royals and top-gallant yards, hauled down the English ensign, fired a blank cartridge, and showed her our right colors."

The muzzles of six cannons staring at him from under the rebel flag quickly convinced the Yankee captain that resistance would be futile. He hove to, backing his foresails to stop. The lettering on the stern identified his ship as the *Alina* from Searsport, Maine.

A boat was lowered over the side. Bulloch was placed in charge. Master's Mate Cornelius Hunt and Midshipman John Mason went along, together with half a dozen men. Mason later twittered in his journal that he was most concerned with the impression the Confederates would make on their first victim because "our boat certainly had no very neat appearance, [with] all the men dressed differently. . . . But the officers were o.k. for we had our uniforms, swords, sidearms, and etc." His embarrassment at the mishmash of dress among the ordinary seamen was eased, he sniffed, when the boat pulled alongside and the captain "received us at the gangway in his shirt sleeves, in true Yankee style."

Sensible enough to wear shirtsleeves at a latitude that was the Southern Hemisphere's equivalent of Honolulu's, Captain Everett Staples was also practical enough to surrender his vessel with no more than a dour, tight-lipped sigh at the quality of his misfortune: the pretty little *Alina*—named for his daughter—was bound from Wales to Argentina with a load of railroad iron. It was her maiden voyage.

For a while it looked as if the *Alina*'s cargo might save her. Staples produced paperwork stating that the iron was owned by a British firm building a railroad in South America. Waddell hesitated. Sending fifty thousand dollars' worth of neutral cargo to the bottom could easily be construed as a hostile act against a noncombatant, and the Confederacy would be held accountable. But the only alternative was to "bond" the Yankee ship, a strangely Quixotic transaction that involved accepting a promissory note from Staples for the value of his ship, then releasing him. The note—due upon a presumptive Confederate victory in the war—would be backed by Staples's word of honor that he would sail immediately for the nearest neutral port and remain there throughout the duration of the conflict, in a wartime version of being "tagged out."*

Waddell's dilemma was further complicated by the rules of the game, which required that if the *Alina* were to be released, it must be with her equipment, cargo, and crew intact. And he desperately needed some of her blocks, supplies, and men.

A drumhead court was convened to condemn her. Waddell, in a bit of legal hairsplitting that would have done the pettiest of kangaroo courts proud, found that since the papers regarding the ownership of the cargo had not been notarized, there was no binding proof it was not American. Through that tiny loophole he sailed the *Alina* to her doom.

"Thus commenced a scene of such indiscriminate plundering as I never saw before or expect to see again," wrote Lining. Staples and his men were allowed to go back aboard and remove their personnel effects, after which "everything which could possibly be of any use was seized upon and put into [the *Shenandoah*'s] boats.

"I was looking out especially for the eatables," the surgeon remembered years later, "and got a very good store of canned meats, and etc. After all the useful things were pilfered, the spirit of plunder still prevailed. Cabin doors were taken down, drawers from under bunks taken out . . . all furniture and crockery was removed, blocks and tackle carried off—In fact, [the *Alina*] proved a very rich mine, as she was brand new and everything in her in very good order and of good quality."

---

*The value of a bonded ship and its cargo was also added to the total amount used to calculate the prize money due a raider's crew at the end of a voyage. Thus, there was no financial incentive to sink a ship if circumstances indicated she should be bonded.

Waddell, for his part, appropriated the barque's chronometer and a newfangled spring-bottom mattress for his bed. Most important, several large blocks were carried off to make the guns functional, as was a quantity of canvas suitable for sailmaking and repairs.

As soon as the Yankee was stripped of everything usable (and a good deal that was not), the *Shenandoah*'s carpenter went aboard to scuttle her. With her hold full of iron, all that was necessary was to knock two large holes through the hull below the waterline and order everyone off. She immediately began to settle by the stern. According to Midshipman Mason, she took less than half an hour to sink. "It was a magnificent sight to see her go down," he wrote.

> The water gained on her little by little and each roll we could see was bringing her nearer and nearer her end. At length she gave a very large roll and seemed to rear right up on her stern, her bows coming up entirely out of water. She was a beautiful little thing . . . all sail was set, even royals and flying jib, and she certainly did look magnificent as she poised herself on her stern for two or three minutes like a fiery race horse and then as if her strength was exhausted she went down with a tremendous crash, the weight of the vessel tearing the masts out of her and then the spars would fly up out of the water as they broke from the ropes. As soon as we saw the *Alina* well down, we got under way . . . and went on our way rejoicing.

They had reason to celebrate. The *Alina* and her cargo were worth valued at ninety-five thousand dollars, and sinking her put the jingle of prize money in the rebels' purse. But while watching the destruction of everything he owned, Captain Staples commented to Cornelius Hunt that "it goes against me cursedly. . . . I know it is only the fortune of war and I must take my chance with the rest. But it's damned hard and I only hope I shall have an opportunity of returning your polite intentions before this muss is over."

All of the diarists aboard the *Shenandoah* remarked upon a similar mixture of feelings while watching the ship go down, Hunt with a flow-

ery-as-usual comparison to "standing beside a death-bed to watch the
sinking away of a soul into the ocean of eternity," Lining describing it
simply as a "beautiful but melancholy sight." But each offered conflict-
ing impressions of its master.

"A black-hearted rascal," thought the doctor. "Mean-spirited . . . a
real Down-East Yankee . . . who will do us all the injury in his power."
Cornelius was more kind, proffering a picture of Staples as a jovial
raconteur eager to relate stories of his own adventures with "infinite
gusto" but not so chummy as to be willing to accept a drink offered him
by Confederate officers celebrating his capture.

A difficult character or not, out of respect for his status as a master,
Staples was quartered in a stateroom and given use of the officers' mess.
The rest of the prisoners, unsure of what would happen next, were
bunked in the forepeak. All were given free run of the ship. "[They] evidently anticipated some unpleasant treatment," wrote Waddell, "and
roamed about the deck, uncertain what to do."

They needn't have worried. They were a valuable commodity, and
after a word from Waddell, Southern hospitality and charm kicked in,
with various junior officers and members of the deck department taking the captives under their wings, offering them tobacco and giving
them personal tours of the ship. Watching this, Waddell noted smugly
that "engaging in conversation with our men was but a prelude to an
enlistment of their sympathies in our cause."

It probably didn't hurt that their guests were all freshly out of a job.
Eight of the twelve men aboard the *Alina* put their marks to the raider's
articles, among them two Frenchmen, two Dutchmen, one Swede, and
an "East Indiaman" (possibly Timorese). Staples and his two mates declined, as did the captain's young apprentice, who had only joined the
Alina to avoid being conscripted into the Federal army and was equally
averse to finding himself in the Confederate navy.

With the addition of the foreigners, the *Shenandoah*'s crew now
numbered twenty-nine. A relieved Waddell noted that the added manpower "produced a remarkable difference in the bearing of the men.

The work pressed heavily still upon them, but we were gathering strength in numbers. . . . [Now] the cry of 'sail ho!' would be greeted with manifestations of joy."

Lining was happy too. Relieved of manual duties, he and his fellow officers could put their coats back on and go back to being gentlemen.

THE NEXT DAY was Sunday, and Waddell, feeling more secure in allowing the men idle time, again declared a day of rest. "Jack is easily entertained," he mused, "and simple in his tastes. After working hours, those who desired amusement collected in the gangways and gave themselves up to dancing, jumping, singing, or spinning yarns."

The picture, quaint as it is, belies an underlying stress. The battery was now functional, but the *Shenandoah* was still a sitting duck. Even with the new recruits, there were only enough men in the "powder division" to operate one gun. And with the havoc wrought by the *Florida* and *Alabama* still fresh in the Union's mind, heavily armed Federal warships cruising the 1,800-mile gap between Africa and South America were a strong possibility. Indeed, even as the *Shenandoah* lay alongside the foundering *Alina*, a large vessel had been spotted bearing down upon them, and it was "hull up" over the horizon before steam could be raised.* The raider scampered away before the stranger was close enough to identify her, but plenty of time had passed for the *Laurel* to have reached Tenerife, where the disgruntled *Sea King* sailors—still smarting from having been promised a two-year voyage that turned into two weeks—would be spreading word of how their British ship had become a Confederate. It was only a matter of time before a Yankee posse started after the *Shenandoah* in earnest.

Worse, and unknown to those aboard the raider, was an ominous

---

*"Hull up" meant close enough for not just the towering sails to be visible, but also the hull itself. For a large ship on a calm day, this might mean twelve to fifteen miles.

shift taking place beyond the horizon. The South was losing the war and the world knew it, forcing the South's European supporters to begin distancing themselves from the sputtering Confederacy. In England, subtle shifts were being made in Crown policies: on the very day the *Alina* went to the bottom, the British consul in Tenerife arrested Corbett for violating the Foreign Enlistment Act.

FIVE

THE WEATHER WENT BAD. Rain fell in heavy squalls. For the next week, water trickling down through the poorly caulked decks made everyone miserable. Between blows the sea was calm and only two sails were chased. Both proved to be British, and with the lack of action came grousing and discouragement. After a month at sea, goldbricking broke out among the crew, with the ship's carpenter trying to avoid work by faking an injury to his foot, then going sullen when Surgeon Lining refused to give him a sympathetic diagnosis. After several days of foul weather Lining himself started to complain that he did not feel well, and began second-guessing his commander when the ship sailed into the doldrums, muttering that it was "a strange proceeding in one who said he wants to save coal" when Waddell ordered steam raised.

On Saturday, November 5, at a latitude 7° north of the equator and just a bit west of the 27th meridian, all of this changed when a sail was sighted just as the sun was going down. Working feverishly, Waddell calculated the current's set and drift before ordering a course change meant to bring the *Shenandoah* up on the stranger at daybreak. It was a carefully reckoned game of variables: Where was the stranger headed? Would he tack if the weather changed? Some worried it was foolhardy, stalking a ship in the night. What if dawn found them approaching a heavily armed Union warship?

In the small hours the wind backed and lay down. By first light the sea was calm. The first rays of the sun curving over the horizon high-lighted a sail straight ahead, right where Waddell had predicted, and he ordered steam raised. By the time the coal-shoveling black gang and engineers had the *Shenandoah* moving, every unoccupied hand was in the rigging, perched in the crosstrees or staring through binoculars.

The *Charter Oak* was a pretty little fore-and-aft schooner, thirty days out of Boston for San Francisco, and she never had a chance. Waddell steamed up within range and ordered one of the small signal cannons fired. A cheer went up when the stranger identified herself with a Yankee ensign.

"The unfortunate part," sighed Midshipman Mason in his journal, "was that there were two 'ladies' on board." Samuel Gilman, the schooner's master, had brought his wife, her widowed sister, and the sis-ter's six-year-old son along for the voyage, marking the Californian as a man of either unusual courage or exceptional foolishness; the *Charter Oak*, at 150 tons burden, was a remarkably diminutive vessel with which to be attempting Cape Horn, especially when one considers that other than a single mate, Gilman's entire crew consisted of three Portuguese men with little or no understanding of their captain's native language. Upon discovering that there were women on board, Waddell was tempted to bond her, but after reviewing the manifest of the schooner's cargo, he ordered her condemned.

"[The women] were an unfortunate complication," Lining mused, "but there was no help for it, no use in bonding, particularly as [the *Charter Oak*] had *furniture* on board." Other than Waddell, who was now resting on the spring-bottom mattress liberated from the *Alina,* most of those aboard the *Shenandoah* were still sleeping on wooden pallets. Even the officers were sitting on crates and eating off their laps. The bulk of the *Charter Oak*'s cargo was made up of "chairs, sofas, bureaus, & etc.," all of which were desperately needed on the raider. Waddell gave the order to burn her.

"If you are going to burn her," giggled Captain Gilman, who was taking the capture with the aplomb of someone with excellent insurance coverage, "then for God's sake save the preserved fruit, for there is a great deal on board." The little schooner's cargo proved to be as unusual as its master. In addition to the badly needed furniture, the looters unloaded nearly two thousand pounds of tinned tomatoes and enough fresh lobster to give every operagoer in San Francisco a case of gout.

After the last boatload of furniture and vegetables had been ferried to the *Shenandoah,* Gilman remembered that there was also a hogshead of ice in the hold, buried beneath an insulating mound of sawdust.* "We were delighted to hear of it," wrote Lining. In the shimmering heat of the tropics, a barrel of ice would be priceless. (Imagine being able to make ice cream or having a cold drink after a month at sea, when everything—skin, clothing, blankets, even food and dishes—was rimed with salt. In 1864, at the height of an equatorial summer, even a glass of simple ice water would have been a pleasure almost beyond imagining.)

The five-hundred-pound cask was wrestled out of the schooner's hold and lowered into a boat, almost upsetting it. So unwieldly was the load that the boat became difficult to control. In trying to come alongside the *Shenandoah* it was swept aft into the propeller.

"How it did for us!" remembered Lining. "[The propeller] stove the boat in and nearly caused the death of two men." Unwilling to give up on such a treasure, the ruptured boat returned to the *Charter Oak,* where the cask was manhandled into another boat, then brought

---

*A hogshead is a wooden cask holding fifty-two and a half imperial gallons.

aboard the raider amid a great deal of shouting and orders to "heave away." None of the diarists aboard the *Shenandoah* recorded the level of disappointment when an eager crowd of overheated sailors gathered around the cask and pried the lid open only to discover the entire contents had melted. The only disappointment expressed was Mason's. And it was reserved for the women captives.

"Our women prisoners were certainly a bore," he wrote, perhaps still remembering the chic belles of France, where he had spent several months before joining the raider. "[They] certainly were the most stupid I ever saw. They were not pretty in the least and could not talk or say a word . . . and they came to meals with the most remarkable dressing gowns on!"

Surgeon Lining was less harsh in his judgments than the twenty-year-old Mason, describing Mrs. Gilman as simply "plane" [*sic*], but her sister, Mrs. Gage, as "a buxom-looking widow . . . with a perfectly auburn suit of hair." The widow's husband, a sergeant in the U.S. Army, had been killed at Harpers Ferry.

Waddell, the only married man among the rebels, was gallant: he presented two hundred dollars in currency found aboard the *Charter Oak* to Mrs. Gilman "on behalf of the Confederacy," under the condition that she share no part of it with her husband. "We all felt a compassion for these poor women," he said, "and had no idea of retaliating upon them for the injuries which General Hunter, Sheridan, Sherman, and their kind had inflicted on our unhappy countrywomen." To ensure the women's comfort, he gave up his cabin to them, then offered Captain Gilman parole, with access to the officers' mess. He was less charitable toward the schooner's Portuguese crewmen: blue army-style overcoats found in their baggage marked them as "bounty jumpers," deserters who had joined the Federal army to claim an enlistment bonus, then slipped away at the first opportunity. Men of such questionable loyalty, he felt, would not be a suitable addition to the *Shenandoah*. He had them thrown in chains.

"It was interesting to watch the meeting between [the masters of the *Charter Oak* and the *Alina*]," he wrote. "The Searsport Yankee had lost money, while the Californian, after a few grimaces, took his capture as a good joke. They did not remain friends long as the Californian found the Yankee 'objectionable and not companionable.' "

Jolly as he was, Gilman was grimly silent when the commander of the *Shenandoah* ordered his little schooner burned. In his memoirs, Waddell, apparently considering that his readers might someday find themselves in command of a commerce raider, gave the following advice on how to burn a ship:

"To prepare a vessel for destruction by fire, first remove all living animals, take out all useful equipment which may be wanted, discover what combustibles are in her hold, such as tar, pitch, turpentine, and see to the removal of all gunpowder. All of these things should be thrown into the sea. Combustibles are then scattered throughout the vessel, bulkheads torn down and piled up in her cabins and forecastle. All hatches are opened and all halyards let go that the sails may hang loosely and the yards counter braced. Fire is then taken from the galley or cooking stove and deposited in various parts of her hold and about her deck. If she is very old she burns like tinder."

And burn she did. It was late afternoon before the *Charter Oak* was thoroughly looted and set ablaze, and once alight, she took until after nightfall to be consumed.

"The wind was light," remembered Waddell, "and the bright flames from the hull, taking in succession each sail, followed the masts to their very trucks, so that the red glare could be seen a long way off, and was a signal of accidental fire or the work of a Confederate cruiser. In either case it would draw assistance."

Leery of attracting a Federal warship, Waddell was yet concerned with his responsibilities to other seamen, which was to leave as little of the schooner's remains afloat as possible so as to offer no danger to the navigation of other vessels. Running downwind far enough to be safe from flying sparks, he ordered the black-hulled raider to halt at the edge of the glow. Drifting with steam up in case an enemy appeared, she lingered until the flames had consumed everything of the *Charter Oak* but the keel and floors.*

THE NEXT MORNING was the first Sunday of November, and as was the Sabbath custom aboard military vessels, all hands were mustered aft to hear the articles of war read aloud. The articles—a sort of all purpose code of conduct meant to remind the ragtag common sailors that they were at the mercy of a military authority—were presented by Lieutenant Whittle, who stood above the assembled crew on the quarterdeck in a uniform of gray wool and brass, a sword at his side. Speaking in a stentorian voice (slowly, one presumes, so that the drawled importance of his words could be understood by the stew of nationalities gathered below him), he repeated the list of offenses and likely punishments:

"For the crime of insubordination, death by hanging.

"For refusing to follow an order, death by hanging.

"For striking an officer, death by hanging."

And so on through the whole gamut of trespasses subject to capital or corporal punishment until the men began to shift on their feet, growing restless at the long-winded recitation of hangings, whippings, brandings, gaggings, tricings, and thrashings available for their discipline. Dismissed, they wandered off in groups, with those new to the military pondering their situation and shaking their heads while the veterans snorted quietly at the notion that any ship so shorthanded as the raider would intentionally cripple, whip, iron, or hang a valuable seaman for the crime of looking an officer in the eye or refusing to follow a foolish order. Only young James Oar, the fourteen-year-old cabin boy who had volunteered from the *Laurel,* stayed behind.

When Lining approached him to ask if he was okay, the wide-eyed

---

*The "floors" of a wooden ship are not the same as those in a building, being instead the beams fastened athwartships atop the keel timber. The "sole"—which would be called a floor by a landsman—is laid atop these.

boy could only stammer, "I say, Sir. Isn't there a great deal of punishing by death in it?"

When Lining repeated the story at dinner that night, Whittle laughed so hard he swallowed a piece of glass.

"Makes me very uneasy about him," Lining wrote, reverting to his role as a doctor. "Gave him a good emetic, so hope everything will be all right."

AFTER THE *CHARTER OAK* came a flurry of captures. In quick succession the *Shenandoah* ran down the *D. Godfrey* of Boston, the *Susan* of New York, and a large full-rigged clipper ship out of New Jersey, the *Kate Prince*. The *Lizzie M. Stacy*, another schooner out of Boston, was last.

On the eighth of November (the same day President Lincoln was reelected) the *D. Godfrey* fell for the subterfuge of a British ensign flown from the rebel's peak. Bound for Valparaíso, Chile, she carried two hundred barrels of prime beef in her hold, as well as a shipment of tobacco. Both were valuable commodities but were buried deep beneath forty thousand board feet of lumber. The plundering rebels could only be grateful for the role the cargo played in the barque's burning.

"She was an old vessel," said Lining, "and she burned very rapidly, making a very brilliant bonfire."

"It was an imposing scene," Hunt agreed. "Darkness had settled around us when the rigging and sails took fire, but every rope could be seen distinctly as upon a painted canvas, as the flames made their way from the deck, and writhed upward like fiery serpents. Soon the yards came thundering down by the run as the lifts and halyards yielded to the devouring element, the standing rigging parted like blazing flax, and the spars simultaneously went by the board and left the hulk wrapped from stem to stern in one fierce blaze, like a floating, fiery furnace."

The loquacious mate's description of the rebels' unwilling guests as they watched the scene from the deck of the *Shenandoah* was equally wordy and fairly oozed with noble posturing:

*That was a vessel which has done her duty well for forty years," said [the
D. Godfrey's captain] to one of my brother officers. "She has faced old
Boreas in every part of the world, in the service of her master, and after
such a career, to be destroyed by men, on a calm night, in this tropical sea,
is too bad—too bad!"*

*"It is but one of the results of the terrible war raging at home," re-
marked one of the ladies who had been a silent witness of the scene.
"Would to God it is over! That the destruction of life and property by sea
and land might cease."*

*"War is a bad thing, there's no denying it," resumed the Captain;
"bad enough on land, where at least you've a solid foundation under you,
but infinitely worse at sea, where it destroys the few planks that you
have learned to trust to keep you from going to Davy Jones's. There is
no sight so awful to a sailor as a ship on fire . . . but there is no
use grumbling."*

Dr. Lining saw less of Rhett and Scarlett in the scene than Hunt,
noting only that "the *Charter Oak* ladies seemed to enjoy the capture
very much, and seemed highly delighted at the misfortunes of their
countrymen."

In spite of Cornelius's romantic ramblings, no one seemed truly
sorry to see the *D. Godfrey* go. Samuel Hallett, the master, had been
planning to sell the ship as soon as they reached Valparaíso, and almost
all of his crew joined the *Shenandoah* shortly after boarding the raider,
including one black man, John Williams, who went to work as a cook.*
A short conversation with the Confederates was all that was necessary
for their conversion. With the new additions, the raider's deck department now numbered thirty-five. The *Shenandoah* was up to nearly half
of her normal complement, but with forty prisoners on board,
Commander Waddell began to worry that trouble might be brewing.
Such a crowd of captives could, if aroused, make a credible rush for

*Various accounts give the name of the *D. Godfrey's* master as Hallett, Hallet, and Halleck.

the ship. Against the advice of his officers, he decided to dispose of the prisoners.

Two days later the log notes the sighting of a sail with the appearance of a Yankee. Steam was raised and the order to give chase was issued. The "Yankee" proved to be a Danish brig. The *Anna Jane* was bound for Rio, and for the consideration of a barrel of beef, one of biscuits, and a fine chronometer from one of the prizes, her captain agreed to carry eight of the prisoners to Argentina.

Captains Staples and Hallett, their mates, and a couple of other potential troublemakers were shifted aboard, "though I doubt," worried Lining, "the wisdom of letting them go at this time, as it is very important for us to keep our movements unknown for some time, and these men may surmise our destination and will certainly describe our ship, her armaments, and etc. [to the authorities]."

Nowhere does Waddell indicate that at this time he was aware that the crack in his authority born of his initial reluctance to begin the voyage shorthanded was growing—that so early in the voyage, his own officers found his judgment suspect. Some, like Lining, found fault no matter what their commander did. When Captain Gilman and his ladies were not put aboard the Danish ship for Argentina, the surgeon griped out of the other side of his mouth, saying that "as any ship that we meet will in all probability be a Yankee, and therefore a prize, I don't see any use in keeping them." In truth, Waddell—ever considerate of the wants and needs of his female passengers—had agreed to keep them aboard in hopes of finding a ship bound for California, in order to see them returned home rather than stranded on a foreign shore.*

A FEW HOURS after saying good-bye to their more recalcitrant prisoners the commander and surgeon found something to agree on. When

---

*Other accounts say the Dane refused to take them out of superstition. In the 1800s many mariners still considered women to be a jinx aboard a ship. "In fact," countered Lining, "they are so comfortable that they don't *want* to leave!"

the brig *Susan* out of New York was overtaken, the deck officer reported to Waddell that she looked like a steamer. Once on deck, the commander declared the distant vessel a "curious looking thing."

"She was one of the funniest looking craft I ever saw," agreed Lining, "very deeply laden, with a wheel on the lee side something like a steamboat." The wheel which had caused the lookout to pronounce her a steamer was in fact a series of buckets attached to a shaft which in turn was fastened to the *Susan's* pump. As the vessel moved through the water, the buckets turned the shaft, which in turn pumped the slow, leaky vessel out.

"An ingenious machine," Waddell pronounced, tongue in cheek. "The patent should be preserved."

Deeply laden with a cargo of Cardiff coal, the brig was bound for the Rio Grande du Sol in Brazil. The odds did not favor her making it.

"She leaked badly, and was the dullest sailer I had ever seen," said Waddell. "Really she moved so slowly that barnacles grew on her bottom, and it was simply impossible for her crew to pump her out as fast as the water made." Three of her deck hands jumped aboard the *Shenandoah* and volunteered to join as soon as the raider came alongside. Even the master, a German named Hanson, offered to throw in his lot with the Confederates. Waddell rejected the overture because Hanson was a Jew, saying none of the other officers would be willing to share their quarters with him.

It did not take long to plunder the *Susan.* There was little on board anyone wanted, other than a pair of dogs, which were taken as pets for the men. After the carpenter was sent on board to knock a hole in the hull, the scrofulous craft settled quickly, going down by the bow. A note in the *Shenandoah's* log set her value, with cargo, at a mere $5,436.

ALL THE NEXT DAY the raider ran south, edging toward the equator before a series of stiff squalls. Lining was feeling low, perhaps as a result of a conversation he had with the captive master Gilman, who described to him how the "Digger" Indians of California were being exterminated. Lining might have been thinking of the carnage being wrought in parts of his own new country when he lamented of the Golden State that "a war is [being] made on men, women and children," agonizing that "none are spared—and it is considered better if more *women* are killed!" In the wardroom, the other officers whiled away the time over checkers and chess. Lieutenant Whittle won consistently at the latter. At sunset, the sky turned a brilliant red.

"Sail ho!" cried a lookout, pointing away to the southwest. Low on the horizon, a large, fast-moving ship was standing away on the port tack. Waddell made a quick calculation and then gave orders for the chase, reckoning a course that would bring the stranger within hailing distance around midnight. Throughout the dark hours of the pursuit, many of the crew—and a few of the officers—muttered among themselves, concerned that so large a vessel would turn out to be a Federal cruiser.

"This was our first night chase," wrote Waddell, "and few eyes were closed, so curious were many to know the character of the stranger. Some doubted if we would ever see her again, while others thought it might be fortunate for the *Shenandoah* if we never did." Of the nervous officers, he added wryly, "Croakers can be found in every class."

A few minutes after midnight, the accuracy of his navigation and judgment proved itself when a full-rigged ship hove out of the darkness into view. Lieutenant Whittle shouted across to ask its identity. A voice shouted back that it was the *Kate Prince,* home ported in New Jersey. Like the *Susan,* she was outbound from Cardiff, Wales, with a cargo of coal.

It being dark and the seas up from the day of squalls, Waddell designated his best men to organize a boarding party. There was no shortage of volunteers eager to join Lieutenant Whittle and Smith-Lee. A ship as large as the *Kate Prince* was a valuable prize, and in theory, at the end of the war, when the total value of all the captured ships and cargoes was to be shared out among the men, there would be, as Cornelius Hunt had written, "wealth, fame, and glory to be earned."

The clipper ship was a plum. A large, juicy plum. Whittle and his gang leaped aboard. What followed next could only be explained as the result of two very different sets of circumstances: either Whittle, Smith-Lee, or both were extraordinarily charismatic men, moving through the crowd gathered at the *Kate Prince*'s gangway with messianic charm, stopping here and there to plant a gracious word or two before disappearing down into the captain's cabin, where they met and instantly wooed a young woman; or (and this seems more likely, since they were only gone half an hour) the *Kate Prince* was a hell-ship, a floating house of misery in the grip of a monstrous despot. Given the news Whittle and Lee brought back to the *Shenandoah*, either scenario is sensible, because of the twenty-one sailors on board the clipper, *all* had declared themselves Confederate sympathizers and asked to join the raider. And the young lady (who was the captain's own wife) was also eager to surrender. She told Whittle she wanted to see the *Kate Prince* burned.

It was a moment of monstrous fortune. To claim a prize valued at forty thousand dollars and nearly double the size of the crew with a score of eager, willing men was not just easy pickings—it was a whole bushel of perfect fruit. But the clipper's cargo manifest held a worm. The coal, bound for Bahia in Brazil, was owned by a British firm. And unlike the *Alina*, the *Kate Prince*'s papers were duly notarized. There was no doubt the coal was a neutral cargo. Waddell had to let her go.

"This, I think, was a great mistake," moaned Lining. "A ship worth so much was ransomed for the sake of a cargo not worth over seventeen thousand dollars at the most. Better to have burned her and let our government settle about the cargo afterwards."

The clipper's captain quickly agreed to the bond, due six months after a peace settlement between the United States and the Confederate States of America. As part of the agreement he also assented to take the rest of Waddell's prisoners, including the *Charter Oak* ladies, who, as Lining put it, "seemed rather unwilling to go; they have been treated, while on board, with every consideration, [and] have never lived so well in their lives."

Morning was coming on as the *Kate Prince*'s master gave the order to get under way. And to show there were no hard feelings, he sent two barrels of potatoes over to the *Shenandoah* as a parting gift.

THE RAIDER'S NEXT "CAPTURE" was even more muddled. Before noon they had overtaken two more sails, a brigantine and a barque, both of which carried English colors, and continued on in pursuit of a third, a barque that gave every appearance of being a Yankee. The log notes that at "12 m." the chase showed "Buenos Aryes" colors.* Suspicious, Waddell ordered a gun fired to bring her around.

"And now took place the most curious [illegible] of circumstances, making the greatest mess I have ever known," wrote Lining. "The barque proved to be the 'Adelaide,' formerly the 'Adelaide Pendergast,' Capt. Williams, bound from N.Y. to Rio with a cargo of flour. It was evident that she had been put under the [Argentine] flag for some purpose, the only question was, was it a bona fide transfer."

Williams, the captain, was not much of a liar and did some "tall swearing" before finally relenting and admitting that the ship was not actually owned by an Argentinian.

"It appears that the barque is the property of a Mr. Pendergast of Baltimore, Maryland," said Lining. Even though Maryland was technically a Yankee state, Pendergast was known to be "a good Southerner, who to save his property from being seized by the Yankees put his barque under the Buenos Ayrian flag, making a fictitious transfer of his vessel."†

---

*"m." stood for "meridian" or "local noon." The most important navigational fix of the day was taken at the moment when the sun reached its zenith before descending into the afternoon. Latitude was determined by the sun's angle above the horizon at that time, while longitude was determined by comparing the time difference between "local noon" and the ship's chronometer, which was set for the Greenwich meridian. The Greenwich meridian is the theoretical north-south line that passes through Greenwich, England, from which all east and west measurements are made. This also explains why raiders always seized a ship's chronometer; it was usually the most precious, easily transported item on board.

†Many Marylanders considered themselves Southerners, even though the slaveholding state never seceded from the Union. Since it was never secessionist, it was also exempt from the Emancipation Proclamation, and slavery remained legal there for nearly two years after the end of the war.

But according to the ship's manifest, the cargo was owned by Messrs. Phipps and Company, a New York concern, which made it Yankee property. Unable to discern from the muddle of false statements and transfers whether he had caught a Yankee or not, Waddell determined to burn her and let the government settle with Mr. Pendergast.

"I was among those who went off to the prize," said Lining.

She had on board a good many Portuguese and their blanc [*sic*] faces, when they were told to take their things and go on board ours, was most ludicrous. She had a great many nice things such as hams, preserved fruits, etc., and we sent them all on board. When we had nearly got through we, or rather Bulloch, discovered a whole batch of letters, and gave them to me to take care of. Fortunately, I had got all I wanted off her, and came on board in one of the cargo boats and gave the letters to Capt. W. On opening them, what should come out but that Mr. Pendergast was not only the owner of this brig, but of the cargo also, and Messrs. Phipps name only appeared to shield them from the Yankee government. Now as Mr. P. was known to be a good Confederate at heart, we did not wish to destroy any of his property. Orders were immediately given to send back to her all that had been taken out of her. This was done, but it was found impossible to restore her to her original state. The cabin was much knocked to pieces in making preparation to burn her—kerosene oil had been thrown over her deck—tar and oil had been poured upon the flour in the forehold to light her quickly—a good many articles taken from her had been lost, or destroyed, and other injury had been done.

"We broke out all the skylights," added Mason. "And all kinds of combustibles [had been] piled up together in order to fire."

Captain Williams was only too glad to be bundled back aboard, even with his ship vandalized and stinking of kerosene. He asked only

for a barrel of sugar—he was low before the rebels pulled him over—
and enough lamp oil to keep away the dark. Brushing aside his captors'
regrets, he explained that insurance rates were still rising as a result of
the *Alabama*'s depredations and the *Adelaide* was not covered. He and
Mr. Pendergast would be happy just to save their ship. There was, however, one thing the Confederates could do for him; if he should be
stopped by a Yankee warship before reaching Brazil it would inevitably
come out that he had been set free by a rebel raider—a circumstance
suspicious enough to reveal his true sympathies, which could result in
the seizure of his ship.

"To remedy this we committed an unlawful act," remembered
Lining. "We bonded the *cargo*, although acknowledging the ship to be
under a neutral flag." The attempt to give Williams a get-out-of-jail-
free card was transparent, he worried, and "if this does not produce
some complication, or row I shall be very much surprised."

In his own memoirs Waddell skips over the embarrassing interlude
in three brief paragraphs. Cornelius Hunt mentions it only in passing.
Lining spoke for everyone after the *Adelaide* sailed away when he said
they were sorry to have left her so splintered and stinking. "But what
could we do? We could only write to Mr. Pendergast apologizing for
our mistake."

Like the *Charter Oak*, the *Lizzie M. Stacey* was a small, sleek
schooner out of Boston. And the next morning at 10 a.m., when her sail
was sighted to the southeast, she proved to be fast. According to a log
note entered in Irvine Bulloch's spare, neat hand, the wind was light
and the weather clear. Even after crowding on a cloud of royals, flying
jibs, spankers, and mainmast staysails, the *Shenandoah* was making only
three knots.

The Confederates swallowed their pride and resorted to the advantage of machinery—"Got up steam, lowered screw," notes the log—but
it still took until nearly four o'clock to catch the *Lizzie*.

"She was a splendid sailer," remarked Hunt, ". . . bound to the
Sandwich Islands, round the Cape of Good Hope." Loaded with

"shooks" of soft pine and thirty tons of iron, the little schooner was to be sold on arrival in Honolulu.*

A warning shot brought her around. A boat under the charge of Lieutenant Grimball was sent to seize her. (The appearance-conscious Midshipman Mason should have been happy; only that morning, for the first time in the voyage, all of the men had turned out in proper gray uniforms. Where the uniforms came from is unclear, but seizing the *Lizzie* with a properly dressed boarding crew must surely have spared him the embarrassment he felt during the ragtag seizure of Captain Staples's *Alina*.) Lieutenant Grimball ordered the schooner's officers to the raider.

Captain William Archer—"the most unapproachable curmudgeon I ever encountered," according to Hunt—stormed aboard. His mate, a wild Irishman, was hard on his heels. Both sneered at Hunt's compliment to them for venturing to sea in such a small boat. Archer shouted, "Shiver me timbers! If there ain't the most lubberly set of sailors afloat on these latitudes that I ever fell in with," adding a tough old nautical oath or two by way of emphasis. "Why day before yesterday, I run across the bows of a big English ship bound to Australia, and all hands made a rush forward when I hove in sight as though I'd been the Sea Serpent or some other almighty curiosity. They invited me to come on board but there was a stiff breeze blowing at the time, and I'd no notion of losing a good run for the sake of showing off a little before a lot of chaps who seem to think nothing less than a seventy-four [gun frigate] is safe to cross the ocean in."

"Faix, and the ould man was right," remarked the first mate aside to one of [the *Shenandoah*'s] men; "the dirthy blackguards wouldn't have appreciated the compliment of a visit from us.

"And what's more, my hearty," the mate hissed at Hunt, "if we'd had

---

*The Sandwich Islands, or "Owyhee" as Hawaii was known, was an independent nation at the time. If the *Lizzie M. Stacey* had made it to the islands unmolested or if the sale had taken place before she departed Boston, she would have been considered a foreign "bottom" and safe from the attentions of the Confederacy. The intended buyer was C. Brewer and Company—still one of the largest and most powerful corporations in Hawaii.

ten guns aboard there, you wouldn't have got us without a bit of a shindy, or if the breeze had been a bit stiffer, we'd given her the square sail, and all hell couldn't have caught her."

"There was truth in this," agreed Hunt. "Had she been armed the *Lizzie M. Stacey* would certainly never have surrendered without a tussle, and with a favorable wind, I am inclined to believe she would have shown us a clean pair of heels."

The *Lizzie* was such a quick sailer that Waddell briefly considered fitting her out with one of the thirty-two-pound Whitworth rifles and sending her out as a wide-ranging scout in search of more victims. But he was still too short of men to spare a crew. Fortunately, with the exception of her truculent master and mate, most of the *Lizzie's* crew showed little reluctance to join the raider. Three of them—two seamen who accepted a signing bonus of six dollars, and the schooner's cook—accepted Waddell's offer. And Charles Hopkins, the cook, was black.*

A light-skinned mulatto from Baltimore, Hopkins was a freeman with no good reason to serve the Confederacy. Northern newspaper accounts later claimed he was brutalized, hung up by his thumbs until consenting, but Captain Archer, who certainly had reasons of his own to despise Waddell and his crew after seeing his ship sunk, declined to confirm this. "I did not see Hopkins hung up," he said. "I saw Hopkins walking about assisting the cook, *after* he was said to have been hung up." The source of the rumor seems to have been Hunt himself, who told another prisoner that Hopkins's shoulder blades had nearly been pulled out (which seems an unlikely abuse to have been suffered by someone who shortly thereafter was seen working with the huge, unwieldy pots and cauldrons used to feed 150 men). Perhaps when faced with the loss of his berth aboard the *Lizzie*, simple survival demanded

---

*An article in the *Creswick and Clunes Advertiser* from 1865 claimed Hopkins and Williams, the black crewman impressed from the *D. Godfrey* a week before the *Lizzie M. Stacey* was captured, knew each other, having parted company at a boardinghouse in New York only a few weeks before. Their surprise at seeing each other, the paper reported, "was quite comical."

he take the job. A bunk on the *Shenandoah* paid eighteen dollars a month.

In any case, the strange fact of a black man volunteering for duty aboard a Confederate ship serves to point up the complicated—and often contradictory—role race and slavery played throughout the war. It was anything but black and white. Though it reached full bloom in Dixie, America's experience with slavery germinated in the Northern states. The first slaves to arrive in North America came in 1619 aboard a Dutch warship that sold twenty "negars" seized from a Spanish "blackbirder" to the colonists of Chesapeake Bay. Within a few years, slave ships operating out of New England had become common. Profits were enormous. Bodies purchased for a few dollars in Africa resold for many times their original price through the auction pens of the West Indies. In the beginning, the majority were delivered to the sweltering cane fields of the Caribbean or directly to the factories of New England, and it was not until 1794, when Eli Whitney's invention of the cotton gin automated the removal of cotton's tiny, clinging seeds and large-scale plantings became profitable, that the vile practice became a cornerstone of Southern society. With profitability came the large plantations and a massive increase in the demand for slaves, and what had been a stream of black flesh moving from east to west across the Atlantic became a flood. By 1860, more than four million Africans were irrigating the South with their blood.

But in the years leading up to the war even Lincoln himself, during his first campaign for the presidency, denied that abolishing slavery would be part of his platform. And after the conflict started a Yankee brigadier named Schleich proposed that the North finance its part in the war by transporting captured slaves to Cuba to be resold.*

Events such as these added greatly to Southern cynicism regarding the North's desire to free the slaves. "For two years they waged war

---

*Schleich, a former Ohio state senator, was a jackass of the first order. A drunkard who once chastised General George McClellan for caring too much about the lives of enlisted men, he was reported to have said, "What are a thousand lives when principal is at stake? Men's lives shouldn't be thought of at such time. [They] amount to nothing."

against the South without attempting to interfere with slavery," growled Waddell. "It was only when they found the negro could be used for killing the white people of the South and serve as breastworks for Northern white troops that they declared him free. . . . they cared nothing for the unhappy negro; they preferred his destruction to that of their white troops."

Meanwhile, General Lee was setting free more than a thousand slaves who had belonged to his deceased father-in-law and planning the manumission of his own. Lieutenant Whittle's own father, Captain William Conway Whittle, had served in the Federal navy before the start of the war and spent two years on the coast of Africa suppressing the slave trade as commander of a sloop of war. In Louisiana, free blacks formed volunteer regiments to act as a home guard against the possibility of a Northern invasion.

But none of this justifies what the Reverend John Wesley called "the execrable sum of all villainies." For every regiment of blacks devoted to the Confederacy, by the end of the war there were entire battalions, legions, *armies* desperate to give their lives for freedom. Whatever image apologists for Southern slavery might wish to foster of "happy darkies" living under benign masters, the fact that more than a million slaves were willing to risk everything to escape to freedom must offset it. Nearly 180,000 runaway slaves served in the Union army, many with unfathomable bravery, in units like the Fifty-fourth Massachusetts Volunteer Infantry, which threw itself time and again against the seemingly impregnable parapets at Fort Wagner in South Carolina. Acts such as these can only be seen as a reaction to what must truly be one of humanity's greatest crimes.

A DEAD WHALE, said Waddell, is "no nose-gay." As he wrote in his memoir, "It is an offensive exhalation too horrible to relate."

He was speaking of the *Edward*, the first whaling ship the *Shenandoah* caught. Three weeks after burning the *Lizzie M. Stacy* and sailing south across the equator, the raider had spotted the whaler drifting, sails furled, lashed fore and aft to forty tons of dead whale. The first thing a crew always did upon killing a whale was remove the jaw and baleen, the initial step in the process of "cutting in" or butchering a captured animal, and the sailors aboard the *Edward*, out of New Bedford, were doing just that when the lookout in the *Shenandoah*'s crosstrees spotted her. After a whale was struck and killed, the carcass was towed alongside, where a chain was passed around the "small," or narrowest part of the body, just forward of the tail fluke, and secured to a stout post. Next, a platform of planks was lowered alongside, from which the crew could shackle another chain around the left pectoral fin. This second chain was shackled to the cutting tackle, a huge two-sheave block even larger than those the *Shenandoah* needed for her guns, riven with rope five inches in diameter. The cutting tackle line was run forward to the windlass, and strain was applied to the fin. Hacking and tearing with huge, heavy blades, the crew would heave at the fin until it came loose at the "knuckle joint," then use the appendage—still connected to the carcass by a layer of muscle and skin—to gradually roll the whale into a prone position. Next would come removal of the "headbone" and its baleen in preparation for a laborious, dangerous operation that used the cutting tackle to strip the skin and blubber from a whale in one long, continuous spiral called a "blanket piece."

At this point it was customary for the man who had first struck the whale to tie a "monkey rope" around his waist to keep from slipping into the frigid water, then lean out over the whale and hack a hole through the flesh just below the spout holes. Another chain called a "head strap" would be passed through this hole, and the head strap would be shackled to a third tackle, which was then hoisted skyward while the "monkey" cut at the two-foot-thick jawbone with an ax, hacking like a lumberjack until it cracked and tore away. It was a gruesome, greasy operation that often saw the ax man plunged up to his neck in cold water alongside the heaving ship but which allowed the two-thousand-pound mass of jawbone and baleen to be hoisted on deck whole. Once on board, the baleen would be peeled from the jawbone, tied into bundles, and stored in the "bone room" until time allowed for it to be brought back on deck for cleaning. On a busy trip, with its unending labor of chasing, striking, hauling, butchering, and "trying out," or rendering, the whales' blubber into oil, this might not be for weeks, and the spoliation of accumulated gum tissue, blood, skin, and blubber clinging to the baleen accounted for much of the odor that assailed the noses of those aboard the *Shenandoah* when she pulled alongside.

"The crew was so intensely occupied with the whale that [we] came within easy range unobserved," Waddell chuckled. In spite of the nauseating stench, he probably felt relieved. It was the fourth of December and the *Edward* was the first American ship they had seen since burning the *Lizzie M. Stacy.*

The run south from the equator had been exhilarating, wrote Lining, with the ship "bowling along most pleasantly" in the southeast trades, hoping to intercept shipping bound from San Francisco to New York via Cape Horn. But once again, the leisure of trade-wind sailing had given way to complaints. Lining and Whittle were having long talks about "matters in general and our skipper in particular," and a disgruntled entry in the doctor's journal noted, "We are going faster now than we have ever done before under sail—But we find whenever night comes on, and she is going her nine or ten knots, [Waddell] begins to get uneasy, can't sleep, gets fidgety, and then takes in sail," slowing the ship's progress for no reason.* Henry Alcott, the sailmaker, had been grumbling and malingering, and when an officer tried to scare him out of it by threatening to have him dropped at the nearest port, the "good-for-nothing, lazy cur" had assented sullenly, "as if he cared not a thing."†

In context, the air of discontent was understandable. The crew had spotted several sails, Hunt noted, "but our captain, for some reason best known to himself, did not give chase to any of them." And so far over the course of the month since the *Shenandoah* had left the Madeiras, they had mugged the wrong ship once, let another, genuinely valuable prize go, and sunk a leaky old coal scow whose only assets had been a pair of mangy dogs; and the *Lizzie M. Stacy* had nearly destroyed them when, after she was set on fire with all her sails set, a sudden gust of wind sent the little schooner surging toward them. There was, Lining dryly noted, a moment of "immense excitement" when it seemed the

---

*In truth Waddell's decision to shorten sail made good sense; it reduced the chance that the already overworked crew would have to be called on deck during the night, which could only have added to their exhaustion.

†Alcott probably deserved more empathy than the officers were giving him. By this time, he had been at sea and at war for several years. At least one of the ships he had sailed on (the *Alabama*) had been shot out from under him, and if post-traumatic stress disorder had yet to be defined, and he was not suffering the depression and lethargy associated with that condition, he nonetheless had a valid claim to being simply tired.

blazing schooner might foul them, until Whittle took the deck and calmly issued orders to back the yards and wore the ship around, dodging the fiery *Lizzie* the way a matador sidesteps a charging bull. Only the *Alina*, valued at ninety-five thousand dollars, had been a worthy prize. The combined value of all the other victims did not equal it.

No one was giving Waddell much credit for having started out with an inadequately provisioned, undermanned ship that was now, through a combination of bluster, luck, and charm (and perhaps a bit of bullying), fully armed, staffed with a crew of forty-one, and stuffed to the gunwales with delectable edibles and comfortable beds. For Waddell, the *Edward* was a timely distraction. Only that morning, before coming upon the whaler, they had spotted a sail that appeared to be Yankee built, hoisted a Union flag as a subterfuge, and stood in chase of it. To further the deception, Waddell ordered his officers and crew to doff their gray caps and uniforms and don every article of blue clothing they could muster. But the effort was wasted; the quarry was Italian. Then the frustrated rebels had a scare when a long, low vessel with the up-and-down stem of a gunboat rose over the horizon.

"Something on deck abaft the mainsail had the appearance of a smokestack lowered," remembered Lining. Like the *Shenandoah*, a lowered smokestack meant a hidden capacity for speed. "We hauled up and stood off on the wind . . . and as the wind was fresh and we were under all sail except studding-sails, we went about ten knots through the water, so we soon left our friend behind and ran him out of sight."

A few hours after they outran the threatening stranger, the island of Tristan da Cunha was sighted forty miles to weather.* The water was red with algae; there were more fish and albatross about; they had arrived on the South Atlantic whaling grounds. At 5 p.m., when the *Edward* was sighted, she never had a chance to escape.

"I lay beside her for two days supplying the [*Shenandoah*] with deficiencies," Waddell wrote. Only four months into a cruise planned to last for four years, the New Bedford whaler was still stuffed with pro-

---

*In sailing parlance, something "to weather" is upwind. Downwind is "leeward" or "looward."

visions of excellent quality. "[We] removed 100 barrels of beef and as many of pork, besides several thousand pounds of ship's biscuit, the best I have ever seen." There was also a great deal of tobacco and soap, both badly needed aboard the *Shenandoah*. There were casks of butter, barrels of flour, and best of all for the ordinary seamen, a deal of new "slops," clothing meant to be parceled out (for a price) to the whalemen over the course of the long voyage as their own wore out.

Seizing the greasy prize did not completely allay the officers' sniping at their commander. During the middle of the second day, while the prize crew was still aboard the *Edward* looting, another sail was seen a little abaft of the *Shenandoah*'s port beam. Waddell gave the order to give chase, but just as they got under way a squall moved in and hid the ship from view. In the excitement, no one had bothered to take an exact bearing on the stranger, and there were a number of differing opinions as to where she lay.

"The captain had his idea and went off in that direction," said Lining. "Whittle, Grimball, and myself thought he was heading to go far astern of her, but the captain thought he was right and went ahead." After half an hour the squall cleared and the sail was sighted just where the officers had said.

"The captain was much put out to find that he was wrong," continued Lining, "and told me he would have given a great deal to have been right, as we seemed so much to rejoice in his mistake." In any case, the pursuit turned out to be in error; the stranger hoisted British colors when they came in range.

Returning to the *Edward*, the rebels finished emptying her. The last things taken were the longboats, two of which were new and replaced Waddell's old and damaged ones. Before the match was struck and the oil-soaked whaler burst into flames, Dr. Lining took the opportunity to go on board the *Edward* to satisfy his curiosity about whaling ships, but he took one good whiff of the horrid smell and came off again.*

---

*Few of the *Shenandoah*'s crew had any familiarity with whaling. Among these was Master's Mate Joshua Minor, who joined the Confederate forces after a Yankee whaler he was work-

Wrapped in the odor of putrid flesh, he had to wonder at the men who lived with the stench every moment of their lives for years on end.

Once on the whaling grounds, whalers rose day after day to put on the same rancid, greasy clothing, then go out in small open boats to chase the huge animals.* For his troubles—which included the back-breaking labor of towing the whale back to the ship, cutting it in, and sweating for hours or days over the roaring try pots used to render blubber into oil, and between whales, the endless boredom and labor of long, dangerous voyages fraught with tropical storms and polar ice—a man sailing "before the mast" (i.e., in the forecastle, where all the common sailors lived, ate, and slept) could look forward to a wage determined as a "lay," or share of the profits, with able and ordinary seamen receiving from $\frac{1}{100}$ to $\frac{1}{160}$ of a voyage's net. Captains, mates, boatsteerers, and coopers were paid between $\frac{1}{8}$ and $\frac{1}{100}$ of the profits, depending on their experience, but new, inexperienced hands and cabin boys had to settle for a "long lay" between $\frac{1}{160}$ and $\frac{1}{200}$. Yankee owners were infamous for increasing profits by cutting corners, and even these minuscule portions would be further reduced by voracious "land sharks," agents who contracted with owners to supply their ships with crews. In addition to being paid a commission for each warm body, the land sharks fattened their own purses by levying exorbitant charges against the seaman for transportation to the ship, food and lodging while in port, and whatever articles of clothing he needed to round out his kit. A man sailing before the mast must even supply his own mattress, a straw pad called a "donkey's breakfast," for which the land sharks took a bite too. And only at the end of the voyage, after the owners had deducted the cost of all food, equipment, supplies, etc., plus charges for wharfage, piloting, agent's commissions, tow boats, watchman's fees, and any other costs they could come up with before determining the net profit, would the lay be di-

---

ing on was captured and sunk by the *Alabama*. Minor worked his way up to an officer's rank aboard the *Alabama* and after it was sunk volunteered for service aboard the *Shenandoah*.
*Between whales, the whalers did occasionally manage to wash themselves and their clothes. The best cleanser available was a strong lye made from the ashes of burned whale skin mixed with human urine.

vided—but not until a final pound was carved from the seaman's flesh by charging him for any tobacco or clothing he had drawn from the ship's slop chest during the voyage. In the years leading up to the Civil War, when prices slumped and most of the world's whale stocks were in decline, the earnings of an ordinary seaman on a whaling voyage averaged less than twenty cents a day—explaining, perhaps, why sailors of a dozen nations did not hesitate to sign on board ships like the *Shenandoah,* even when they were engaged in a civil war. Most were as overworked as black field hands, under similarly deplorable conditions and with as little chance to escape. For the common sailor, signing onto a whaler was often an act of desperation. Of the *Edward*'s crew of twenty-five, most asked for a berth aboard the raider, but only one, a British cooper, was allowed to join. "The rest were Yankees, whom we did not want," noted Midshipman Mason, "or Dagos [Portuguese] who are not worth having."* Waddell had them all thrown in chains, then ordered the helmsman to steer for Tristan da Cunha Island.

WADDELL DID NOT BOTHER dropping anchor after the *Shenandoah* rounded the northwest corner of the island at 7:30 on the morning after the *Edward* was burned. The weather had turned foggy and calm, and now the three longboats they had replaced with the *Edward*'s whaleboats were towing easily along behind. Ahead, the precipitous green wall of a mountain rose into a bank of low clouds. At the mouth of a valley spilling down from the mountain a dozen simple grass-roofed houses squatted on a bench of level land. In the middle of the village, a British flag strung from a pole hung motionless in the still morning air. It was the cruiser's first landfall since Madeira.

---

*Waddell remembered the crew of the *Edward* as being made up largely of Kanakas, or Sandwich Islanders. Mason's reference to Portuguese may be more reliable, since his notes were written within days of the events, while Waddell's were in some cases recorded years later. It may also be that neither took much care to distinguish between the races—a particularly narrow outlook for a mariner, since both Hawaii and Portugal had much longer and more important seafaring histories than the Confederacy.

"[This] was the island of Tristan da Cunha," wrote Midshipman Mason, "a small part of which only is inhabited." Two other islands adjoining it, Nightingale and Inaccessible, were both uninhabited. "It has about thirty-five inhabitants all told," he continued, "and they never see anyone but the whalemen who come in there from time to time to recruit and to get fresh provisions."

Waddell ordered the engine stopped two miles from shore. "Ready the boats," he commanded. Whittle instructed the prisoners to gather what little clothing they had been allowed to salvage from the *Edward.* While the prisoners were being loaded into the longboats, a small boat pulled out from shore. Within minutes it was alongside.

"In charge of this boat was a *Yankee,*" groaned Mason. "For you are sure to find some of that race all over the world." The boatman offered to sell them fresh fruit and vegetables. Waddell grumbled that "he was after trade." (In fairness, the despised Yankee boatman had lived on the island for nearly twenty-five years, having deserted a whaling ship to escape the deplorable conditions.)

Lining was a bit more charitable, remarking of the peddler and his companions only that "they are entirely cut off from the world, and live in the most primitive style. . . . They know nothing of wars or rumors of war, and so dense was their ignorance of what was going on in the world around them, that it was impossible to make them understand anything about the war in America."

Hunt agreed. "It was the first time any of the Islanders had seen the flag that floated at our peak, and to what nationality it belonged they could not imagine. Nor was their astonishment in any wise diminished when we informed them that our ship was a Confederate cruiser, and we had thirty-five prisoners which we proposed contributing to their population"—which led to the following remarkable exchange*:

"And where the devil did you get your prisoners?" asked one of the mystified villagers.

---

*Most accounts give the number of prisoners landed as twenty-eight.

"From a whaler not far from here," replied one of the *Shenandoah*'s officers.

"Just so, to be sure; and what became of the whaler?"

"We burned her."

"Whew! Is that the way you dispose of what vessels you fall in with?"

"If they belong to the United States; not otherwise."

"Well, my hearty, you know your own business, but my notion is that these sort of pranks will get you into the devil's own muss before you are through with it. What your quarrel with the United States is I don't know, but I swear I don't believe they will stand for this kind of work."

The villagers' astonishment, Hunt recalled, "and their conviction that our calling was not likely to be a very safe one," did not stand in the way of what he and Waddell saw as the islanders' mercenary, Yankee-like proclivities: a bargain was made to buy fresh beef from the island for eight cents a pound, to be paid for with flour at the rate of seven.

"In this he got the advantage of us," said Lining. "Selling us his beef at a high rate and getting flour cheap." The sharp dealing did not stop Waddell from putting in an order for as much milk, sheep, fowl, and garden provisions as the islanders could spare.

In truth, the island's small population was composed not only of New Englanders, but also Englishmen, South Africans, immigrants from Saint Helena Island, and a Dutch castaway named Peter Green who had anglicized his name from Peter Groen after being shipwrecked there in 1836 and becoming the de facto governor of the colony. Waddell had to negotiate with Green for the maintenance of the prisoners.

Surgeon Lining recorded that "in consideration of these twenty-eight prisoners being put upon the isle, [we sent in] four barrels of beef, four of pork and 1,680 pounds of bread." He also sent a note ashore to the captain of the marooned prisoners telling him that the victuals were for their use, "because I did not want it ever said that we left them on a nearly destitute isle to the charity of such poor people."

Hunt had an altogether different take on the ethics of marooning prisoners. "Heretofore," he said,

> [our prisoners] had been transferred to some prize selected for the purpose and sent on their way . . . but now for the first time we had left our captured foes on an island in the South Atlantic, thousands of miles from their homes, where they might have to remain for many weary months, ere a passing ship would take them off. . . . None of us were quite satisfied with the part we were necessitated to play, but I question whether our Yankee acquaintances stood much in need of our sympathy. After all, they had the free range of a charming island, where reigned perennial summer; and besides, there were a number of the gentler sex in want of mates . . . and where there are pretty women so circumstanced, there can sailors be happy.

By two o'clock a light breeze was fluttering out of the northwest and Waddell gave hurried orders to get under way. It had been over a month since the sinking of the *Alina,* time enough for word of the *Shenandoah's* depredations to have reached Federal warships in the South Atlantic. After clearing the island, Waddell instructed the helmsman to hold a course of "east by north and a half north" to make it appear they were sailing for Cape Town at the southern tip of Africa. Once out of sight below the horizon, he ordered the ship's heading altered to "south by east and ¼ east" and steered for the "Roaring Forties," a belt of fierce winds and giant waves that churn unimpeded around the bottom of the world. By blowing past Africa, he hoped to lay a false trail and reach the whaling grounds of the South Pacific off Australia.

The subterfuge was timely. Behind him, on the coast of Brazil, Captain William H. Clark of the U.S. man-of-war *Onward* was composing a dispatch to Secretary of the Navy Gideon Welles:

From Bahia, Brazil

Sir: I have the honor to inform you that after provisioning ship for six months at Rio de Janeiro, by request of the U.S. minister and Commander Rodgers of the U.S.S. Iroquois, I proceeded to Santos [Brazil], at which port I received news of the presence of the rebel pirate Shenandoah on this coast. . . . She captured the American ship Kate Prince in latitude 2 degrees 30' north, longitude 28 degrees 30' west, on the 12th day of November, and as she had an English cargo, bonded her for $40,000.

In Santos, Clark had been confronted by the frightened master of the *Kate Prince,* who begged Clark to convoy him to such a distance off the land as might be necessary to prevent the *Kate Prince* from being captured again. Clark, evidently a man of some courage, was game for both convoy duty and pursuit of the rebel, in spite of a warning from the American minister to Brazil that "the *Shenandoah* is said to have two guns of longer range than the *Onward* and if this is so the pirate has only to place herself to windward of the *Onward* and beyond the reach of her guns to render the destruction of your man-of-war certain."

Waddell had another advantage over the *Onward.* Clark had pulled into Santos in search of drinking water for his crew, but the rebel carried a coal-burning water maker capable of distilling freshwater from salt water, allowing her to stay at sea as long as her supply of coal held out.*

Five days after Captain Clark arrived in Santos, Commander C. R. P. Rodgers of the USS *Iroquois* made port in Montevideo, Uruguay, where he too learned for the first time of the existence of the rebel steamer, through an article in a Brazilian newspaper.

The war years had been hard on Rodgers's *Iroquois.* She had been launched in 1859 at a cost of slightly more than a quarter of a million dollars, and already the five-year-old ship's boilers were decaying and

---

*The water maker was a fantastic technological innovation. On older vessels, water carried in wooden casks quickly grew so foul that it became necessary to treat it with rum to make it palatable. A mixture of three parts water to one part rum was known as "grog."

encrusted with salt. Her canvas was minimal for a vessel her size, making her slow under sail, and the enlistment of a number of her seamen was running out. But her eleven-inch guns were more than a match for anything the *Shenandoah* carried, and if that were not enough, she also carried a hundred-pound "Parrot" rifle with a far greater range than the rebel's, as well as a sixty-pound rifle and a matched pair of forty-two-pound guns. If the *Iroquois* ever caught up with the rebels, her superior armament would hammer the *Shenandoah* to pieces. On December thirteenth, Commander Rodgers dispatched a message to Secretary of the Navy Gideon Welles informing him that he was "leaving without a moment's delay."

While Rodgers was slapping a makeshift patch on the *Iroquois*'s boilers, life grew quiet aboard the raider. Lining sighed, "The monotony of sea life begins again." The weather was misty but pleasant as the ship hammered south. Nonetheless, the doctor was in a "great funk." Waddell too was unhappy, and throughout the first night after leaving Tristan da Cunha could not sleep for thinking he heard a noise in the propeller wheel.

"So last night he went up to find out what it was," wrote Lining, "and sent Mr. O'Brien [the engineer] to do the same." Nothing could be found to account for the noise. And no one besides Waddell could hear it. To some of his underlings the commander's worrying seemed a sign of strain—or perhaps a lack of the mettle needed to deal with it. Fortunately, in addition to responsibility, the command of a vessel also carries with it the power to issue orders in the face of general disbelief, and after a second night of listening to the grinding between his ears, Waddell ordered the engineer to accompany him on a follow-up inspection. His sensitivity to the thousand tiny creaks, groans, and vibrations of his vessel was vindicated after they triced up the propeller. A crack was found running through a brass sleeve at the coupling.

Like most commanders, Waddell did not often share his thoughts with lesser officers, and from across the divide an uninformed Mason worried that "mysterious reports [are being] whispered about that we are no longer a steamer, that the screw was irreparably damaged."

Without propulsion, the crew worried that the raider would be an easy target for a Union cruiser. The *Iroquois* might be undercanvased, but in light airs, even patchy boilers had the advantage over a damaged screw. And if a Union warship did not find them, the chance of catching any more prizes was much reduced.

"For a long time it was uncertain whether the crack did not extend through the whole coupling, had which been the case the propeller would have been useless to us until another was cast." On closer inspection, Lining hoped for a better diagnosis; others muttered that the damage could be repaired only back in England.

Engineer O'Brien and his assistants went to work. It took two days to cut the roof off the engine room and rig up the spanker boom for a crane. The entire assembly—shaft, coupling, and wheel—was hoisted on deck. Everyone was relieved when Chief Engineer O'Brien decided that the crack did not extend completely through the coupling and could, with a bit of improvisation and the addition of several large screws, be prevented from failing completely.* But any such repair, O'Brien warned, would only be temporary. To depend on the jury-rigged coupling was to risk permanent damage to the stern post if it failed.

Cape Town was the only place short of Melbourne where permanent repairs could be made. And Cape Town was the first place any Union cruiser trailing them would look. "After turning the subject over in my mind," wrote Waddell, "I decided it best to cross the Indian Ocean under sail, hoping to keep company with good luck, for certainly I had been favored in overcoming difficulties during the seven preceding weeks."

His optimism was not shared by everyone. Australia was six thousand miles away. Years later, Waddell admitted that concerns other than purely military matters may have entered into his decision. "I desired to reach Melbourne in time to communicate with a mail steamer which

---

*The damage to the *Shenandoah*'s coupling was preexisting; O'Brien found signs of eight previous screws that had been concealed by the *Sea King*'s sellers.

would leave on the 26th of January." The regularly scheduled steamer was a rare opportunity to exchange letters with his wife.

Others too were pining for home, with some showing signs of the depression common among men living lives devoid of women. Still suspended in his funk, on December 11 Surgeon Lining wrote: "Sunday again, and how far from all my friends. . . . It has been three months exactly since I saw ['Miss Mary' and 'Miss Reid'] but I can see them now, how they looked . . . with their hair parted on the side of their heads, and how they had been amusing themselves dressing it. . . . When will I see them again?" Earlier in the voyage he had complained of pain in his eyes and not feeling very well. He spent entire days without rising from his bunk. During the hubbub over the damaged coupling, he scribbled in his journal that there was "nothing of interest going on," though they were shouldering the seas aside in what must have been an invigorating run. On three successive days, using the noon navigational fixes, Midshipman Mason logged distances of 165, 213, and 194 miles. Lieutenant Whittle, as always, was a stalwart, helping young Mason study German when he could. Assistant Surgeon McNulty was developing a taste for rum.

"But as yet we are all good friends," wrote Lining, "and have no quarreling. . . . Smith-Lee is the life of all . . . all the time getting off some joke or other on McNulty, who he referred to as 'a little deaf, but great in curing diseases of the ear.' "

On December 13 the raider crossed the 40th parallel, sliding into the Roaring Forties on a gentle breeze. One hopes they enjoyed it. By midnight the breeze had freshened to force 6 and Lieutenant Grimball was noting in the log "heavy seas," large waves and winds up to 33 miles per hour.

SEVEN

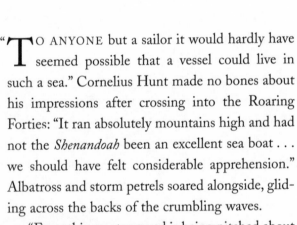

"TO ANYONE but a sailor it would hardly have seemed possible that a vessel could live in such a sea." Cornelius Hunt made no bones about his impressions after crossing into the Roaring Forties: "It ran absolutely mountains high and had not the *Shenandoah* been an excellent sea boat . . . we should have felt considerable apprehension." Albatross and storm petrels soared alongside, gliding across the backs of the crumbling waves.

"Everything not secured is being pitched about in fine style," said Lining. The seas had inflicted a string of misfortunes on Lieutenant Chew. "His *chez,* as he calls it [an upright closet taken from a prize] had capsized and made a perfect wreck of it. I went on deck to tell him of it, and his trunk, which he had up airing, made another capsize and sent some letters which he very much valued into the deep. With his trunk still overturned and with the wind blowing his things about, there he stood gazing at his letters, to the great danger of everything else going." Chew, a good-natured Missourian who was one of everyone's favorites, was a magnet for disasters. When accidents happened, they happened on his watch, and once, when the ship took an unexpected roll, Chew went sliding across the poop deck in a most unofficerlike fashion, only narrowly saving himself from a tumble over the side through some undignified scrambling. Waddell, who was watching, just shook his head in silent judgment.

"Everybody uncomfortable," wrote Lining. "Ship very uneasy. Shipping a good many seas."

It was Mason's first experience of bad weather at sea. "One night I was on watch from eight to twelve," he remembered, "and I had gone up on the poop to heave the log, when from bad steering or something or other she came up suddenly and took a tremendous sea over the starboard rail in the waist.* This tremendous volume of water came right off with a tremendous roar and as I watched it from the poop it seemed to carry everything before it." Two immense water casks weighing a thousand pounds apiece were picked up bodily and carried away, lashings and all. Young and inexperienced enough to revel in the excitement, the midshipman had a great laugh when a medicine chest crashed to the floor beneath his hammock, flooding the already awash room with vapors from a broken bottle of ether. The hammocks used by the ordinary seamen and junior officers were ideal in such weather, gimballing themselves to the heel of the ship. Senior officers leery of the indignity of scrambling butt-first in and out of the swinging nets were decidedly more uncomfortable in fixed bunks, which pitched and heaved with every corkscrewing motion of the ship. "Could not sleep," moaned Lining, "but just rolled around in my bunk, so this morning my neck and shoulders are perfectly sore." The plaintive entry ended with "blowing pretty heavily. . . . Nothing of interest going on."

---

*"Heaving the log" did not mean throwing the logbook overboard. Instead, a piece of wood attached to a long coil of line was pitched over the side and allowed to run free. The line was knotted at precisely measured intervals. Mason counted the knots as the line was hauled back, and the number of knots determined the boat's speed. Thus the use of the term "knots" for boat speed instead of "miles per hour."

Waddell too was having trouble sleeping. In the huge following seas, the ship's rudder kept slamming side to side, "making a most terrible row, jarring the whole after part of the ship, and making me think, sometimes, that the whole thing will be wrenched off."

"It makes such a noise that the captain would give $5,000 had he never taken command of this ship, so much is he worried and bothered," wrote Lining. Extra men were stationed at the relieving tackles in case the wheel ropes parted. The tackles restraining the heavy cannons were doubled and secured. Backstays and preventer-braces were set up to reinforce the mast and prevent an accidental jibe, and an order was issued to batten down the hatches. On the sixteenth, for the first time during the two and a half months of the voyage, readings of the barometric pressure were entered in the log. "We are taking on seas on both sides and up forward to the house," groaned Lining. "What a miserable thing a rolling ship is."

"To get a meal in a Christian fashion [is] the next thing to impossible," complained Hunt. Every time the Malay steward managed to get a dish on the table, the ship would give a heavy lurch and scatter the contents across the deck. On one occasion, after a soup tureen was pitched to the deck, a second, larger wave came "pouring down upon us like a cataract, and the remnant of our dinner previously disposed around the cabin floor by the first wave, was by the second, submerged under a couple of feet of water."

Roaring along under mizzen staysail, flying jib, and royal topsails, the cruiser flew at such speeds that by noon of the next day she had covered 243 miles. Shortly after noon on the seventeenth a wave of "mountainous dimensions" rose up behind the ship and surged down upon her "like a very demon of the ocean intent upon our destruction." The avalanche of water trembled the ship to a halt.

"Fore and aft the water stood level with the top of the bulwarks," Hunt continued, ". . . and she would in a few brief moments have sunk to rise no more, had not our dauntless crew in obedience to an order from the officer of the deck [Lieutenant Whittle], uttered as cooly as though it was the most ordinary occasion instead of a matter of life or death, sprung forward with axes, and dashed out the ports," thus freeing the water, "which was pressing us down, like the hand of doom, into the treacherous bosom of the Atlantic."

The gale raged for three days, driving the ship past Africa at speeds that often hit eleven knots. By turns the officers logged fast-moving squalls, snow, hail, and sudden breaks in the clouds that sent sparkles of sunlight dancing across the waves. Waddell, who worried over every detail, continued to have trouble sleeping. When he snapped, he took it out on the accident-prone Lieutenant Chew.

"Our first day in the Indian Ocean came to be celebrated by a most disagreeable row," was the way Lining put it. "Last night Chew had the mid-watch, and as it was blowing pretty heavily, and a big sea running, the Captain got a little uneasy, and about 9 p.m. sent for the first Lieutenant, and told him to go and tell Mr. Chew . . . that he would not be called for his watch but that Mr. Minor, the Master's Mate, was ordered to keep it."

Whittle had to wake Lieutenant Chew up to tell him, and the next morning, still stinging under the insult of being replaced by a junior officer, the second lieutenant went to ask Lining what he should do.

"Of course, [he] feels very much hurt about it," recalled Lining, who had already been discussing the matter with Chew's colieutenant, Dabney Scales. "And I gave him my opinion very freely, for I thought his dignity and position as an officer would be injured unless he did something.

"He then went and talked with the Captain, who gave him no redress or satisfaction, saying that he would do it again should circumstances arise to make it desirable, in his opinion." In other words, Waddell did not trust Chew with his ship. With his competence thus questioned, Chew asked to be relieved from duty and said he would prefer to leave the vessel.

"There I think [Chew] was wrong," offered Lining, "as I would allow no man to run me out of his ship under such circumstances." Had Waddell and Chew been equals, it was the sort of insult which might have led to a duel. As it was, Chew had no choice but to swallow hard.

Chew's watch came and he was not called. "Neither was anything said to him," remembered Lining, "but we saw the Captain and Mr. Whittle in most earnest conversation." As the ship rolled and slammed through the seas, talk of the affair raged through the wardroom, with Whittle later telling Lining that Waddell had complained that "all his old friends had deserted him," and that "everybody had turned against him."

"How childish and foolish that is," scoffed Lining, "for if he would only act rightly, we would all be with him." Whittle persisted in his role as peacemaker, engaging his commander in animated conversation out of earshot of the other officers. Forty-five minutes later, Lining reported, "Mr. Chew was sent for, and in a short time [came down] with his face all lit up and said that he was to be called to keep his watch.

"What the exact nature of the conversation was, I know not, but one of the provisos was that in very heavy weather Mr. Whittle was to keep watch with him." Clearly, Whittle had taken on extra duty to keep peace in the ship. Everyone was relieved, as Lining said, because "any such row between a captain and an officer always breeds discord in a ship . . . and I want nothing like that during this cruise."

ALONG WITH THE COOLING TEMPERS came better weather. On December 19 Lining's journal entries returned once again to "nothing of any interest going on," and the twentieth was "one of the most delightful days as far as the weather is concerned, that I have almost ever seen." On the twenty-first (the longest day of the year in the Southern Hemisphere) a chess mania came over the ship, with everybody sitting about the sunny decks in little knots. Midshipman Mason passed the time between games by giving French lessons to Lieutenant Grimball and Assistant Surgeon McNulty. That night the temperature began to fall.

The twenty-second was the coldest day yet. It was "too cold to be comfortable on deck," according to Lining, and on the twenty-third it was even colder and blowing half a gale. Lining spent most of the day in bed trying to get warm and "feeling quite badly, I don't know from what cause." Again, he sighed to his diary, there was "nothing of interest going on." Mason was more upbeat, buoyed by a youthful approach to the holiday, even though "our ship is in a most discouraging condition [with] nothing in order . . . and only a third of a crew. In spite of all this, I am comparatively speaking perfectly happy."

Christmas Eve dawned bright and clear. The temperature was forty-two. Over the last twenty-four hours the barometer had plummeted, losing more than three-quarters of an inch of mercury. Mason came on deck at 4 a.m., just as the sun was rising; the sky was a violent red. It was, he said, "certainly one of the most magnificent sights I ever saw." Some of the more experienced hands contended that the unusual cold was a sign of icebergs in the vicinity. At night, ice was more treacherous than a hidden reef.

Mason went on: "Before eight o'clock the sun was so hid by the clouds that I could not get a [noon navigation] sight." (For which he was not sorry, as this gave the young navigator-in-training nothing more to work out than the ship's dead-reckoning position.)*

The wind, which was very light that morning, freshened rapidly. Before noon the royals and flying jib had been pulled down and the topgallants taken in. As the wind built, the mainsail was hauled up and furled, the foresail was reefed, the jib was hauled down, and the topsail was double-reefed. The half gale of the previous day grew until it reached full proportion, and the seas, according to Lining, were "running heavier I think than any I have ever seen, not even excepting those round Cape Horn." When Mason finished with his work and went below, he wrote, "Oh! How thankful I am that I have no watch for it is now blowing quite strong and raining hard. . . . In my limited experience at sea I have never seen anything to equal this and several of the officers who have been at sea for a great many years say they never saw

---

*"Dead reckoning" is a corruption of the abbreviation "ded. reckoning," for "deduced reckoning." In using dead reckoning, a vessel's position is estimated using a formula of time, speed, and direction applied to the vessel's last fixed position.

such tremendous seas as we have seen this afternoon. . . . I never dreamed that the sea or the waves as we call them ashore could raise so high."

In spite of the weather Mason's spirits were high. He was excited by the prospect of a proper Christmas dinner. Charles Hopkins, the black cook from the *Lizzie M. Stacy,* had slaughtered a couple of "puny looking" geese purchased on Tristan da Cunha for the wardroom and butchered a pig brought along from London for the men. At midnight on Christmas Eve, everyone not on watch gathered in the smoky, dimly lit wardroom to wish each other Merry Christmas. Hunt described the scene as "profoundly miserable," and complained that "instead of receiving the time-honored salutations from family friends and bright-faced girls, whose lips give so sweet an intonation to the old phrase, I heard it from rough-bearded men." Disheartened, he whimpered petulantly that in place of preparing for a gay holiday, "I donned my sou'wester and moodily made my way to the deck to stand a four hour watch."

The dawn of Christmas Day gave him no reason to celebrate. The wind, which had been out of the northwest, suddenly backed, coming around to the southwest and increasing. The barometer bottomed out at 29.59. The opening entry in the day's log, written in Chew's shaky hand, notes "gales and squally, very heavy seas running." At 5:30 he wrote, "Wind increasing, shipped several seas." Waves were starting to break over the ship.

Surgeon Lining was more expansive. "Christmas at sea," he began. "[What] a great beginning did we have! At almost 6 a.m. we shipped such a sea that it came up nearly to the rail, washed one man over the lee rail into the sea, but fortunately the next sea washed him back again." The immense wave flooded the decks and nearly shivered the ship to a halt. With the decks awash and the ship in danger of foundering, Whittle once again rose to the occasion, grabbing an ax and leaping into the flood, knocking out the port shutters to allow the water to run out.

"The sea stove in the engine room skylight," gasped Mason, "showering water down on the engine. Everything was adrift in the steerage—chairs, books, table, sofas, sextants, and everything swimming about in a most admirable confusion."

"In the meantime," added Lining, "the sea had come aft, burst open the ward-room door, and completely flooded the ward-room. Some of it even washed up on my bunk."

The water was bitterly cold. The log throughout the morning is difficult to decipher. Any effort to write legibly under such conditions was wasted. Several items (whether rammers, sponge, or eight drums is difficult to tell) were logged as "lost overboard." Twenty minutes after a second "buster" slammed aboard, Waddell ordered a close reef in the main topsail.* At 6:20, he concluded that "to continue the course would be almost suicidal" and ordered the ship run off before the waves. So severe was the beating that at 7 a.m. all hands were mustered aft for a drink of rum.

"To a landsman it may seem the height of recklessness to serve out any intoxicating beverage at such a time to a ship's company," explained Cornelius Hunt, "but the omission of such an item in the routine of their lives would probably engender a general feeling of dissatisfaction more to be dreaded than any trifling excess in which they would be likely to indulge."

"The squalls of snow and hail during the gale were frightful," Waddell added. Even at that hour of the morning the liquor would be revivifying. Lining joked quietly of the near disaster and later remarked that he "never saw such good humor manifested—no cursing, all laughing, and joking about our misfortunes."

Mason's youthful spirits went up and down like the swells, speaking first of his "infinite disgust" at how things were "getting rather bilious," then dwelling on how the sight of a huge sea frothing above the fore yards was "a most magnificent thing to behold . . . [but] I should enjoy it a thousand times more were it not for the discomfort and danger

---

*"Reefing" means to reduce the exposed surface area of a sail. To "close" or "deep" reef a sail meant to furl it to its smallest working size. The next step would be to furl it entirely or take it down.

which are indispensable parts of a gale of wind. . . . it is indeed wonderful how such a frail thing [as a ship] can stand such rough treatment. No one could believe it without experiencing it themselves."

The wonder, Lining thought, was not only in what the ship could stand, but in what could be accomplished by its men, especially the cook and the galley department. "Who would think that a ship which had not dropped anchor for sixty-seven days could have for dinner goose, fresh pork, nice corn beef, fresh potatoes, mince pie, and etc. . . . they deserve a great deal of credit, all hands, cook, steward, and boys." Ruminating on the meal, he spared a thought for his loved ones back in the beleaguered Confederacy. "How I wish I could give them a little of my plenty," he worried. "What an awful thing this war is, and how terribly those at home have suffered."

Hunt was not so impressed. "Our cook, good conscientious man that he was, put all his science in requisition, and strained his resources to the utmost, to achieve a good dinner, but the old goose upon which he tried his skill, was, I verily believe, the identical fowl that Commodore Noah took with him on his first and last cruise. All that fire could do to render digestible that tough old specimen, was done, and in due time we grimly devoured him, but not before he had been several times rescued from his native element beneath the table, where he had been tossed by the heaving of the ship."

"Most of the dishes left the table for the deck," conceded Waddell. "But notwithstanding the disappointment at the loss of a good dinner, there was still life enough to enjoy it as an incident of the sea."

Hunt did not agree. All in all, he grumbled, "my Christmas in the *Shenandoah*, off the Cape of Good Hope, [was] the most miserable travesty of the festival I have ever celebrated." More, he intoned: "My solemn advice to the world at large, is never go off the Cape of Good Hope in a cruiser to enjoy Christmas."

ON MONDAY the wind died away but the seas continued to be quite heavy. Exhausted by the storm, Mason slept for ten hours. On the twenty-eighth another gale struck, but after the ferocious Christmas blow, he reported, it seemed nothing, and "one feels much more at ease." He might have been less serene had he known that a Union warship was steaming in their wake. While the *Shenandoah*'s beleaguered crew was grabbing at snatches of much-needed rest, Commander C. R. P. Rodgers of the USS *Iroquois* was dropping anchor off Tristan da Cunha Island in Falmouth Bay. After leaving Brazil, he wrote to Secretary of the Navy Welles: "I went with all dispatch to Tristan da Cunha, at which anchorage I arrived on the 28th and found that the *Shenandoah* had touched there just three weeks before to land the officers and crews of the whaling bark *Edward*, of New Bedford, captured on the 4th of December and burned the next day . . . and the *Lizzie M. Stacey*, of and from Boston, captured and burned on the 13th of November."

After taking the marooned prisoners on board, Rodgers sailed the same evening, saying he would "push forward with all possible dispatch." Fortunately for the rebels, the false scent Waddell had laid for the Yankee bloodhounds worked; Rodgers plotted a course for Cape Town.

The Union commander had fallen for the feint, but with newspaper headlines around the world screaming of the new rebel "pirate," American shipping was scrambling for cover. Back in England, James Dunwoody Bulloch had written that "the announcement now made public that another Confederate cruiser is at sea cannot fail to have a depressing effect upon the foreign commerce of the United States by increasing the rate of insurance in and upon American bottoms." He was correct. Insurance rates took another leap. And with foreign manufacturers becoming increasingly reluctant to entrust valuable goods to Union bottoms, more and more Yankee owners were facing bankruptcy and offering their vessels for sale overseas. As far away as the Pacific, others, not knowing where the marauder might strike next, simply ordered their captains to scamper into the nearest port and stay there. Fear of the *Shenandoah* was rippling out across the oceans of the world in great waves.

ON THE TWENTY-NINTH, Waddell wrote that the wind moderated as rapidly as it had risen and swung to the south, "bringing with it an occasional squall of fine rain and leaving an ugly cross sea that seemed undecided where to expend itself." Heavy seas broke against the hull, driving fine spray through open seams into the berth deck. The men's hammocks were soaked.

"A wet watch is unpleasant," commiserated their commander, "but to nod in a chair or turn into a damp bed is even more so." The morning passed slowly. The ship corkscrewed under shortened canvas and wallowed in the rolling seas. At 9 a.m. the queasy monotony was broken by a lookout's cry of "Sail ho!"

Coming up astern, the approaching sail alternately appeared and disappeared between curtains of blowing rain. The *Shenandoah* was bowling along, close hauled on the starboard tack under double-reefed topsails and reefed foresail, main, staysail, and fore topmast staysail. Despite the speed she was making, the other vessel, a medium-sized barque, was even faster.

"[They] came up with us quite rapidly," remembered Lining, "and at two p.m. was hull up, but we paid little attention to her."

Not thinking it likely the sail was a Yankee's, said Mason, the Confederates went about their business, "but as she came up to us, our suspicions were excited and finally we hoisted the English flag as a sort of a feeler [and] to our infinite delight she replied."

For a long moment the stranger's faded flag could not be made out. Everyone with a spyglass or lorgnette climbed into the rigging and watched surreptitiously. As she drew in range there was "a stifled outburst of delight." The flag was red, white, and blue.

"Here was a surprise," chortled Lining. "A Yankee ship about to catch *us*."

"The trouble now was to get alongside of her," said Mason, "she having the weather gauge on us, and we had no steam up, not even any fire in the furnaces nor water in the boilers. But our minds were soon relieved from any uneasiness on this subject by the maneuvers of our friend, who not suspecting our true character, came right up to us and when we jammed our ship up into the wind [to stop] he passed around our stern, thus putting us on his weather beam"—right where the *Shenandoah* wanted him.

Lining chuckled. "[She] sailed right into our clutches in a most unsuspecting manner." As the stranger passed, an officer on the Yankee's poop deck held up a blackboard, a common method for a passing ship to request confirmation of its longitude. In answer, Waddell ordered the false English colors struck and the Confederate flag raised. The startled Yankee took one look at the *Shenandoah* lying dead in the water and decided to make a break for it.

Mason picked up the thread. Having a heavy spread of canvas on, he said, the nimble Yankee immediately spun on its heels and ran, showing them its stern. "He began to gain on us like the mischief, and when we fired the little twelve-pounder, a blank cartridge, he did not seem disposed to heave to."

The order was given to cast loose the two forward rifle guns, but the makeshift nature of the rebels' armament nearly stymied them. "There were no breeching bolts," groaned Mason. There was no way to lock the breech of the gun after a shell was inserted, "so we had to lash an anchor stock outside of the port as a toggle to lash the breeching to."

The delay in readying the guns nearly allowed the Yankee to get away. By the time the gun crew was ready to fire, Lining said, "we thought we had lost him. . . . he was almost two miles away and going very rapidly through the water, while we were lying perfectly still hove to. There was every reason why he should try to escape and we would have found it very difficult to have caught him."

For the unpracticed gun crew to hit the speeding bark two miles away in rolling seas would have been remarkable. Many aboard the cruiser were resigned to its escape. Then to everyone's surprise, said Mason, "just as we had made everything ready to give him a shot from the Whitworth gun he commenced hauling up his mainsail and we were saved the trouble of chasing." Why the Yankee master should suddenly decide to surrender was a mystery. Lieutenant Whittle ordered Bulloch to ready a longboat and fetch the master.

Captain William Green Nichols was in a snit when he came aboard the *Shenandoah*. The master of the *Delphine*, out of Bangor, Maine, on a voyage from London to Burma with a cargo of rice-polishing machinery, was, as Cornelius Hunt said, "a good deal chagrined when he first came on board of us and discovered to what an incipient man-of-war he had surrendered. He had expected, when he came off to us, to find a cruiser with all her guns in working order, and men to work them—a craft, in fact, that in five minutes' time would be ready to blow him out of the water." Eyeing the jury-rigged gun toggles, Green noted the polyglot, undersized crew, then "bitterly lamented that he had not at least made the attempt to show us his heels."

Hunt understood. Like the *Delphine*'s master, Hunt was "very much inclined to the opinion that had he shaken out his canvas, going at the rate he was, he would have given us the slip." What Hunt could not have understood was the complexity of Nichols's problem. A bluff, careful, middle-aged man, Nichols was one-third owner of the *Delphine*, but the prospect of financial loss was the smallest part of his consternation. In the mid-1800s, it was common for captains to have a personal stake in their ships, and the ever present possibility of loss was accepted. Nichols's *real* problem was that he was married to Lillias Pendleton Nichols, whose father, Phineas Pendleton, owned the rest. And Lillias was a stubborn, determined woman, possessed of the same granite-hard will that had placed her progenitors in positions of power and prestige among some of the saltiest communities on earth. In 1860 nearly a fifth of Maine's population were mariners, and of these, 759 were masters. Tiny Searsport (Lillias's ancestral home) had only 1,700 inhabitants, but nearly 150 were captains. And many were Lillias's relatives. Her mother, Wealthy Carver, had five brothers, all captains (a sixth having died too young), and a good many ships plying the waters of the globe had been built in Carver shipyards. In short, the only thing preventing Phineas Pendleton's daughter from obtaining a master's rank was her gender. The personality required was plaited into her DNA.

Lillias saw no reason to surrender to a ship of the upstart rebel navy. When the Stars and Bars had fluttered up the *Shenandoah*'s backstay, she had exploded, lashing the *Delphine*'s crew into flight. Only the dark muzzles of the Whitworth rifles coming to bear on his ship had had more effect on Captain Nichols than her tongue.* Now, faced with the absurdity of his surrender, he was no longer sure which was worse. Desperate to save himself, he lied. When Waddell questioned him, he claimed his wife was delicate, of a nervous disposition and quite frail.

"It may cause her death to remove her," he told the rebel commander. "The report of the gun has made her very ill." Unknowingly, Nichols had struck the only chord that might elicit a sympathetic response from Waddell, who was, as Mason wrote of his commander, "an exceedingly tender-hearted man, [who] believes everything one tells him." The officers worried that their commander's chivalry would dispose him to bond rather than destroy the vessel.

"I heard [Nichols's] account of her sickness," recalled Lining, "and came to the conclusion that she was not as sick as he made out, but that he wanted to make her his handle by which to get off." At Whittle's insistence, Waddell reluctantly agreed to send the surgeon to examine her. Lining reported back that Mrs. Nichols was "in a perfect state of health and the ruse unavailing."

Waddell ordered a whaleboat readied. The seas were still high, but a chair was prepared, a whip fitted to the main yard, and very soon Mrs. Nichols, fully outfitted in bustling petticoats and clutching a birdcage on her lap, was hoisted aboard. The first thing she said to Bulloch when she came on board was "I suppose you are going to steal my canaries, so you had better take them at once!" Once on deck, she fell to giving orders to the men as they brought first her six-year-old son over, then

---

*Assistant Surgeon McNulty was more charitable toward his fellow Yankee, remembering him as a "plucky fellow" who had "showed his high heels for some time" and not come to until "the third solid shot almost cut away his fore rigging." McNulty's statement, however, was made nearly thirty years after the fact, in 1893.

her stewardess. The starboard cabin, next to Waddell's, was readied for their occupation.

"I was in the act of leaving my cabin," said Waddell, "and they were being conducted to the 'ladies' chambers,' [when] Mrs. Nichols asked in a loud, stentorian voice if I was the captain and what I intended doing with them. . . . I was surprised to see a tall, finely proportioned woman of twenty-six, in robust health standing before me, evidently possessing a will of her own, and it soon became palpable she would be the one for me to manage, and not the husband." Doing so would not be easy. In addition to her iron will and sharp tongue, Lillias possessed a nineteenth-century woman's most potent weapon. She was absolutely beautiful.

"A finer looking woman I have seldom seen, physically," whistled Lining.

Mason, who was lurking nearby, agreed. "[Captain Nichols's] wife is quite a pretty woman," he scribbled, "but rather a strong minded one . . . and I rather think she wears the breeches."

As it turned out, Captain Nichols was not only henpecked but superstitious, and the catalyst for the surrender of his ship lay not just in the hands of the *Shenandoah*'s gunners, but in his son's. Shortly after the *Delphine* departed London, Dr. Lining explained, "One of the German sailors on board the *Delphine* had given the little boy a bible saying 'This then is an English Bible for you.' The little boy, knowing he was an American, thought the English language might be different from his own, and had taken it to his father and asked, as any boy confident in the all-knowing infallibility of a father would, . . . 'Here, Papa, is an English Bible. Can you read it?' "

To show he could, Nichols opened the Bible at random and lit upon the tenth verse of the twenty-seventh chapter of Acts, in which Paul is about to set sail on the Mediterranean Sea. Concerned that the journey was taking place during winter, when the shallow Mediterranean is most hostile, Paul advised his fellow travelers, saying, "Sirs, I perceive that the voyage will be with injury and much loss, not only of the cargo and the ship, but also of our lives." Nichols, certain the passage must presage some misfortune about to befall the *Delphine*, turned pale and shut the Bible.

"And from that time," snickered Lining, "he gave himself up as lost. . . . It certainly was a strange coincidence and will always make him a believer in omens."

Superstition or not, the omen was correct. Waddell ordered the *Delphine* burned.

THE WEATHER was still rough, making it too dangerous to remove many items from the captured barque. The crew was allowed to remove some of their clothing, but other than the chronometer and sextants, the only things seized from the *Delphine* were a number of books, a nanny goat, its kid, and some pigs. While the prize crew condemned the *Delphine*, Mason and Brown amused themselves by catching albatross on baited hooks. The feet, once skinned and tanned, would make curious tobacco pouches. It took until after dark to fire the ship.

"At about 10:15 p.m. we saw the fire break out fore and aft," said Lining, "and in a short while she was wrapped in flames."

Hunt, as usual, was more loquacious, describing "the first forked tongue of fire, issuing from the companion-way of the fated barque, warn[ing] us that the destroying element had commenced its work. Rapidly the flames gathered headway, casting a fierce, lurid glow over the heaving bosom of the ocean; from doors, windows, and hatchways they burst forth like the vengeful spirits of destruction, wound up the spars, stretched out upon the yards, swiftly enveloping shrouds, sails, and halyards in one splendid, fiery ruin . . . a holocaust to the God of War."

It took Hunt almost as long to depict the burning of the vessel as the actual destruction took. Lining noted simply, "Never have I seen a vessel burn so fast," adding that it was a beautiful sight.

The conflagration brought a new set of concerns. Eleven o'clock came and still the boat bearing the prize crew had not returned. "We began to grow uneasy," worried Lining, "and to think that some accident had happened to the boat, either that she had been turned over when the men were getting into her, or that the boat's crew were drunk and could not pull."

The last, if the crew had gotten into a stash of liquor aboard the *Delphine*, would be bad enough, but the first was an abiding nightmare of every sailor in the Southern Ocean. The worst fear of a man drifting in the water or clinging to the bottom of an overturned boat was not drowning, but the ever present clouds of albatross, gulls, and petrels that were reputed to swoop in on helpless castaways and batter relentlessly at their heads and hands until exhaustion set in. Once a man was too tired to lift his arms, his scalp and ears would be torn to bits. More than one life belt had been found floating with its ties undone, cast away by a sailor who preferred to slip beneath the waves rather than have an albatross pluck out his eyes.

The clock was nearing midnight when the boat was seen approaching. The water had been so rough that it had taken several tries to get away from the burning ship without capsizing. Lining must have been counting the minutes. He noted the time as exactly 11:35.

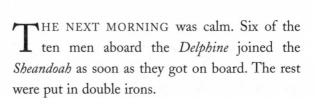

EIGHT

THE NEXT MORNING was calm. Six of the ten men aboard the *Delphine* joined the *Sheandoah* as soon as they got on board. The rest were put in double irons.

"On the whole," said Mason, "we now have a most promiscuous crew." With the addition of three Germans from the barque, the *Shenandoah*'s sails were now being handled by men from Germany, Britain, France, Sweden, Denmark, Malaysia, Ireland, Scotland, Hawaii, and oddest of all, "some three or four live Yankees from Maine." These last, according to the midshipman, were "amongst the best men we have." One—a large, stout, good-looking fellow who had spent two years in the Union army—Mason singled out in particular, and said wonderingly of him and his Northern brethren: "What induced them to ship [with us] I don't know."

The mate of the *Delphine* drew less approbation. When Grimball asked him if there were any meats or preserved fruits aboard the barque, he snapped, "Good God, man, are you hungry?" Worse, when Waddell inquired if there was any money on board (no doubt meaning to turn it over to the "lady of the ship" as he had done for Mrs. Gilman with the currency found aboard the *Charter Oak*), the mate was impudent, offending the officers' sense of courtesy by barking, "Money! What the hell do you think I'd be doing with money at sea?"

Lining declared the mate "uppish" until a stern word from the *Shenandoah*'s hulking boatswain rendered him "exceedingly meek."

Lillias too underwent a change as complete as the weather. After refusing breakfast and lunch, she decided to come out to tea. Laughing and talking, she "flew out" only once, rising to some remark made against her husband while her little boy scampered about playing with the kid goat. The testosterone-addled Southern boys ate it up. One young rebel gushed that "Mrs. Nichols . . . is quite a handsome woman, has a genteel look about her, almost a refined face." Then almost as if remembering that she was, after all, the enemy, he silently chided her for "once in a while coming out with some ungrammatical expression which dispels the illusion." By the end of the day, Mason, whose job it was to go into her cabin in order to wind all the captured chronometers, was pronouncing her "delightfully clean" and "not such a Tartar as I first thought.

"She always dresses neatly, even very well," wrote the fashion-conscious junior officer. "But what is still more important, she dresses in good taste. In appearance she is quite queenlike."

Having smiled her way to royal status with Mason, she turned her attentions to the rest of the men. When it came to flirting, Lillias could put Scarlett O'Hara to shame. Even Waddell fell under her sway, becoming less standoffish and for her entertainment overturning a long-standing edict against playing cards aboard the ship.*

---

*It was not uncommon for a captain to forbid all forms of cards, dice, or other competitive entertainments, since the passions aroused by a losing streak or cheating could easily lead lead to trouble or even violence in the already rough-and-tumble environment aboard a ship.

"I have just had the distinguished honor of playing a rubber of whist in the Captain's cabin," prattled Mason. "It is most positively prohibited . . . but in the Captain's cabin it is allowable as the 'skipper' is monarch of all he surveys."

With so much charm and gentility caroming about the ship, some of the Confederates were reminded of how deprived life on the deep could be, and at midnight gathered in the wardroom to greet the New Year with toasts to sweethearts and "the cause."

Waddell, after a few drinks, mourned: "How many of my boon companions are gone to that bourne from whence no traveler returns?" Then he grew resentful, chewing at his role in the conflict and what he saw as its cause.

"[The Yankees] fought on a calculation of profit," he growled. The North's sole purpose in prosecuting the war was not, as stated, to free the slaves but to dominate the South financially. "This fact never left my mind, and reconciles me to the destruction of the property which was captured." The *Shenandoah*'s rampage, he felt, was fighting the Union "more effectually than if I were killing the miserable crowds of European recruits which they filled their armies with."

Later, alone in his quarters, Surgeon Lining hoisted another drink to "my little darling, whom I would like so much to see." After ruminating on how only a year earlier he had been sailing the Mediterranean, bound from Marseille to Genoa, and was now in the middle of the Indian Ocean on his way to Australia, he asked rhetorically, "And where will I be a year from now? Only 'Echo' can answer—Where?"

THE NEW YEAR went sour early on. The first day of the year was also the first Sunday of the month, and according to Lining was "the first fair and delightful day that we have had since we have been in the Indian Ocean." The weather, he hoped, was a harbinger of things to come. But at one o'clock the next morning a deckhand fell down an open hatch and was knocked senseless. Two days later the weather turned overcast. The wind increased until the ship was doing eleven knots and a large pod of killer whales—"blackfish" the sailors called them—surrounded the ship. Their towering dorsal fins flashed in the stormy light. In the forepeak, bickering broke out among the over-worked sailors, and someone "made a monument" out of Seaman Sylvester's nose. Quartermaster Hall appeared with two black eyes. Mason reported that even the pigs were not getting along. "They kept up a tremendous noise last night," he noted in his diary, "and this morn-ing in the midwatch I went forward and noticed them lying apart in their pen." The pigs captured from the *Delphine* were huddled apart from the *Shenandoah*'s. "They did not seem to relish the idea of being obliged to mess with rebels," quipped Mason. "Or perhaps our good Confederate pigs were insulted at being obliged to take in the Yankees."

As the ship strained eastward under single-reefed topsails, breaking seas washed her decks fore and aft. On the fifth, Waddell's smoldering distrust of Lieutenant Chew's abilities rose once again to the surface.

"Waddell called Chew into his cabin," recalled Lining, "and offered to make him a kind of prize master, by giving him charge of all the prize chronometers, sextants, and etc." To do this, Waddell explained, Chew was to be relieved of his watch duties. "Chew was weak enough to fall into the trap," said Lining when the lieutenant accepted the po-sition. "He thus lowered himself from an officer of the deck to a winder of six chronometers." Joshua Minor, the chief master's mate, was to keep the lieutenant's watch.

"How Chew consented to it, I cannot see," wrote Lining. "He is certainly not the man I thought."

The lieutenant was not the only person affected by Waddell's deci-sion. As midshipmen, both Mason and Brown outranked Joshua Minor, and to have him elevated above them was a swipe at their com-petence. But when they protested to Waddell through the executive of-ficer, the commander responded with an acerbic remark about "what his officers would *let* him do before long."

The next day Waddell spent several hours writing out new appoint-ments for all the officers in what Lining and several others thought was a transparent effort to "get around the imputation contained in Brown and Mason's protest." Chew was given a "promotion" to the newly minted position of "ordnance officer." Whittle again had a long talk with his commander, but it was unavailing; Waddell was intransigent, and as a result Lining was "very much afraid that we are going to have trouble in this ship before this cruise ends."

The only bright spot in the increasing gloom seems to have been Mrs. Nichols, who according to Lining was becoming "far more satisfied and sociable, talking freely to all around her." Such was the effect of her attentions that the majority of the officers seemed oblivious of what was going on in the forepeak. After another whist party, Mason, in comparing the Yankee enchantress to the dowdy *Charter Oak* captives, found himself unable to express himself in English and burst into French, swooning: "Mrs. N. does not have as much to say as they did . . . [but] what she says is *beaucoup plus spirituel and plus a propos.*" Even the melancholy Dr. Lining, whose journal often contained entries of "nothing of interest going on" began making sparkling observations of "another bright and heavenly day!"

"She is a much better woman than at first I thought," the surgeon doted. And his married commander seemed to agree. "She has tamed down somewhat," Waddell harrumphed, "and I rather admire the discipline she has her husband under." Earlier he had bragged that "a refractory woman can be controlled by quiet courtesy, but no flattery," but the change in Lillias's demeanor seems more likely to have been due to a pretty woman's ability to catch more flies with honey than the commander's patronizing attitude.

While Lillias was setting the hook, Captain Nichols was working himself into a lather. "[He] is infernally jealous," Lining sputtered, "and allows no one to talk to her that he does not come poking around." After Nichols interrupted Lillias's attempt to show Lining some photographs of her home and sisters, the surgeon sneered that the *Delphine*'s master was a "fool and an ass . . . to be obliged to suspect his wife and to have to keep his eyes on her to prevent her going wrong— I shall now go on talking to her to plague him, if nothing else."

Nichols need not have worried. From Lillias's perspective, there was far more to fear than some Confederate tampering with her virtue. Upon sighting the remote island of St. Paul, halfway between Cape Town and Australia, Waddell had made a small joke she interpreted as meaning they were to be marooned there. The notion of being deposited on a volcanic rock a thousand miles from nowhere frightened her.

"The tears with which her eyes were heavy furnished me with a ready clue to the apprehension under which she was suffering," said Cornelius Hunt. When asked where she had gotten the idea that the master of the *Shenandoah* would maroon an entire ship's company on such an out-of-the-way spot she hesitated a moment, then with a furtive glance at Hunt said: "Why, they tell the most terrible stories at home about the outrages committed upon defenseless men and women by your rebel cruisers. The papers have been full of them and I naturally supposed they were founded on fact.

"I could not restrain a smile at the naiveté with which our lady prisoner admitted the entertainment of a pretty well-defined conviction that she was in the hands of veritable pirates," wrote Hunt, ". . . but I suppressed any stronger demonstrations of merriment, and upon expressing my desire to see some of the literature to which she referred, she brought from her state-room a file of an illustrated New York publication, wherein was a marvellous narrative, written by a lady with a multitude of initials. I subsequently read it through, greatly amused, I must confess, at its stupendous absurdities. In the course of the story the Confederate cruiser Alabama was introduced, and her officers and crew represented as a pack of rascals, whom Morgan the buccaneer or the leader of the Indian Sepoys would have expelled from their several commands, lest they should become contaminated by evil associations."

Lillias, in her own way, seems simply to have been taking out a little insurance and paying the premium with her charm. Stirring up a storm of hormones among the young men was an effective way to remain on the ship. As Lining noted, "her presence on board served to relieve the monotony."

ON JANUARY 9 the *Shenandoah* sailed across the meridian exactly opposite the globe from Charleston, South Carolina. They were as far
from home as it was possible to get, but in a burst of forced optimism,
the doctor said he preferred to believe that "every mile that I go east
now brings me so much closer to home." He might have been less ebullient had he known that the *Iroquois* was astern. On the same day the
Confederates found themselves halfway around the world from home,
Commander C. R. P. Rodgers arrived at the Cape of Good Hope and
realized he had been misled. In Cape Town he found that "nothing was
known of the existence of the new rebel cruiser *Shenandoah,* but a report had been circulated that the *Sea King,* with Captain Semmes on
board, had been lost near the Canary Islands." Knowing the distorted
rumor to be untrue, Rodgers informed his superiors by dispatch that he
was "now taking in coal, and shall sail as soon as possible."

"As soon as possible" probably meant several days. The *Iroquois* had
arrived in Cape Town with only one day's coal on board, badly leaking
boilers, and a malfunctioning air pump needed to keep the gaseous engine room inhabitable. And even if the leaking boilers could be plugged
and the air pump repaired, he reported, the enlistments of several of his
men had expired during the monthlong passage from Uruguay. "I have
invited them to reship for the cruise," he wrote, "but they have declined
to do so. The allure of the large bounties now being paid to recruits at
home and their little hope of prize money on a foreign station render
them anxious for their discharge."

He had already lost several men to desertion and needed sixteen
sailors, marines, and firemen to fill his complement. Worse, he wrote, a
machinist in Rio had assured him that his weak boilers could withstand
no more than fifteen pounds of pressure, and he would have "no hesitation in believing that they are wholly unsuited to the performance of
the duty in question." In spite of this, he believed the *Shenandoah* was
likely to head for the East Indies to prey on Yankee merchantmen, and
it was his duty to pursue her. Crippled and undermanned, Rodgers
nonetheless demonstrated an almost poetic flair for tenacity when he

wrote that "thither, therefore, I shall follow her with all dispatch, for in spite of the defective motive power of the *Iroquois*, I shall not abandon the hope that she may have the good fortune to arrest the progress of this new buccaneer."

MEANWHILE, back on the cruiser, Lillias may have been keeping up the officers' spirits, but outside the radius of her warmth the rest of the ship was suffering. The steward took sick and Lining worried that he might lose him. Bulloch's eyes became so inflamed he could not use a sextant. A debilitating toothache flattened one of the mates, but without anesthetic, the searing pain was too awful to pull it. Waddell was plagued with constant headaches and feeling "very blue." With so many medical worries on his mind, even an evening of backgammon with Lillias could not prevent Lining's journal entries from lapsing into "nothing of interest going on."

On the eleventh the wind died. The sails hung slack, reflecting their own image in the water. When the wind returned, it came from the northwest, stemming the ship's progress toward Melbourne. The headwind, some felt, was a message from Providence; altering their course to accommodate the wind would allow them to lay a comfortable heading for Cape Leeuwin, sixteen hundred miles west of Melbourne. At that time of year the cape was a center for Yankee whaling. "Have been trying to induce the Captain to run along the western coast before he goes into Melbourne," wrote Lining. "But he has his head set for port and is stubborn."

The headwinds grew stronger. On Sunday there was no muster or reading of the articles of war because the decks were awash, the ship bashing head-on into heavy seas. Monday was Whittle's twenty-fifth birthday, but the occasion was marred by a block that fell from the rigging and struck one of the prisoners. "If it had struck him directly it would have killed him on the spot," said Lining. Instead, the glancing blow only opened a nasty gash on the prisoner's head.

At midnight the wind fell calm again. The next day at noon,

Waddell ordered steam. "An extravagant waste of coal," thought Lining, and one that would have unhappy consequences. The coupling had failed a second after the initial Tristan da Cunha breakdown and been repaired by the addition of yet more screws; now the second repair was failing, and the engineer was worried the bearings and sternpost would be damaged by the wobbling shaft. "The chief engineer told the captain that he would not like to run the engine unless absolutely necessary," wrote Mason, "but not withstanding this warning the Captain in his impatience continued.

"Previous to our arrival off the Australian coast, everyone thought we would go first to the whaling grounds . . . [but] it seems the mail arrangement was known to the skipper and he was bent upon catching the January mail, all of which we did, but it certainly cost us dearly."

Years later, Waddell remembered things differently, claiming a course *had* been laid for Cape Leeuwin "but a change in the weather prevented the contemplated visit." There was an easterly wind, he said—"the most unfavorable quarter for us"—and a current from the west threw the ship from her course. "It was absolutely necessary that the vessel should be docked and not withstanding the injury which may already have been done, or might follow, to the bearings by the use of the propeller, I desired to reach Melbourne in time to communicate with the steamer."

"He thought it very important to catch the mail," conceded Mason. "Saying the news would be of much importance to [Confederate secretary of the navy Stephen P. Mallory] in making out his report for the meeting of Congress." Waddell also argued that news of the *Shenandoah's* exploits would have a tremendous effect on morale throughout the South, but Mason countered that "as the country must have heard of our performances off the South American coast, I cannot help thinking that it would have been better policy to have concealed our whereabouts from the civilized world for a month longer."

He was right. On January 12, Union secretary of the navy Gideon Welles sicced the commander of the USS *Suwanee,* armed with ten large guns, on the raider, saying that "information has been received to the effect that the piratical steamer *Shenandoah* has been destroying American shipping. . . . Every exertion must be taken to overtake her, and if successful, to destroy or capture her." Welles authorized the *Suwanee*'s commander Paul Shirley to follow her "anywhere in the West Indies or the Caribbean Sea, on the coasts of South America, Europe, or Africa, to the East Indies or the Pacific." Mindful of the international outrage that had followed the ramming and capture of the *Florida* in the Brazilian port at Bahia, Welles narrowed the worldwide mandate only by cautioning Shirley that it would be best if the *Shenandoah* was not attacked in a neutral country's waters.

Waddell was several steps ahead of his pursuers, but so great was his eagerness to catch the mail steamer that it blinded him to an easy capture. The embarrassing episode began on the seventeenth, when a large ship was sighted and ordered to heave to with a shot from the twelve-pound gun. Lieutenant Chew was sent over with a boarding party. Everything was in order. The ship's papers proved her to be the *Nimrod*, American built but flying English colors. She had been sold by her Yankee owners to avoid bankruptcy. After the boarding, the new captain—"a grand looking fellow, with tremendous white whiskers, which gave him something of the general look of a venerable polar bear"— came off in his gig for a visit to the *Shenandoah*, bringing with him a case of brandy, a gift for the Confederates, he said, with whom he felt a kindred spirit. He was married to a woman from New Orleans and grateful to the raiders for making it possible to obtain the *Nimrod* at a bargain price.

"Bully for him!" crowed Lining.

"The compliment was fully appreciated," added Hunt, and the brandy was excellent, with "a scene of festivity which followed on board the Shenandoah that I shall not soon forget. . . . For weeks afterward his name was often coupled by our officers with enthusiastic praise, and I only trust he has as pleasant reminiscences of his visit to the rebel cruiser."

The *Nimrod*'s visit was the last pleasantry for some time. That night the propeller "carried away" (meaning the shaft coupling broke again), and by daybreak the *Shenandoah* was once again bowling along under canvas, with plenty of wind in her close-reefed topsails. By nightfall it was blowing half a gale and the jib stay parted in a gust. Waddell fretted over everything, pestering the mechanics at the propeller and interfering with the boatswain's efforts to fix the stay. When Nichols made a snide remark about his anxiety, Lining noted, "Old 'Wad' worked himself into a rage," yelling that Nichols was a fraud and a liar before retreating to his cabin embarrassed by his loss of self-control.

The next day was calm, the one after that fair and breezy. That night a comet blazed across the sky. Lining tried to interpret this as a harbinger of good news, but the omen failed: "We had three sail in sight this morning," he sighed. "One of them looked very much like a Yankee, but the Captain disagreed."

"We were steaming about nine knots at the time," Mason threw in, "[and] we could see this vessel most distinctly—indeed she was not more than two miles from us."

As Captain and Mrs. Nichols looked on, Waddell declared the stranger to be the *Nimrod,* the same English ship the rebels had overhauled and boarded a few days earlier. Lining shook his head in disagreement. It was January 22, and "I, unfortunately, mentioned that the mail left Melbourne on the 26th, thinking that would make the Captain not try to get in there by that time." His warning had the opposite effect. So determined was Waddell to catch the mail steamer that he ordered more throttle, willfully blind to the fact that the ship alongside them was larger and of a completely different rig than the friendly *Nimrod.* He also failed to notice that Lillias and William Nichols were, in their own words, "shaking in their shoes for fear we would stop her," because they *did* recognize the stranger. It was the *David Brown,* a five-topsail yard ship out of Maine. And it was owned by Lillias's father. They stood on the deck, holding their breath, until they were sure the *David Brown* was safe.

The next day the Yankee was in sight again but Waddell was "running for the mail and would not turn out of his way for anything." He ordered the ship's speed increased to eight knots.

"This, I think, is culpable for two reasons," wrote Lining. "One being that it is a waste of coal and a danger of breaking our machine, the other that by no means ought we to get in before the steamer sails, as it will spread word of our arrival all over the world."

Emboldened by the air of discord brought on by Waddell's insistence, Lillias threw off her cooperative facade. When presented with a parole form containing an agreement "not to serve against the Confederacy or to give any information tending to the injury or detriment of the ship," she refused to sign. Her husband, the *Delphine*'s mate, and the remaining crewmen signed willingly, said the doctor, "but when it came Mrs. N.'s turn, she let loose with her tongue, pitching into her husband for telling her to sign it and say nothing."

"I do not intend to hold my tongue," she snapped, "nor do I consider myself bound by anything I am going to sign. I *will* talk, for at least they cannot stop my tongue!" Snatching up a pen, she stabbed a signature onto the form and turned on Smith-Lee. "Is there anything you want my little son to sign?"

"No, M'am," he replied coolly. "We are much more afraid of you than we are of him."

"She went out in a towering rage," Lining laughed. "Not to have the vials of her wrath poured out on me, I kept quiet."

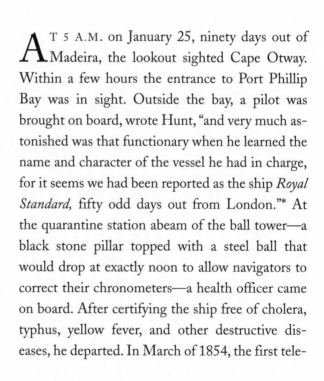

NINE

A T 5 A.M. on January 25, ninety days out of
Madeira, the lookout sighted Cape Otway.
Within a few hours the entrance to Port Phillip
Bay was in sight. Outside the bay, a pilot was
brought on board, wrote Hunt, "and very much astonished was that functionary when he learned the
name and character of the vessel he had in charge,
for it seems we had been reported as the ship *Royal
Standard,* fifty odd days out from London."* At
the quarantine station abeam of the ball tower—a
black stone pillar topped with a steel ball that
would drop at exactly noon to allow navigators to
correct their chronometers—a health officer came
on board. After certifying the ship free of cholera,
typhus, yellow fever, and other destructive diseases, he departed. In March of 1854, the first tele-

*Pilots are local mariners brought on board to act as guides in ar-
eas where an in-depth knowledge of currents, tides, and hazards
is vital to the safe operation of a ship.

graph in the Southern Hemisphere had been constructed alongside the ball tower to connect the small waterfront community of Williamstown, built on the flats just inside the Port Phillip heads, with Melbourne. The wire began singing immediately of the cruiser's arrival.

In 1865, the soup of Melbourne's political opinions mirrored those of England. Founded less than thirty years earlier by a mixture of businessmen, freed convicts, tradesmen, and miners, it had exploded into a colony of fifty thousand souls who were by turns ardently pro-Union—or at least antislavery—or in love with all things Southern. Thirteen years earlier miners forty miles away in Ballarat had staged a rebellion of their own to demand democratic rights. That uprising had easily been trounced by a small number of bayonet-wielding redcoats, but it left Australia's miners—many of whom had migrated south after the diggings in California played out—finding it easy to identify with the Confederates, whom they saw as being in a fight for self-determination. On the opposite side of the fence were a number of merchants involved in shipping, many of them Yankee expatriates. And these last found strange bedfellows among a band of paramilitarists who thought Australia was under imminent threat of an attack from North America.

"There is no doubt," wrote an editor for the *Sydney Morning Herald* in the first year of the Civil War, "that the chance of invasion of this country by American privateers has roused up the spirit of self-defence." The nationalists had begun readying for an invasion as early as 1856, and by 1862 the Parliament in Victoria had spent nearly a million pounds on harbor defenses. Yet when the Russian warship *Bogatyr* visited Port Phillip, the battery at Queenscliff had been unable to return a cannon salute from the visitor because they had forgotten to buy ammunition. After that embarrassment the ministers demanded a more effective resistance be put in place, and the entrance to Melbourne's harbor was now guarded by a number of bobbing cannons mounted on floating platforms.* The HMCS *Victoria* was the only armed vessel in

*In the end, the only bombardment ever suffered by Melbourne was an incident of "friendly fire" by the HMS *Nelson,* a British warship that accidentally shelled a home in St. Kilda. No one was killed, but the navy never explained the incident either.

the harbor when the raider entered, but neither she nor anybody else was pointing artillery at the *Shenandoah*. Instead, Melbourne was in a mood to party. And for a country still enthralled by the romantic exploits of the *Alabama,* a visit by a Confederate ship was reason to celebrate.

"[We] created an immense sensation," wrote Lining. "Steamboats came off to meet us, throwing things aboard, and boats sailed around us filled with persons eager to see a Confederate." Waddell blustered that he had been expecting the reception because "it was from generous and brave hearts who believed in the righteousness of our cause."

Hunt called the scene "one of excitement . . . that baffles all adequate description. Crowds of people were rushing hither and dither . . . and ere we had been an hour at anchor, a perfect fleet of boats was pulling towards us from every direction." In short, as the *Shenandoah* steamed slowly toward the anchorage at Sandridge it seemed as if all of the vast island continent's residents had turned out to greet them, with everybody on the streets whistling "Dixie."

Among the things thrown aboard the *Shenandoah* from the circling steamboats were newspapers, offerings from friendly Melbournites who knew that one of the first things any crew returning from a journey desires is news from home. And after three months at sea, the rebels had plenty of war news to choose from; Melbourne had three newspapers—the *Age,* the *Herald,* and the *Argus*—and all carried regular dispatches from California, along with occasional pieces from Richmond. Much of the news awaiting the Confederates was bad. Southern forces had abandoned Washington, North Carolina, to the Federals. The Arkansas garrison under General Price had been routed. The most glaring defeats were in the Shenandoah Valley, where the Confederates were in wretched condition, retreating and leaving General Sherman's forces free to pierce deep into Georgia. Masow and Milligville had been taken, Griffin, Hillsboro, and Monticello burned. Macon was threatened and Savannah was expected to fall. More and more, the weakened and bleeding South was resorting to a guerrilla warfare that amounted to near thuggery. A gang of Mosby's raiders dressed in stolen uniforms had insinuated themselves into a column of Yankee cavalry and on a given signal drawn their pistols and shot ten Union troopers dead. In New York, a plot to set fire to a museum and eight major hotels had failed, resulting in the capture of the saboteurs and an order from General Dix for the summary execution of any Southerners detected in the city. The son of the African explorer Dr. David Livingstone had been kidnapped (presumably by the rebels) from the vessel on which he was serving with the Third New Hampshire Volunteers.

Confederate victories were few and scattered across a broken landscape. A dispatch from Louisville spoke of ten thousand rebels under General Breckenridge driving the Union forces from Bull's Gap, Tennessee, and a band of bold Confederates had pulled off a successful raid all the way up north in St. Albans, Vermont, but everywhere else they were losing ground.

"We have heard of the re-election of Mr. Lincoln," Waddell wrote in a letter home, "and the sinking of the *Florida*." With the loss of the *Florida*, the *Shenandoah* was now the only Confederate cruiser still afloat. But after so long at sea, the pleasure of making harbor was greater than the weight of bad news, he said, and he was "getting along boldly and cheerfully." In an apparent reference to the size of his crew, he added, "I will get all the men that I want," before closing with a chipper wish that the recipient would "give my love to all the ladies."

Love—and the ladies—were on everyone's mind. To all appearances, the Australians loved the Confederates dearly, mobbing onto trains, wagons, yachts, and rowboats by the thousands for a visit to the harbor, where they hoped to get a glimpse of the "rebel pirates." In return the young rebels developed a crushing ardor for the Aussie gals. After a day of fending off visitors while awaiting permission from the Victorian government to begin making repairs and taking on supplies, they'd thrown open the gangway to a riot of visitors in a scene that inspired Lieutenant Chew to write he had "never seen such an excitement as this poor converted merchantman created. Thousands upon thousands came off to see her." Even though workmen had immediately begun caulking the cruiser's leaky decks with pitch, he estimated that ten thousand people came aboard in one day. "Every part of the ship was thronged," he said, "and many steamers were refused permission to come alongside because there was no standing room on our decks."

Best of all, he felt, was that "among our fair visitors there were many very pretty girls. . . . Upon every steamer's approach we would look out for pretty faces and if found we stood near the gangway so as to take them in charge. If they were particularly agreeable, we took them aft to the cabin and requested the pleasure of a glass of wine with them."

Although he fancied himself something of a ladies' man, Lining felt left out, grumbling that "there were very few pretty girls" among the visitors, except one in particular he thought "quite so." Miffed at seeing this beauty cut out of the herd before he could make his move, he groused of some "great lump of a fellow who kept tagging after her like a schoolboy and gave very few others a chance."

Such jealousy was not confined to the cruiser. In an acerbic letter to that evening's *Herald,* one anonymous writer complained that "young females who go in for cheap sentiment and electro-plated ware were generally anxious to defile their boots with nasty pitch this morning in order to gaze on the ultra-marine chivalry of the South. . . . this is all very well on the part of the stupid and frivolous girls, who read sensational novels . . . [but] women have something higher and better to do in the world than to go sight-seeing in such doubtful quarters."

To accommodate the crowds, extra trains were put on the Melbourne–Sandridge line. More than seven thousand passengers made the trip in a single day. The throng of rowboats and small ferries crowding around the steamer became so boisterous that a small whaleboat capsized, spilling two men and a woman into the water. The men came aboard dripping, but the woman, embarrassed by the cling of her soaking crinolines, refused.

"They were everywhere," complained Lining, "poking into everything, and even while at dinner we had difficulty in keeping them out of the ward room." There were, he acknowledged, some very pleasant people, but also a great deal of "riff raff."

The cruiser's arrival sparked a battle between Melbourne's newspapers, with the first broadside being fired by the pro-Union *Age:* "We cannot regard the Shenandoah as other than a marauding craft," raged the conservative broadsheet, "and her officers and crew than as a gang of respectable pirates. . . . Her vocation is not to fight, but to plunder; not to vanquish enemies in a fair struggle, but to destroy unarmed antagonists; not to shed the blood of her crew in their country's defence, but to fill their pockets with prize money."

The *Herald* preferred the South and referred to Waddell's subordinates as "a fine and determined looking set of officers," and the crew as "a happy and apparently well-contented lot, [who] express great confidence in their commander, and are well-pleased with the service in which they are engaged." That service, the *Herald* acknowledged, was to "burn, sink, and plunder," but "we cannot but recognise and fraternise with the brave men who uphold their country's flag at the risk of being hanged at the yard-arm." Here the *Argus* joined in, lambasting Lincoln's Federal government as "a government which has kept no faith with her enemies and wherever it has been possible to do so with safety, has broken every promise to its friends—a Government which under the pretext of a Crusade against slavery, has committed crimes against civilisation more detestable than slavery."

While the newspapers were exchanging blows, another paper skirmish was opening up between Waddell and the colonial government. One of the first things he had done after dropping anchor at Sandridge was to send Lieutenant Grimball ashore in a small boat bearing a message for the governor of Victoria, with a request for permission to begin making the necessary repairs and take on coal. Also, he wrote, "I desire your Excellency's permission to land my prisoners," and he promised to observe the neutrality.

Sir Charles Darling had begun his political career as an aide to one of the most detested governors in New South Wales's history, and had been awarded the governorship of Victoria as much for his position among the aristocracy as for any merit. Before migrating to Victoria, he had been the governor of Jamaica, where the difficulties of governing an unyielding people had imbued him with such a strong belief in Henry David Thoreau's dictum that "the government is best which governs least" that now, at the pinnacle of his bureaucratic career, he often found it best to do nothing. When doing nothing was impossible, he did the next best thing: he delegated.

After stalling as long as he could, Darling called a meeting of his executive council. The council first decreed that the *Shenandoah* had only forty-eight hours to resupply, then relented and said she could stay until the cracked propeller band was fixed. Governor Darling also directed his commissioner of trade and customs, James G. Francis, to contact Waddell and ask him to describe the nature and extent of his requirements vis-à-vis repairs and supplies. As for the prisoners, Francis wrote, "his Excellency desires to be furnished with a list of the prisoners in question," and followed this up with a letter to the U.S. consulate in Melbourne asking if the Federal government would take responsibility for the prisoners.

Waddell replied that he had engaged the services of Messrs. Langlands Brothers & Co. to examine the propeller bearings and to undertake repairs, but said nothing about the prisoners.

Francis wrote again, asking for a list of supplies required "together with one of the prisoners, as I requested in my previous communication."

Waddell shot back an order for "brandy, rum, champagne, port, sherry, beer, porter, molasses, lime juice, and light material for summer wear," then added sheepishly that "in regard to a list of prisoners, I have to communicate that all those persons whom on the high seas I considered my prisoners left my ship without my knowledge, in shore boats, soon after my arrival in this port."

It had been impossible to keep them on board. Some, including John Williams, the black cook impressed from the *D. Godfrey,* had leaped overboard and swum for shore, while others slid away among the hordes of visitors. Of the "deserters," only Lillias Nichols had faced her captors, waking Waddell at daybreak by berating her husband in a loud voice from the cabin next door. "If those chronometers and sextants were mine," she had shouted, "I guess I would make him give them to me!" She also insisted that a case of books taken from the *Delphine* be returned.

"They were getting their things together for an early departure," sighed Waddell. "They were told they could go on shore, but they would not be allowed to use any of the steamer's boats."

A shore boat was called. Lillias, along with her husband and luggage, was placed aboard and shoved clear, but not before a final squall with Lieutenant Whittle. Offended by her unbridled language, he hurled her copy of *Uncle Tom's Cabin* overboard. Her departing words were "I wish that steamer may be burned!"

Francis brushed aside Waddell's excuses: "I again renew my request to be furnished with a list giving the number of and particulars with respect to the prisoners."

Waddell replied, "I cheerfully furnish a list of those persons who were my prisoners on the high seas at your request, and at the same time wish to inform you that a list *was* furnished; [to] Mr. MacFarlin, chief officer of her Majesty's customs for Williamstown as far back as the 25th or 26th of January, in official form"—only with this letter, too, he omitted to enclose the list of prisoners. Francis's response was a scathingly blunt demand. Nonetheless, when Waddell finally complied, he continued to imply the failure was with Francis. "Sir," he wrote, "I have the honor to acknowledge your communication . . . calling my attention to *another* list of prisoners which you desire. I cheerfully furnish this second list, and have the honor to be, very respectfully, your obedient servant."

By then it did not matter. The prisoners themselves were already sitting in the office of the American consul, William Blanchard. Mindful of having signed a parole that enjoined them from divulging anything detrimental to the cause of the Confederacy or the ship, several declined to give any information beyond the circumstances under which they were captured. Lillias was not among them. She roared into Blanchard's office and demanded to make a statement.

After recounting the details of her capture, Lillias noted that Captain Waddell had treated her with kindness and consideration, then got down to the business of swearing "that while on board said steamer, I was frequently in conversation with the said Waddell, who frequently told me that he came out in the *Laurel* steamer from Liverpool to a place off Madeira, and that the *Laurel* was waiting three days for the *Sea King* . . . and that the said steamer *Shenandoah* was formerly the *Sea King*, built at Glasgow; and that the *Laurel* and *Sea King* steamer met off Madeira, and that the guns and ammunition then on board the said steamer *Shenandoah* were brought out by the said steamer *Laurel* packed in boxes."

Lillias's statement gave Blanchard all the ammunition he needed to open fire on the Confederates. It was, he concluded, sufficient evidence to have the vessel seized for being in violation of Britain's Neutrality Act. And if more was needed, he had sworn affidavits from other escapees testifying that the words "Sea King" were emblazoned on the ship's bell and galley cutlery. Nor had it had taken newspaper reporters long to notice the poorly obscured letters "ING" on the transom.

William Blanchard was a determined man. He quickly assembled a package of affidavits, newspaper articles, and other papers regarding the arrival of the "pirate" in Australian waters and forwarded it to Charles Francis Adams in England, with a copy to the American consul in Hong Kong requesting "that a [warship] might be put on her track as soon as possible." By rushing, Blanchard managed to get the dispatches aboard the same departing mail ship Waddell had been in such a hurry to catch.

"As soon as I had reason to believe that the *Shenandoah* and the *Sea King* were one and the same ship," he said, "and that she had not entered any port since leaving England, I took the position towards the authorities here that she was not entitled to any of the rights of a belligerent as contemplated in Her Majesty's neutrality proclamation, and that she could not change her nationality at sea." In a letter to Governor Darling, he carefully reiterated the argument.

HER MAJESTY'S GOVERNMENT was being painted into a corner. At the outset of the war, when the demands of the cotton trade had driven Lord Palmerston's cabinet to play fast and loose with Britain's neutrality, turning a blind eye to clandestine Confederate activities against the North had seemed appropriate. Now the war was turning against the South, and England and the other European powers wanted to distance themselves from the loser. Seizure would amount to a de facto admission that the law had been broken, but allowing the *Shenandoah* to continue burning and plundering would reinforce charges that the British government was illegally abetting a belligerent. Great Britain—and her Australian colony—ran the risk of being "hoist on their own petard."*

Faced with an issue of such complexity, Sir Charles did what skilled bureaucrats have done throughout history. He dithered. He waffled. Then he forwarded Blanchard's protest to a panel of legal advisers and notified the American consul that he could not act until he received their opinion. He apparently hoped that if he kept his head down, stalling might give the raider time to get out of town and relieve him of any necessity to act. After giving the raider permission to coal and repair, he made himself scarce.†

On the *Shenandoah*'s first full day at anchor, Waddell had made an appointment to visit the governor in his office shortly after noon. "Wanting a tail," wrote Lining, "he appointed Grimball, Scales, and myself to go ashore with him to make the official call."

The governor was not in. Waddell, considering himself a representative of the Confederate government, decided it would be undignified

---

*A petard was an explosive device hung on the end of a long pole used by a besieging army to blow open a closed door. If the charge exploded prematurely, its applicant might be speared by the pole and flung into the air. Thus, to be "hoist on one's own petard" was to be killed by one's own device—or fall victim to a failing plot.

†Sir Charles's hands-off style of governing also made him wildly popular among the independently minded citizens of Victoria. Tagged as "the people's governor" for his reluctance to issue orders that might interfere with their daily living, he was eventually recalled from his post by a British government unhappy with his laissez-faire and populist sentiments.

to wait. As they were leaving, they spotted Darling going the other way in a carriage.

They didn't try to stop him. Waddell was eager to get the repairs started as soon as possible, but the rest of the men wanted a holiday. After missing the governor, they headed for a popular Melbourne watering hole, the Scott's Hotel. There, according to Lining, they laid aside their swords and "started to drink with every fellow, with the consequence that 'John Collins' decidedly knocked some of the party." (Meaning, one presumes, that they got roaring drunk.)

Regulars at the saloon immediately set about organizing a reception for the *Shenandoah*'s officers at the Melbourne Club, an exclusive private retreat that had been offering Victoria's more successful ranchers, merchants, and miners a chance to mingle with statesmen and politicians since 1839. The dinner came off at seven o'clock, and according to Midshipman Mason, "a remarkably fine one it was, being attended by sixty members of the club. . . . all the first people of the town, all the members of parliament, the judges, and etc., etc. were amongst the members."

Lining agreed. "Everything went off remarkably well—there was no putting of fellows 'under the table' and our crew, especially, behaved very well."

"The dining room was a most magnificent apartment," Mason gushed, ". . . and the dinner was excellent, with all sorts of fine things, wines, and etc. I enjoyed myself very much, but in a reasonable manner!"

To Mason's right sat "Dr. B.," a "jolly old fellow who was very kind and polite." While stewards in scarlet waistcoats and velvet breeches circulated in and out of the dining room bearing platters of roast beef, "Old Sawbones" bent Mason's ear with an enthusiastic discourse on a subject dear to the heart of anyone accused of piracy. "He entertained me during the whole course of the dinner with a dissertation about hanging," said Mason, "contending that instead of placing the knot behind the ear as is usually the custom, it should be put behind the neck immediately upon the neckbone where the fall would snap the neck off and thus produce instantaneous death, whereas with the old custom of placing the knot behind the ear always five and sometimes ten minutes were required to produce death."

The doctor had been allowed to experiment on condemned criminals and bragged to Mason that he had never had a death under five minutes with the old system, but with his own, death was always instantaneous.

"So much for hanging," said Mason. "The sum of it all is that if I am to be hung, I shall beg the executioner to put the knot behind my neck."

FOR WEEKS, factional letters and articles crowded every newspaper in Australia. Feelings and verbiage ran high. Throughout, efforts by the *Age* and its supporters to brand the *Shenandoah* a criminal enterprise seem to have had little or no effect on the Southerners' popularity. In spite of the smears, life for the officers became a nonstop round of parties. Invitations to parties and balls continued to pour in from all sides.

"Whenever and wherever an officer appeared on shore," said Cornelius Hunt, "he was forthwith surrounded by a little conclave of sympathetic admirers. Had we accepted a tithe of the invitations we received to indulge in spirituous comforts, we should all of us, from the Captain down to the toughest old shellback in the forecastle, have been shockingly inebriated during the whole period of our sojourn." More important, the swashbuckling image touted by the press carried great cachet with the ladies. Hunt noted that a large percentage seemed to entertain the notion that human beings were sometimes destroyed with the vessels. Titillated damsels often inquired solemnly of the Confederates how their Yankee victims bore themselves as the flames of a burning ship engulfed them. "But notwithstanding the hard character they were ready to ascribe to us," he chuckled, ". . . the ladies in particular were well pleased when they could secure the attendance of a grey uniform."

In favor with the ladies or not, Hunt cautioned that "it must not be supposed that the entire population favored us." A strong element among Melbourne's citizens favored the Union cause, and these "looked upon us as contumacious rebels, seeking to overthrow, by the most unjustifiable and atrocious means, a generous and beneficent government. And could they have retaliated upon us some of the depredations we had committed upon their merchant marine, our gallant ship would certainly have proceeded no farther."

What he meant was that along with Blanchard's efforts to have the raider seized, other, more covert efforts were being made to sabotage their voyage. These ranged from plotting direct attacks against the ship to entrapping the rebels into violating Britain's Neutrality Act.

"Every effort was made to entangle me in legal difficulties," said Waddell. "I received forty-seven letters, a large majority of which were bogus applications for service in the Shenandoah." The applicants were certainly Union toadies, British subjects sent by Blanchard to lure Waddell into violating the neutrality. According to Hunt, one of the smoothest attempts came at the hands of an old woman who came aboard with her little son, with a plea so touching it aroused suspicion. "She was a Southern woman, she said, and her little boy had been born in the Sunny South, and she desired Captain Waddell to take him as the only contribution she had to offer to her country."

Waddell snorted. "She was referred to the attorney general in Melbourne . . . and directed not to renew the application unless provided with a certificate setting forth her indispensable right to enter the lad in the service of the Confederate States. . . . The plot was well laid, but having failed, the old woman and her hireling never returned."

Rumors reached the ship that Union sympathizers were planning to blow up the *Shenandoah* by attaching a torpedo to her bow.* Whittle posted armed lookouts, and night after night, rowboats approaching under cover of darkness turned away after being challenged.

"I had employed a carpenter to make and put up a bureau in my

---

*Before the invention of submarines, a torpedo was not a self-propelled bomb but more like what is today called a "mine."

cabin," Waddell said, "and while he was engaged about it, fitting it to the side of the vessel, he told me he had heard in a restaurant some Americans discussing the feasibility of smuggling themselves on board, and after the steamer was at sea to capture her." The commander was in bed when he received this intelligence and told the carpenter that "if it is attempted they will fail, and I will hang every mother's son of them."

Blanchard's other schemes were more transparent. He offered a hundred dollars to anyone willing to desert, along with protection from arrest. (So great was the power of a ship's master over ordinary seamen in the 1800s that even those impressed against their will were subject to capture and return if they had signed a ship's articles.) Eighteen crewmen, including Williams, the black cook from the D. *Godfrey,* an Irishman, and "sixteen dirty Germans" accepted Blanchard's offer, but when one of his emissaries tried to seduce Peter Wiggins, the *Shenandoah*'s quartermaster, he refused.

"They tried in every manner possible to involve us in a quarrel with the government," added Lining. "And having persuaded, or probably bribed, a number of our men to desert, they finally succeeded in making a sort of case against us [when] one of these deserters made affidavit that we had enlisted a man by the name of Charley after getting into port, and that he himself had seen Charley sign the shipping articles."

"Charley" came closer to ending the voyage than any of Blanchard's plots.

Governor Darling's advisers were growing impatient. A report from the engineering firm Langlands Brothers & Co. recommended that the ship be dry-docked. Repairs were estimated to take ten days—far too long for Darling's peace of mind, or Waddell's, the first because the longer the raider lingered in Melbourne, the more likely it became that the government would be forced to act, and the second because every day spent in harbor gave his already slender crew another chances to defect. Worse, from Waddell's perspective, a protracted stay also increased the odds of being discovered by a Union gunboat. By now the

Iroquois had discovered that the *Shenandoah* was not in Cape Town and was on her way to Batavia (now Jakarta in Indonesia), only a few days away. And the departing mail steamer would soon be spreading news of the raider's arrival in Australia.

Nevertheless, the repairs were vital. There was no choice but to tow the raider the two miles from Sandridge to Williamstown and begin unloading her stores. Everything down to the last shovel of coal had to be removed in order to lighten her enough to be lifted onto the cradle. On the second day, there was a near disaster.

It had been blowing a stiff gale from the northward all day, blowing so hard that the crew had to put out extra hawsers. At 10 p.m. the wind backed to the west and grew stronger. At eleven the stern lines parted. An hour later the bow line snapped, driving the raider sideways against the breakwater.

"I don't think I ever saw the wind blow harder than it did about midnight," said Lining. As the crew labored to protect the ship from the rocks with coils of heavy line and bales of hay, a fierce gust nearly blew him off the forecastle. The pilot of a steam tug coming alongside to tow the cruiser off ordered the attempt aborted. Only by pinning one of the lightering barges between the ship and the rocks was damage averted.

At daybreak the storm relented, but it took another three days of winching and tugging to pull the *Shenandoah* off the breakwater and winch her up the patent slip. Once she was high and dry, the repairs proceeded slowly, even with work gangs laboring around the clock.

Darling's executive council, fearing the colonial authority would appear to be openly assisting a belligerent, refused the Confederates use of any government-owned equipment during the repairs. Yet even as it refused to expedite the ship's repairs in any way, the council was continually pressing Waddell to name his departure date.

But while Waddell steamed over the government's pestering, Blanchard too was meeting with frustration: after more than a week of debate, Governor Darling's legal advisers had issued an opinion stating that the raider could not be seized for piracy.

The stymied consul's next attempt was to have the *Shenandoah* indicted by the admiralty court, which functioned as a separate authority. Armed with a briefcase full of affidavits from former crewmen aboard the *Alina*, the *D. Godfrey*, and the *Lizzie M. Stacey*, he stormed into the Crown law offices and confronted the magistrates. Under pressure, the jurists claimed that while the conversion of the *Sea King* appeared to be illegal, they could not act because the law had not been broken in Australian waters.

"[The magistrates] seemed to admit that the *Shenandoah* would be liable to seizure and condemnation if found in British waters," he said, "but would not admit that she was liable to seizure *here*, unless she violated the neutrality while in this port." As a sop, they promised that if the raider did violate the neutrality, they would take immediate action. An hour later, when he returned to the consulate, this final statement proved to be music to Blanchard's ears.

John Williams, the black cook from the *D. Godfrey*, was waiting in Blanchard's office, where he signed an affidavit testifying that he had served as cook "under compulsion and punishment on board said *Shenandoah* from the day of my capture until Monday, the sixth day of February, 1865 . . . and that when I left the said *Shenandoah*, on Monday last, there were fifteen or twenty men concealed in different parts of the ship who came on board since the *Shenandoah* arrived in Hobson's Bay." These men told Williams they had come to join the ship. He had cooked for them for several days before he jumped over the side and swam away, and swore there were three others—two in the galley and one in the engine room—already wearing Confederate uniforms. One of the galley hands went by the name of Charley.

Blanchard immediately sent a copy of Williams's affidavit to Governor Darling. Darling forwarded it to the office of the crown solicitor. There, the minister for justice and attorney general decided to interview Williams personally, promising that "[should] evidence sufficient to support a charge of misdemeanor against any of the persons concealed on board the *Shenandoah* or against any of her officers be found," the government would proceed immediately.

Blanchard next renewed his plea to have the *Shenandoah* seized because of the nature of her origin, but was again rebuffed by Darling, who said he had "furnished no new ground for an alteration of the views respecting the presumed character of the *Shenandoah*, which have already been communicated to you."

Finally the consul got lucky. Two of the *Alina*'s former crewmen, both of whom Waddell had scorned as "dirty Germans," signed affidavits swearing that when they abandoned ship on February 12, after three weeks in harbor, the cooking was being done by a new hand named Charley. Charley, they said, had joined the ship in Melbourne. He was a twenty-two-year-old Scotsman known to the Melbourne police as James Davidson. He could be found working in the galley, wearing a Confederate uniform.

Confronted with sworn testimony of such exactitude, Governor Darling had no choice but to relent. He forwarded Blanchard's letters and affidavits to the attorney general with a note directing him to "take whatever steps are requisite to ensure a strict adherence to Her Majesty's Proclamation of Neutrality."

A warrant was issued for Charley's arrest. Superintendent Thomas Lyttleton of the Williamstown police was chosen to serve it.

LINING LATER REMEMBERED that when he got back to the ship, he "found it in a great commotion." He had been to Williamstown, paying a parting call on new friends in anticipation of leaving. The repairs were expected to be finished the following day. When Superintendent Lyttleton arrived with the warrant, Lieutenant Grimball refused to let him serve it. Commander Waddell was ashore, he said, and Lyttleton would have to satisfy himself with inspecting the ship's articles, where he could see for himself no cook named Charley was listed.

Lyttleton insisted. Grimball resisted. After a brief argument, the superintendent agreed to come back when Waddell was on board.

"When the superintendent returned I received him kindly," said the commander. After introducing the subject of his visit, Lyttleton cautiously asked, if he introduced a witness to identify Charley, would the witness be arrested? That is, if the witness was a deserter from the *Shenandoah?* Lyttleton thought he had an ace up his sleeve. One of Blanchard's German deponents had agreed to finger Charley, but only if the consul promised he would be protected. He was waiting on the pier with a police escort.

Waddell deemed the question ludicrous. "I replied the deck of the *Shenandoah* was Confederate territory, and every violation of the law committed on her deck would be punished by the laws which governed the ship. Therefore if any deserter from the *Shenandoah* appeared on her deck, it mattered not under what circumstances, such arrests would be made."

Lyttleton argued that it had been sworn under oath that there were British subjects on the ship who had enlisted in the Confederate service. Waddell denied this emphatically. More, he said, "I pledge to you on my word of honor as an officer and a gentleman that I have not anyone on board, nor have I engaged anyone, nor will I while I am here."

"I'll use force if I have to," countered Lyttleton. "I must execute my warrant."

"His application to search the vessel was refused," said Waddell. "And he was informed should the Victorian government attempt so great an outrage, the *Shenandoah* would be defended at every risk to life."

Lyttleton left. At 5:30 p.m. he returned, accompanied by a body of policemen and a corps of artillery. This force took up positions on the pier, encircling the stranded ship with armed men and small cannons. Governor Darling issued a proclamation that no more work was to be done on the ship.

"It was a display of intellectual and military weakness I was not prepared to witness," thundered Waddell. "For the *Shenandoah* lay helpless on the slip, where it appears she was decoyed for the purpose of insult."

Lining, like his commander, was outraged. "I don't know if I have ever felt more humiliated in all my life as when I saw policemen on each side of the ship, with guns in their hands, keeping guard over us, while we lay perfectly helpless on the slip. Everybody seemed to share this feeling, even the men, and a general wish was expressed to resist if possible." They swore to fight, though being unable to train their guns, there was little they could do to resist artillery with carbines and cutlasses.

The standoff grew tense. Sidearms were distributed. Word filtered across the bay into Melbourne that the cruiser had been seized. Waddell assembled his officers in his cabin for a war council. In his opulent chambers, Darling did the same.

"Captain Waddell called Whittle, Grimball, Smith-Lee, and myself in," said Lining, "and requested our opinion of what he had better do. It was decided that under no circumstances should a search be permitted, that a letter should be written to the government denying that the man was on board, but refusing any search." But before sending the letter, the surgeon suggested an officer be sent to search the ship, "in order that we might be perfectly correct in what we stated."

"The master-at-arms was ordered to make the desired search and no one but the ship's company and the hired mechanics were found on board," added Mason. He was chosen to go ashore with the letter. Immediately after his departure, Irvine Bulloch knocked on the cabin door and asked for Lining. What he had to say nearly spilled the wind from the Confederates' sails.

"He came to me and told me that he knew of some stowaways being still on board, and asked me what he had better do," said the doctor. "I told him of course to go and tell Whittle." Whittle ordered Grimball and the master-at-arms to find the stowaways. Their commander had given his word, he said, and when Grimball returned to report that he had indeed found four stowaways, the lieutenant made a command decision: after darkness came, the stowaways were to be smuggled from the ship.

In his own chambers, Governor Darling was casting about for a way to defuse the crisis. His advisers argued that it was vital that the government demonstrate it was able and willing to exercise its authority, but an actual attack would be tantamount to declaring war against the

Confederacy. On the other hand, the police could not be withdrawn without making it appear the rebels were being allowed to bully his government.

Darling's solution was to announce the vessel had never in fact been seized, only the wharf, and that the company of rifle-toting policemen and artillery were sent not to enforce the warrant but to ensure that in their sympathy for the Confederacy, the residents of Williamstown were not allowed "to set at naught the prohibition [against further work] and defy the authority of the government by assisting the crew of the *Shenandoah* to launch the vessel."

He was right about the public sentiment: the engineer and several workmen told Waddell they were willing to stay on board and continue working in exchange for meals. And while the *Shenandoah*'s crew peered across the bulwarks at the waiting policemen and fondled their weapons, the *Herald* reported that "Melbourne was in a complete fever of excitement. . . . The streets of the city were crowded with persons anxious to hear what has been done with the *Shenandoah,* and groups of the species *gobemouche* were to be met with at every turn, exchanging their stock of information and occasionally fabricating news on their own account."

In the interim, Darling began trying to blame the escalation on poor communication between his functionaries and an overzealous police force. Francis, however, pushed for a tougher stance, and in response, Waddell—arguing with the same finely nuanced sense of law that had allowed him to sink the *Alina* for failing to notarize its cargo manifest—sent a note to the governor claiming he should not be accused of refusing the warrant, because the warrant had been for the arrest of Charley and there was no such person on board. He had refused only the *search*, he argued, and had done so to preserve the dignity of his vessel, which he considered to represent "the majesty of the country whose flag she flies." More, he offered, "Our shipping articles have been shown to the superintendent of police, all strangers have been sent out of the ship, and two commissioned officers . . . have reported to me that after making a thorough search, they can find no person on board, except those who entered this port as part of her complement of men."

In return, Darling offered a face-saving compromise, arguing that if there was no such person as Charley on board, Waddell should still allow the warrant to be executed so the authorities could prosecute Blanchard's claimants for swearing to false information.

According to Mason, "The captain then decided to take the bull by the horns, and accordingly, at about nine o'clock at night, an officer was sent with a communication to Mr. Francis informing him that unless the embargo was removed by the time the tide was high the next day, when the ship would be ready for launching, the captain would haul down his flag, send home his crew and officers, and leave the ship in the possession of the authorities." Doing so would put the government "in the same predicament as the fellow who drew the elephant in the lottery."

Darling was saved the inconvenience of finding himself in possession of a 225-foot raider by the sudden appearance of Charley, just as the tide turned and began rising. At about 10 p.m., an hour after Waddell's officer departed for the governor's office with the ultimatum, Constable Alexander Minto of the Williamstown water police watched four men climb from the dry-docked raider into a rowboat. When he paddled over to ask what they were doing, they claimed to be laborers.

Officer Minto was no fast thinker. Before it occurred to him to question their story, the quartet had already rowed out of sight. But after giving a bit of thought as to who they might be and what they might be doing, he sprinted ashore and ran as fast as he could the few blocks to the Williamstown railway station, where he found two of the men already waiting on the platform. The other two were hiding in a restroom. One was James Davidson, aka Charley. All were placed under arrest and marched to a confrontation with Superintendent Lyttleton.

"They told me that they had been on board a few days unknown to the captain," claimed the superintendent. "And that as soon as he found they were on board, he ordered them to go on shore." At eleven o'clock the next night Waddell received a letter from Commissioner Francis:

It has been reported by the police that at about ten o'clock last night four men, who had been in concealment aboard the Shenandoah left the ship, and were arrested immediately after so leaving by the water police. It appears from the statements of these men that they were on board your vessel when their presence was denied by the commanding officer in charge, and by yourself subsequently, when you declared that there were "no persons on board this ship except those whose names are on our shipping articles. . . . I am in a position to state that one of the four men previously alluded to is ascertained to be the person named in the warrant. I am also able to observe that, while at the moment of the despatch of your letter it may be true that these men were not on board the Shenandoah, it is beyond question that they were on board at the time it was indited.

Waddell was busted and he knew it. His pulse must have skipped a beat when he read the next paragraph:

Nevertheless, as the only person for whose arrest a warrant was issued has been secured, and as you are now in a position to say, as commanding officer of the ship . . . that "there are no persons on board this ship except those whose names are on our shipping articles, and that no one has been enlisted in the service of the Confederate States since my arrival in this port," His Excellency the Governor has been pleased to revoke the direction issued yesterday suspending permission to British subjects to aid and assist you.

In other words, they were letting him off the hook. But Francis was blunt: "It is expected that you will exercise every despatch to insure your departure."

Charley was not as lucky: for attempting to violate the Foreign Enlistment Act, he was sentenced to ten days.

Hauled out for repairs at the Williamstown dockyard, Melbourne, Australia, in February 1865. Note Confederate flag (possibly retouched) flying from her mizzen gaff and fresh caulking between her planks.

TEN

A T FIVE O'CLOCK a steam tug arrived to drag the raider from the pier. Groaning winches lowered the ship to the waiting tide. The bill came to fifteen thousand dollars, but this did not bother Waddell and his officers. Instead, they were gloating over the suddenness of their newfound freedom.

"The police and militia folded their tents like Arabs and stole away," crowed Lining. Whittle added, "We were now the masters of the situation; they were at the mercy of our guns." Only the HMS *Victoria*, an old single-gun frigate, stood between the pissed-off rebels and the city. Waddell ordered the guns armed with shot. Fortunately for everyone, the Australians knew how to smooth ruffled feathers: they threw a party up in Ballarat and stocked it with pretty girls. The railroad supplied the Confederates with free passes, and the entire population turned out to greet them beneath a triumphal arch of roses. The ballroom at Craig's Hotel was decorated to the hilt.

"It was a decidedly recherché affair..." said Hunt. "With the wealth, beauty, and fashion of Ballarat out in full force."

In Lining's opinion, the sweetest-looking girl in the room was the daughter of the mayor, though he judged two married ladies to be "splendid . . . fair, fat, and thirty." Bulloch struck up with a young lady from Geelong. A fair admirer squeezed Smith-Lee's hand. The dancing went on until 4 a.m., and the next afternoon, Bulloch was still kissing his Geelong lady. At seven, Lining, Grimball, and Chew straggled into the railway station, accompanied by the married ladies.

"Many a grey uniform coat lost its gilt buttons that night," wrote Hunt, "but we saw them again ere we bade a final adieu to Australia, suspended from watchguards depending from the necks of bright-eyed women. . . . God bless the gentle women of Melbourne and Ballarat! They are remembered gratefully by the officers of the ship."

TWO DAYS LATER, clutching their buttonless jackets closed with one hand, their pants held aloft with twists of twine, the officers assembled to salute the *Shenandoah*'s departure from Melbourne. It was the eighteenth of February, the weather mild and clear. Lieutenant Chew had the watch.* When the boatswain piped the men up to hoist the anchor, they threw themselves at the windlass with alacrity. Twenty-five days had passed since their arrival in Australia, and with the exception of McNulty, who had been so reluctant to leave that Mason and Scales had to be dispatched with orders to use force to bring him back aboard if necessary, all were glad to be under way.

Blanchard, on the other hand, was unhappy. Extremely unhappy.

---

*No one ever mentions how Lieutenant Chew regained Waddell's favor after having been relieved of his watch and demoted to "winder of chronometers" in the Indian Ocean. He simply reappears as officer of the watch upon leaving Melbourne.

For the twenty-four hours preceding the raider's departure he had been subjected to an incredible runaround. After an informant came to him with information that men were gathering on the Williamstown pier waiting to be ferried out to the raider, he had taken the informant to the Crown law offices, where the solicitor had refused to take a deposition, saying he was late for dinner. Next Blanchard tried the police, only to be shrugged off and directed to Parliament. From the Parliament building, the attorney general had sent him to another magistrate's office, this one a mile away, where that magistrate too had refused to take the informant's statement, saying it was the responsibility of the Williamstown water police. Upon hearing he would be required to return to Williamstown, the informant had grown afraid of encountering the men he was tattling on and had run away.

Worse, while Blanchard had been running this gauntlet of bureaucratic unconcern, he had spotted the *Shenandoah* sidling up to a British supply ship, the *John Fraser,* for a load of coal. That the collier was named for a senior partner in the firm that acted as the Confederacy's bank in Europe was not lost on the consul, nor was the fact that it had departed London almost simultaneously with the *Sea King* only to arrive on the far side of the world just in time for the resupply, in a coincidence Waddell described as "singular," but which the consul simply logged as more evidence of British calumny. (In his report to Lincoln's secretary of state, Blanchard complained bitterly that "there are eyes that do not see and ears that do not hear, and I fear that this port is endowed with such a portion of them as may be required to suit the occasion.") He might have felt even worse had he had known how close the *Shenandoah* had come to being captured. On the same day Waddell gave the order to hoist the anchor, Commander C. R. P. Rodgers of the USS *Iroquois* was writing from Ceylon to say he had learned of the rebel's stay. "I should sail for Melbourne immediately," wrote Rodgers, "if I could hope to reach that place in time to overtake the *Shenandoah.*"

But as the route from Ceylon to Australia was in the teeth of the southeast trades, he could not expect to arrive until after the raider had sought "some new field of pillage and destruction." Instead he would sail for the Sunda Strait, near present-day Singapore, where the convergence of islands and currents created a natural bottleneck for American ships laden with the treasures of the Far East attempting to make the return voyage to California. And for the three and a half weeks the *Shenandoah* lay anchored in Sandridge, the ten-gun USS *Suwanee* had been steaming at full speed toward the Pacific. By the end of the month, five vessels—the USS *Santee, Suwanee, Wachusett, Iroquois,* and *Wyoming*—would join the chase, aided by the Pacific and European squadrons.

But while the pursuing Yankee topmen were shaking out every last stitch of canvas and sweating stokers were cursing out one more knot, Waddell—hearing the steady thump of the steam engine beneath his feet and the hiss of the bowstem cutting the waves—was ecstatic. Reveling in the bright blue sea, he grew so swept up in the feeling of freedom that he burst forth with an unexpected shard of rhyme.

"While the stars that oversprinkle / the heavens seem to twinkle / with a crystalline delight" may or may not have artistic merit, but given that on the night the *Shenandoah* departed a full silver moon hung shining overhead, it is probably forgivable for even the most hardbitten sea captain to be driven to rhyme, or for his crew, in their celebratory distraction, to have let their ship run nearly headlong into disaster. Soon after the steamer's head was brought around to a course for Bass Strait, the dark shadow of a landmass suddenly loomed off the bow. It was only through a series of quick and furious maneuvers that the ship was saved.

No sooner had the adrenaline introduced by this near disaster begun to burn low than another, perhaps even greater surprise erupted. Muffled clangs and scraping were heard from within the hollow iron bowsprit, and first one, and then another, and another, strange man crawled out. Others began appearing in small bunches, coming up from hiding places belowdecks. "They made their appearance from every conceivable place where a human being could conceal himself," wrote Hunt. "Fourteen of their number crept out of the bowsprit, which was iron and hollow, and where they had come very near ending their existence by suffocation; twenty more turned out of some water tanks which were dry; another detachment was unearthed from the lower hold!"

Soon a mob of forty-two stowaways was milling about the deck.

"How such a number of men could have gained our deck unseen was a mystery to me then and is still," Hunt later claimed. "But there they were, and the question now was how to dispose of them."

The question was disingenuous. After desertions, the *Shenandoah* had left Melbourne with a complement of only thirty men, far too few to allow the continuance of its mission. And there was no possibility of returning to Melbourne.

"Of course, we could not go back to put these men ashore," said Lining. "So there was nothing to be done but enlist them."

The stowaways were quickly mustered aft and the captain was sent for. From there, the affair took on an air of farce, with Waddell making his appearance and without preamble demanding to know of the new hands what country they belonged to and their intentions.

"The old sea-dogs chuckled, rolled their tobacco, and hitched up their trousers," said Hunt, "and with one accord, protested that they were natives of the Southern Confederacy, and had come on board thus surreptitiously for the purpose of joining us.

"There was something absolutely refreshing in the effrontery with which that motley crew had first stolen on board, at the moment of our leaving port, and then claimed the privilege of remaining, on the ground that they were our countrymen. I verily believe half the nations of the earth had contributed to this proposed accession to our numbers, but sailors are genuine cosmopolitans, and as a general thing, change their nationalities as readily as they do their names."

Waddell tallied his newly fattened crew. The increase "placed upon our decks seventy-two men, all quite homeless and accustomed to a hard life, more in search of adventure and fun than anything else." There were even representatives from New England, and it was "droll indeed to find a genuine Yankee on the deck of a Confederate warship, manifesting delight in the destroying of his countryman's property."

In general, Waddell was correct in his regard for the new men, but of two he was mistaken. The first was Captain John Blacker of the British steamer *Saxonia,* now anchored in Melbourne Harbor, who had grown so enamored with the Southern crew and their cause that he was willing to throw off the prestige of his own command to pitch in with the Confederates. All he asked for was a position as Waddell's clerk. The second introduced himself as George P. Canning, an aristocratic refugee who had snuck aboard accompanied by a black manservant. And of all the odd characters to stride the *Shenandoah*'s decks—the polyglot wanderers, Russian refugees, African American volunteers, descendants of Southern aristocracy, and Yankees willing to burn their own ships—George P. Canning was one of the most mysterious.

"THERE IS SOMETHING in the history of this man that none of us knows," Lining would later write. "In fact, we know nothing about him."

What they did know was that he came aboard suffering from a gunshot wound to the chest, a wound he claimed to have received at the Battle of Shiloh while serving on General Polk's staff. But according to the records of the National Archives in Washington, no Canning ever served on Polk's staff. Nor does the name George P. Canning appear anywhere else in the records. Indeed, there are indications that Canning, who carried himself with an aristocratic aplomb, wrote with the hand of a gentleman, and spoke with a bit of Southern accent, was born in 1837 not as George P. but as George Boutrenne (or Baltriune) Canning in Rotherhithe, England, and raised in France. Boutrenne had two brothers: Alfred (who immigrated to Australia and became a member of Parliament) and Rafton, who was so similar to Boutrenne in personal history and appearance as to pose a puzzle; a descendant of Canning's interviewed for this book contends that Boutrenne and Rafton may have been one and the same man, a hypothesis advanced by French census records that indicate both Boutrenne and Rafton married foreign women, fathered only sons (Rafton's named George and Georges's named Rafton), and lived at addresses only a short dis-

tance apart. But the kicker came in 1936, when, in assembling and la-
beling old family records, brother Rafton's son came across a tintype of
his presumed uncle George and wrote across the back that "the likeness
to my father is so remarkable that [mother says] it might *be* considered
as that of Rafton Canning, my father." And Rafton's son George, in
preparing the information for his own death certificate years later, listed
his own father's name as George instead of Rafton. It is also known that
George P. told his Australian brother that his wound had been received
in the Crimea, where once again there is no record of him having ever
served. Through her own tenacious research, Kim Salisbury of Bixby
Knolls, California (the descendant previously mentioned) has come to
believe that Canning's wound may have been the result of bigamy; that
Margaret—a Southern woman George P. told some of the *Shenandoah*'s
officers he was married to—may have shot him after discovering he was
maintaining a second household only a short walk from their home in
Paris. The conjecture is reinforced by old French records that show
Boutrenne's son Rafton was born in the local shire officer's residence,
which would be somewhat akin to being born in a sheriff's office.
("Was she under arrest?" asks Kim. From there Margaret disappears
from the family records. Her children, including young Rafton, were
raised by an aunt.)

　　But the mystery of George Canning may wander even further
afield, driven by the "singular coincidence" of a supposed Confederate
veteran showing up on the scene almost simultaneously with the arrival
of the British coal ship *John Fraser*. Was there more to George P.
Canning than a man fleeing domestic turmoil? Why wait to be smuggled aboard with the riffraff of Williamstown, when as an ex-member
of a Confederate field officer's staff he would surely have been wel-
comed aboard at his own convenience? Being accompanied by a black
manservant only added to the veracity of his story, and with his background in France (where the Confederacy continued to try to obtain
fighting ships), it seems the mysterious Sergeant Canning may in some
way have been connected with James Dunwoody Bulloch's spy ring,
which, now that the South's war efforts were collapsing and the

European nations were withdrawing their diplomatic support, may have been trying to smuggle various agents from the Continent. Why else would a man shot through the lung even *consider* going to sea? And why would a commander enlist him?

This, of course, is pure conjecture. All that is known for sure is that George P. Canning came aboard shot through the right lung, accompanied by his sidekick Weeks (for whom he insisted on equal pay), and, though weakened and gasping, somehow inspired Waddell with enough confidence to be made a sergeant of marines.* As for the other stowaways, said Hunt, "we really needed their assistance, and as they had come through no connivance of ours, we determined to consider it providential and they were enlisted. . . . Good men and true they proved, and very useful before our cruise ended."

Waddell ordered the *Shenandoah*'s course held until ships inbound for Melbourne could report his direction, then resorted to his customary dodge of laying a false trail by bringing the ship's bow around to a southeast heading. The breeze was light and baffling, making it difficult to hold a course for their next destination; they hoped for Yankee vessels off the whaling grounds off Middleton, Lord Howe, and Norfolk Islands.

It took hours of drifting and tacking to clear Cape Howe. It was, said Lining, as if the ship itself were sorry to leave Australia.

"We [the officers] still looked back and spoke of what we would be doing if we were there," he wrote, mulling that "when I look back, I can hardly determine whether I can look back with pleasure or not, for I certainly had some very pleasant hours in Melbourne, and as surely some very disagreeable ones—at any rate, we are all glad to be once more rid of the vexations which we experienced there."

After all the balls, politics, love affairs, and frustrations, they were finally under way.

---

*Marines were the police of the ship, armed and trained to deal with mutiny or insurrection. It was also the task of the marines to be the first to board an enemy vessel in close-quarters combat.

ELEVEN

F ROM THE OUTSET, each of the *Shenandoah*'s officers referred at various points in his journal to the nobility of the Southern cause and to honor. And because Waddell was commander, his sense of honor was the most finely tuned (or at least the most loudly trumpeted). But the appearance of forty-two stowaways on the deck appears to brand him as a liar. With one or more officers on watch at all times and armed guards patrolling the ship twenty-four hours a day, it is inconceivable that so many men could have sneaked aboard and secreted themselves without being noticed. Yet in the privacy of his journal each officer remarked at the "surprise" of finding the men on board—a surprise difficult to digest in view of various verbal nudges (such as Mason's continuous referral to the "stowaways" in quotes), which instead create the impression of a coordinated effort to mislead anyone who might later delve into their reminiscences. In any case, the protests, oaths, and words of honor presented to Commissioner Francis, Inspector Lyttleton, and Governor Darling regarding the presence of Charley or other illegal enlistees on board are rendered hollow by (1) the very presence of so many stowaways and (2) Waddell's casual statement in his earliest letter home that he would "get all the men that he wants." (And if further evidence were needed, a classified ad placed in the *Argus* during the raider's stay advertised for "respectable young men to be generally useful to travel up to new country," giving the address of a boardinghouse commonly used by sailors. Respondents were asked if they had any experience with big guns.)

In other words, the Confederates' honor was elastic. When it was pragmatic to do so, they lied. And the closest they had come to the glory of battle was a drunken brawl at Scott's Hotel, where as Hunt said, they were "just sitting down to a sumptuous repast when an individual entered, invited himself to join us, and forthwith commenced a tirade upon rebels and the Southern Confederacy, making use of such language as gentlemen seldom submit to in silence." Assistant Surgeon McNulty had leaped to his feet and knocked the loudmouth out with one punch, but in an instant the fight had become a classic barroom brawl, with "glasses and decanters being turned into missiles, and knives and pistols drawn." Fortunately, nobody was seriously hurt in the melee, and while the rebels did finish up the affair with a certain panache by lining up in formation and marching away singing, it was hardly the stuff of heroes. And the disparity between what the officers said in the privacy of their journals and did in real life was not the only contradiction in the records. Mason, Lining, Whittle, and Chew all scoffed at reports that the *Shenandoah*'s crew routinely brutalized their victims or forced unwilling prisoners to join them. Each in turn denied that the captives ever suffered anything more offensive than being placed in irons. Yet a volunteer named John Maclean, who had left the ship in Melbourne saying he declined to serve a country that so ill-used its prisoners, had written a letter to the *Argus* swearing he had seen men whipped, gagged, struck with marlinespikes, and having tobacco juice spit in their faces. The raider, he said, was "a hell on the sea."

But there is no denying that the fellows of the *Shenandoah* must have been in some way charismatic. As many recruits from the raider's victims stayed on board in Melbourne as deserted or swam away, at least one victimized owner had offered to sign the ship's articles, and Captain Blacker aboard the British steamer *Saxonia* took the extraordinary step of deserting his own command to join.

Like any society, a cross-section of the *Shenandoah*'s crew would undoubtedly have revealed pious men and scoundrels, decent men and rakes, and others who were a blend of each. The only inarguable thing about the rebel "heroes" was that they were having a tremendous effect on the world's economy. Since the start of the conflict, the *Alabama, Florida, Shenandoah,* and others of their "piratical ilk" had sunk nearly 250 Union ships, driving insurance rates so high that another 700 were sold into foreign ownership, effectively destroying the hegemony of the American merchant fleet. When the *Iroquois* sailed into Batavia, Commander Rodgers found the port full of American vessels too frightened to venture outside the harbor. As far away as Hong Kong and Peru, the tattered remains of the Northern trading fleet sat at anchor. Yankees everywhere were too spooked to move.

The ocean the raider sailed into north of Australia was a void. A steady wind out of the north and west forced them to tack back and forth through miles of empty space, and they passed Fiji and the Ellice Islands without spotting a single sail.

North of Fearn Island, a revolving cyclone had come spinning down out of the upper latitudes and blasted them with northeast winds, enveloping them in a storm Lining called "one of the hardest gales I ever have seen in all my life." Tremendous seas and squalls of blinding rain hammered the ship, and when the double-reefed storm trysail blew out, the crew struggled for hours to replace it with a heavy tarpaulin. It was a miracle no one was killed when a huge sea roared aboard and tore the starboard howitzer from its lashing, then sent it tumbling across the deck to destroy a section of the portside bulwarks.

"I had never in twenty-three years' service seen such a succession of violent squalls," remembered Waddell. "She was enveloped in salt mist and tossed about by an angry sea like a plaything." With innumerable uncharted islands lurking downwind, there was no choice but to lie to under a deep-reefed mizzen staysail and keep fire in the boilers in case it suddenly became necessary to claw off a hidden reef.

The storm lasted four days. Behind it came a breathless calm, and for days the sky was as hot and empty of wind as the horizon was of sails. The humidity soared, broken only by heavy midday showers. By the middle of March Lining was complaining that "[there is] nothing in sight, not even a bird. In fact, this region seems to be the abomination of desolation, as the very birds have deserted us."

"Indeed," Mason sighed, "I believe we have found a portion of the world that no mortal has ever explored."

Without targets to pursue, ennui began to eat at everyone, and in the forepeak the sailors bickered, saying Waddell was driving them crazy giving orders, then countermanding them. He would order the boilers fired, then suddenly grow concerned about using precious coal and have them banked again; extra sails were ordered set when there was no breeze. After days of aimless drifting, the heat and boredom drove the ship's carpenter and one of his cronies to worm their way down the shaft alley into a storeroom, where they broached a barrel of rum and siphoned off fifty gallons. For the next several days, the stupor of men dozing about the deck was no longer induced solely by the blazing sun. Three months had passed without chasing a Yankee sail.

Finally, on March 20, Waddell relented, saying they would head for Drummond Island in the Cannibal (or Gilbert) Island chain, where he thought a small fleet of whalers might be working.* He waited until sunset, then ordered steam raised.

They traveled for three days. As they drew closer to the equator, the sun grew so hot it bubbled the pitch from the decks, and the touch of bare metal could singe one's skin. At eight o'clock on the evening of the

---

*Many of the island names used by mariners in the 1800s have disappeared from common usage. Drummond is now charted as Tabiteuea, or as Surgeon Lining wrote it, "Taputeouea," its original indigenous name.

twenty-third, they reached a point only a few miles from Drummond Island and stopped, drifting all night, waiting for daylight before approaching the island. There, Lining wrote, "the captain says he expects to take at least seven whalers." But when a sail was sighted, it was not what anyone expected.

"The boat was a canoe formed by pieces of wood sewn together and having an outrigger to keep it steady," said Lining. In it were three natives, "all perfectly naked and frightfully tattooed." They were, thought the surgeon, "a horrid looking set of devils, more like monkeys than men." It took a while to coax the natives alongside, although they had clearly come to trade. Their craft was heaped to the gunwales with colorful fish and fresh fruit. All they wanted was tobacco—proof, thought some of the officers, that they had been in contact with Western sailors.

Using a variety of gestures and grunts, Waddell attempted to question them about Yankees in the area but received only uncomprehending stares. Everyone was surprised when one of the older sailors stepped forward and said he could speak their language. (Several Malays had joined from among the raider's victims, and since the residents of the Gilbert Islands are more akin in appearance, language, and custom to some of the native groups of Malaysia than they are to their Polynesian neighbors, it seems reasonable to presume the unexpected interpreter was one of these.)

"Through him," said Hunt, "we inquired of them if any whalers had been there lately, and learned that there had not within the last three months." (This may also explain why they were out of tobacco.)

"So our visions of seven ships on fire were dissipated," continued Lining. "The captain was so disgusted that he would not remain even for the other canoes which we saw coming off . . . but started off under steam to the north and west." In a burst of anthropological curiosity, Lining begged Waddell to stay, to allow him to go on shore "that I might see the people in a state of nature, having had no contact with civilization or missionaries."

But it was Lining's lucky day, because Waddell refused. Fifteen years earlier, in 1851, John Bowman, a journalist from California, had described the island's residents as "the most savage kind . . . clad in coats of mail and helmets made of the skin of a horny kind of fish, with weapons of the most frightful character, formed from the teeth of some of the voracious monsters of the deep." One seaman had been carried off by the savages, and in revenge the leader of Bowman's expedition shot the chief of the Drummond Islanders dead and set their town on fire, destroying three hundred houses. Bowman observed dryly that the islanders reacted by showing "little of the characteristic hospitality usually found among other savage tribes." (This did not prevent him from remarking that the women, though murderous, had "delicate features [and] slight figures, and are generally pretty," which may also have had something to do with Lining's sudden interest in the island's primitive sociology. Nonetheless, the *Shenandoah* sailed on.)

The next day, a Saturday, the doctor was still sulking when the ship reached a latitude only twenty miles south of the equator, grumbling that "we are nearly out of the South Pacific in which we expected to catch so many prizes, and where we have caught not a single one—all owing, I believe, to bad management." By noon on Sunday they were nine miles north of "the line," and he moaned of "apathy having taken the place of enthusiasm and any feeling of pride in the ship." All he cared for now was to have the cruise over and a chance to get back to a shoreside life.

Crossing back into the Northern Hemisphere brought wind and—almost—a change of luck. By midday a steady breeze was bringing some relief from the oppressive heat. At five o'clock the quartermaster sang out that he saw a ship hovering on the horizon off the lee bow. Lieutenant Grimball, too, thought he saw it, and as Surgeon Lining came on deck to see what all the commotion was about, Waddell turned to him in a triumphant manner and said they had a prize. Lining also believed he saw the sail in the distance. Within minutes everyone from the forepeak to the poop deck was swearing up and down they were looking at a Yankee ship. But no sooner had the raider altered course to pursue the stranger than it disappeared, "and all our looking could not make us see it again." Some began to mutter that it was a "Flying

Dutchman," a phantom visible only to those who are in some way doomed. The next morning at daybreak, all hands were hard at work searching the horizon, desperately hoping to spot the sail and break the curse. But the day passed without finding it. Wednesday brought pouring rain, reduced visibility, and even less chance of spotting a sail. All hands were engaged in making use of the downpour to scrub out hammocks and clothes when a lookout cried that there was a sail, a real one this time, broad off the lee bow. Waddell gave the order to stand in chase.

It took well into the evening to overhaul the phantom. Once in range, it hoisted a Hawaiian flag and was brought around with a shot from the signal gun. Captain Hammond of the schooner *Pelin*, five months out of Oahu on a trading expedition for oil and tortoise shell, was waiting at the rail as the boat under Bulloch's command drew alongside. Suspicious of the drawling Southerner, Hammond did not quite believe Bulloch's claim that the *Shenandoah* was the Union steamer *Miami* and was reluctant to share any news. But while the rebel examined the schooner's papers, either Hammond or one of his subordinates mentioned that there might be whalers at Strong Island, 120 miles away, or lying at Ascension Island, where there had been several when the schooner stopped there three weeks earlier.

"Having fine trade winds," wrote Lining, "we made a splendid run and about 1 pm made Strong's or Oualan Island a little on our lee bow."

Nowadays the only island in the vicinity of 5° north, 163° east—the coordinates given in the log—is Kosrae, in Micronesia, which also fits the doctor's description of Strong Island as "high, seemingly nearly round, and almost eight miles in diameter," with a central cone that appeared to be volcanic in origin. The island was covered in lush vegetation, and numerous huts nestled in among the coconut groves lining the shore testified to a healthy native population. "Like [Drummond Island]," wrote Hunt, "it is in reality a most charming spot, as far as its physical features go . . . producing spontaneously all the luscious fruits of the tropical zone, [but] it is also the abiding place of a similarly degraded race, but one remove, if any, from cannibalism."

Describing rounding the island under steam, the petty officer rambled on that when "viewed from the distance . . . it seemed a very Arcadia, where man might forget the cares and turmoils of the busy world with which the Anglo Saxon race are so characteristically familiar, and taste for himself the delights of the old pastoral days . . . [but] a closer inspection would have revealed, not pastoral simplicity, but all the revolting practices of savage tribes, sunk in unregenerate barbarism."

Still, Lining wanted to go ashore. And again Waddell refused. The only thing the commander cared about was that steaming completely around the island had revealed no Yankee sails. He ordered a course for Ascension Island.

Ascension Island was a mirage. Before the nineteenth century, it floated in and out of history in a now-you-see-me-now-you-don't fashion that began in 1521 when Magellan managed to sail through Micronesia without spotting a single island.* The first "discoverer" of the island now known as Pohnpei or Ponape was Alvaro Saavedra, who spotted it seven years later in the same way most Spanish explorers found new places: by blowing wildly out of control through uncharted territory until they fetched up against something hard, then going ashore and claiming it for queen and country (often to the puzzlement of the inhabitants). The English pirate Francis Drake dropped by in 1579 on his way to ravage Spanish settlements in the Philippines, and a few others stopped now and then to plaster the lump of volcanic basalt with a series of names—John Bulls Island, Harpers Island, William the Fourth, Ascension, and even Senyavin Island—but for the most part nobody cared much about the place until whalers started stopping there in the early 1800s to top off their water casks.

In the wake of the whalers came Christian missionaries, and the two were not a good mix. After months at sea, the whalers were often

---

*The Ascension Island of the *Shenandoah*'s voyage should not be confused with the Ascension Island in the South Atlantic, which lies nearly two thousand miles north of Tristan da Cunha Island and is still referred to by that name.

more interested in the island's copper-colored women than they were in its freshwater streams, and the devout gentlemen of the Micronesian mission considered the sailors' appetite one of the biggest barriers to saving the natives' souls. Missionary brothers Luther and Theodore Gulick once wrote a letter to the owners of New England whalers accusing their sailors of seducing the island's women, declaring that "most of the ships which you are sending to this ocean are the most disgusting of moral pesthouses. Not only are the sailors given to every crime, but the captains with nearly all their officers practice in these seas vices similar to those which brought destruction to Sodom and Gomorrah." Their accusations were vigorously denied, and the captains and crews dropping anchor at Ascension Island told Luther and his brother to piss off. The opportunity to trade a plug of tobacco for the company of a slender nymph was too good to pass up.

Eventually, the missionaries realized that their charges were never going to forgo tobacco, nor would the sailors give up the condolences of the flesh. A peaceful, almost friendly truce ensued, and in the years after the Gulick brothers departed, it even became the habit of some of the New England captains and officers to drop in on their successors for the pleasure of a "gam" with someone from home. By the time the *Shenandoah* rounded up and furled all sail before standing in toward the island under steam, the feud, in true Ascension fashion, had disappeared.

As the sun rose on the morning of April 1, 1865, only the top of the twenty-five-hundred-foot peak that makes up the island's interior was visible above a band of thick fog. By eight o'clock, the rising sun went to work on the obscuring mist, and it too disappeared. A boat was seen pulling out from the island. Behind it lay four ships in the harbor. The first was flying Hawaiian colors. The others had the Stars and Stripes at their peaks. For the first time in more than eight thousand miles, the rebels had hit the jackpot, and the missionaries and the whaling captains had helped them do it; it was they who had sent the approaching boat out as a friendly gesture made under the mistaken impression that the *Shenandoah* was a survey vessel in need of a pilot. Thomas Harrocke, the Englishman in charge of the pilot boat, was an escapee from the penal colony at Sydney. He had been thirteen years on the island and settled down with a native wife.

"I could scarcely conceive a more degraded looking object," Hunt wrote later of Harrocke. "He had adopted, preforce, no doubt, the habits of the islanders; his body was tattooed with all manner of fantastic designs, and he spoke his mother tongue with hesitation and difficulty. . . . so far as I could learn, he was treated with kindness and consideration by the savages among whom his lot had been cast, but the torrid climate, with unnatural and perhaps oftentimes disgusting food, had made sad inroads upon a naturally robust constitution, and it was plain to see that he was descending by slow but sure stages to the grave.

"Thus far we had displayed no bunting," he continued, "and as would have been naturally expected, one of the first questions our pilot asked on coming on board was in regard to our nationality." Unsure where Harrocke's sympathies lay, the rebels told him their ship was a Union cruiser. He agreed to take them into the anchorage for thirty bucks.

Waddell, growing suddenly suspicious at the good fortune of finding so many Yankee fish in the island's barrel, strapped a pistol around his waist and accompanied the pilot to the forecastle, where he warned Harrocke he would be shot at the first sign of a trick. Were he a Union sympathizer, he could easily run the raider aground on a hidden reef. A puzzled Harrocke signaled the helmsman to proceed. Once safely through the narrow entrance, Waddell ordered the anchor dropped in fifteen fathoms of water, in a position that would effectively block anyone trying to enter or leave. Four boats were lowered, manned with two officers and six armed sailors each. When all was ready, the signal gun was fired and the Confederate flag run up. At the report of the cannon, a crowd of natives watching from shore panicked and ran for the bushes.

Mystified by the proceedings, Harrocke stood watching the departing boats for a moment, then stared at the flag. Finally, turning to the officer of the deck, he asked what flag it was, why the gun had been fired, and what the boatloads of armed men were about.

"All answered in a word, my hearty," responded the officer. "Those four ships are prizes to the Confederate government."

"And what the hell is a Confederate government?" asked the astonished pilot.

"The best and biggest half of what was the United States of America," the officer boasted. "The Yankees didn't sail the government to suit us, so we cut adrift and started on our own hook."

"The devil! What are you going to do with your prizes?"

"Set them on fire by and by, after we have taken what we want out of them."

"Well, you and the Yankees must settle that business to suit yourselves," huffed the tattooed Englishman, "but if I had known what you were up to, maybe I should not have piloted you in. I don't like to see a bonfire made of a good ship!"

It did not take long for the boats to come back. Lieutenant Grimball had seized the *Edward Carey* of San Francisco, Chew and his crew the *Pearl* from New London. On boarding the *Hector* of New Bedford, Smith-Lee and Mason had been surprised to find a "strapping big Negro" as chief mate.* Lieutenant Scales took the *Harvest* of Honolulu and brought back with him the first mate. The captains of all four whalers were away, visiting a missionary from Massachusetts in the next bay.

"The armed boats were dispatched with orders to capture the vessels and send their officers, ship papers, log books, instruments for navigation, and charts to the *Shenandoah*," said Waddell. He emphasized that the charts were vital. The whalers' were much more detailed than

---

*The New England whaling industry was one of the first arenas where African Americans stood a chance of being treated somewhat equally. A large percentage of vessel owners were Quakers, to whom slavery was anathema. Despite the surprise of the *Shenandoah*'s officers, it was not unusual for blacks to rise to positions of authority. According to Mason, the *Hector*'s third officer was a "darkie," too.

his own, and "with such in my possession, I not only held a key to the navigation of all the Pacific Islands, the Ohkotsk and Bering seas, and the Arctic Ocean, but the most probable localities for finding the great Arctic whaling fleet without a tiresome search."

The captains returned near sunset, apparently well relaxed by their "jollification" with the missionary; they rowed straight up to the *Shenandoah* before they noticed anything was amiss. "Their astonishment may perhaps be imagined when they discovered a cruiser in that remote sea bearing a Confederate flag," chuckled Hunt. "For a moment they rested on their oars as though undetermined what to do, then put about and pulled toward shore."

It only took a few minutes for one of the *Shenandoah*'s boats to overtake them and return with the Yankees in tow.

"The captains of the three Yankee vessels could give no good reason why their vessels should not be confiscated," said Waddell, and the *Edward Carey*, the *Hector*, and the *Pearl* were condemned. The *Harvest*, sailing under Hawaiian colors, was more problematic; several of the *Shenandoah*'s officers thought her flag genuine and recommended releasing her as a neutral. Waddell disagreed.

"The captain of the Oahu vessel could not produce a bill of sale and could not swear he was cognizant of her sale to a Honolution," he argued. In addition, "New Bedford" was still painted on her transom; she carried an American register; her mates were all American; and according to the log she was still under the command of the same captain who had taken her on whaling voyages before the war broke out. The log gives the combined value of the four condemned ships and their cargo as $117,759, and tellingly, of this amount the *Harvest* made up nearly a third. (Reading between the lines, one also senses more resistance in the seizure of the Ascension whalers than the *Shenandoah*'s earlier victims. For the first time in the voyage, Waddell had the masters put in chains. And of the whalers' 130 sailors, he recruited only 7—4 Portuguese, 2 Yankees, and an African American. The others, he sneered, were "composed of Honolutions, a timid, mongrel race, easily imposed upon and cheated, but suiting the purpose of such men as command whalers."* Given the choice of coming along with the rebels as prisoners or staying with the natives of Pohnpei, all stayed.)

Before looting and burning the captured ships, Waddell, ever aware of his stature as a representative of the Confederate government, decided it would be best to engage in a bit of international diplomacy by soliciting permission to do so from the Pohnpeian "king." Immediately after quarters the next morning he sent Harrocke ashore to King Ish-y-paw with "my earnest solicitation for his health, peace, and prosperity, and a strong desire to have him visit one of President Jefferson Davis's ships." Within an hour, seventy wildly decorated war canoes put out from shore, the king himself seated in the captain's gig with Harrocke, surrounded by a retinue of advisers. A dark, well-made man of forty, Ish-y-paw had got himself up for the occasion with a head-to-toe rubbing of coconut oil, a simple headband, and little else.

"They are rum looking chaps," said Mason. "They wear no garments of any kind but a belt with long grass which hangs about the upper part of their legs." The king's retinue wore head wreaths of sweet-smelling yellow flowers, while the only additional sign of authority decorating the king was a colorful woven belt worn at the level of his "inexpressibles." The women, marveled Mason, were no more modest than the men, going about bare breasted with only a square of yellow cloth over their shoulders. Men and women alike had had their earlobes pierced and stretched to such a degree that the mutilation afforded the king a convenient place to store a long-stemmed clay pipe. And like the king, Lining noted, the whole lot was "sloshed down with oil until they shone and smelt!" Everyplace they touched or sat was left with a greasy mark.

Waddell invited His Majesty and his attendants to his cabin, where diplomacy was postponed until after a round of schnapps. Using

---

*It should be noted that the islands of Hawaii are one of the most remote landforms on earth and the original Hawaiian settlers got there by sailing open canoes across thousands of miles of open ocean. King Kamehameha, the islands' most famous ruler, once lifted an eight-hundred-pound stone and could snatch hurtling spears out of the air. A "timid mongrel race" indeed.

Harrocke as an interpreter, he then introduced the topic of conversation.

"I said the vessels in port belonged to our enemy, who have been hostile to us for forty years—"

"Then you don't like each other," interrupted the king.

"No. It is incompatible with virtue that the South should ever be reconciled to the North. Blood has been spilt, life has been taken, our countrywomen have been outraged and the unprotected have been driven into the forest for shelter while their homes are destroyed by fire."

Waddell went on to explain that his chief, President Jefferson Davis, had ordered him to destroy the enemy's vessels wherever they were found, "and if your majesty's laws of neutrality would not be violated, I will confiscate the vessels [and] present their contents to your majesty . . . and when your tribe has finished with them I will take them to sea and burn them."

Confused for a moment by the concept of neutrality, the king nonetheless recognized a good deal when he heard one, and it took only a brief conference with his attendants to agree. He asked only that Waddell not fire his cannons at the whalers, since he worried a wild shot might injure someone on shore. He also suggested a nearby reef would make a handy site for the burning, instead of going to the bother of towing the emptied ships out to sea. Waddell sealed the bargain like any modern power does when dealing with an undeveloped nation: he offered the king an arms deal, then screwed him. If Ish-y-paw would agree to post a few of his warriors to guard the cables connecting the *Shenandoah*'s stern to the shore, Waddell would give him several cases of dangerously antiquated muskets seized from one of the whalers.

"I said to his majesty, 'my fasts on shore are very insecure; a wicked person could cut them . . . and a flaw of wind might drive her on the rocks." Several men from the whalers were already on shore, having deserted as soon as their vessels were seized. The king accepted the offer and sent the muskets ashore along with orders to begin guarding the cables immediately. What he did not know was that the muskets were so old and neglected that they were dangerous.

"I would have preferred the muzzle to the chamber as far as danger is concerned," Waddell chuckled. Their Yankee owner had meant to sail to the Arctic and foist them off on unsuspecting Eskimos in trade for furs. In return, the trusting and grateful king offered Waddell his princess, the daughter of his second wife, who Waddell contended was "downright ugly, the first really ugly woman I ever saw." As for the offered princess, he pled the excuse of being already married.

On April 3 the destruction commenced, with first the *Pearl,* and then the *Hector* and the *Edward Carey* turned over to the natives for looting.

"And what a time they had of it!" laughed Mason. "Not having sense enough to rig a tackle and hoist out the casks of flour, meat, sugar, and molasses, they broke them all open in the ships' holds, loosing half and making a most horrible mess."

"Such a rare occasion for wholesale plundering had never occurred before, and was not likely to again," said Cornelius Hunt, and the natives made the most of it. All day long they swarmed over the vessels "like driver ants upon a dead carcass." The islanders filled their canoes with bits of iron, harpoons, whaling lines, and every bit of loose planking they could find. Bulkheads were knocked down and towed ashore as flooring for the huts, and the canvas sails were cut away in long strips. Mason nearly laughed himself sick at one poor fellow who climbed to the royal yard and in trying to cut loose the sail sliced through the royal lift, "which of course cock-billed the yard and left him swinging about between wind and water, much to his astonishment and discomfort." Soon, the three Yankee ships were so thoroughly emptied that they began to ride higher in the water, allowing the natives to tear the copper sheeting from their bottoms.*

---

*Before the invention of antifouling paints, copper sheeting was fastened to the bottom of sailing ships to prevent the growth of moss and barnacles, which drastically effect the efficiency of a hull's movement through the water.

"The natives placed a value on that metal," remembered Waddell, "and I was informed some of it would be used for pointing spears and arrows, some converted into breastplates and shields, and some traded with neighboring tribes." The thoroughness of the sacking was suitable, he felt, as the whalers "had been accustomed to ill treat the natives and cheat them, besides introducing loathsome diseases."

One by one the stripped whalers were towed to a reef and readied for burning. On Monday the *Pearl* went up in flames. Tuesday it was the *Hector* and the *Edward Carey*'s turn. The last, as it had no whale oil on board, was difficult to light, but when it finally caught it burned beautifully, illuminating the night like an erupting volcano. Natives dancing in the glow of the flames along the beach gesticulated wildly, unable to understand why so much wealth was being destroyed but enjoying the spectacle immensely.

Satisfied with this work (and apparently confident that no Union warships were going to make a sudden appearance), an uncharacteristically relaxed Waddell surprised everyone by declaring five days of liberty. From the fifth through the ninth of April, everyone not on watch was free to explore the island. The officers took turns organizing parties of native guides with canoes to visit a large complex of ruins a few miles up one of the rivers; Whittle and Lining spent a day trying to shoot migrating plovers off the reef; others fished or visited with the "primitives," and nearly everyone, officers and men alike, got tattoos.

"Nearly every one of us had something put on his arm," said Lining. "Which was done with four prongs of some thorny tree put upon the end of a stick, which was stuck into the flesh with a short piece of cane." The operation was painful, but produced a result that was quite artistic.

On the tenth the *Harvest* was brought alongside the *Shenandoah* to be emptied of everything the Confederates had a use for. First came the water casks, recently topped off with fresh Ascension water. A load of coal was hoisted into the raider's hold. Barrels of molasses, flour, meat, and bread came off, followed by a few casks of whale oil. Forty pairs of matching blue pants made Sergeant Canning happy; he needed them as uniforms for his marines.

Throughout the day, high spirits prevailed. Bulloch, Lining, and two of the petty officers slipped away to play hooky, armed with fishing poles and lines. Had they known what was taking place on the opposite side of the world, they might have been less ebullient. Micronesia lies west of the International Date Line. In other words, the tenth of the month there is still the ninth on the East Coast of North America. And April 9, 1865, was the day Robert E. Lee rode up to the courthouse at Appomattox, Virginia, sat down at a small table across from General Ulysses S. Grant, and surrendered.

TWELVE

T HE *HARVEST* went up in flames, the eleventh vessel destroyed by the *Shenandoah* in six months. Within days of Lee's surrender the Confederacy was in collapse, making the whaler the last arguably legitimate target for the raiders. When King Ish-y-paw presented Waddell with two dead chickens and a dozen coconuts to deliver to President Davis, the *Shenandoah's* commander accepted graciously, unaware that at that moment the intended recipient was already fleeing the Confederate capital in Richmond. With nearly a million dead and wounded (one out of four military-aged men in some parts of the Confederacy, one in twenty for the North), the home the men aboard the *Shenandoah* dreamed of returning to was little more than a smoking ruin. And things were about to get worse.

At daylight on the thirteenth the hawsers tying the raider's stern to the shore were taken in, the anchor was raised, and she steamed out of the harbor. Then she shook out her sails and set a course of north-northwest. The weather was fine and clear, the wind steady out of the northeast. On the fourteenth the log opens with "moderate breezes." At ten it was "clear and pleasant." At noon the ship's position was 9° north, 155° east, logging an impressive 210 miles of travel during the previous twenty-four hours. At 2:30 the wind started to increase and the order came to haul down the outer jib and give the mizzen topsail a single reef. The watch was called to furl the main. But the most interesting entry was made at three o'clock: "speed eight knots, wind at force four, the barometer holding steady at 29.87." The entry is written in Irvine Bulloch's hand and is important because three o'clock in Micronesia is 10 p.m. in Washington, D.C. And at the moment Bulloch was making the entry, a twenty-eight-year-old actor named John Wilkes Booth was creeping up the back stairs at Ford's Theater, stepping quietly into the box where Abraham Lincoln was sitting with his wife trying to enjoy a performance of *Our American Cousin,* and putting a bullet in the president's brain.

THE WIND HELD AT NORTHEAST. Waddell bypassed Guam on a course for the area between 17° and 20° north, where merchant ships riding the great conveyor belt of the northeast trade winds shuttle from the west coast of North America to Hong Kong. (The return voyage begins farther north, from 39° to 45°, where the wind bends and flows back from the southwest.) The temperature hovered in the eighties, rising into the nineties when the sun was overhead. "In all the course of my sea life," wrote Waddell, "I never enjoyed more charming weather." For the next ten days he was content to stand on the deck gazing on "that wonderful creation, the deep liquid world," wonderfully oblivious of the fact that Lincoln was dead, the Confederacy was imploding, and he and his command were the sole remaining vestige of the Confederate military. The sailing was so pleasant that he ordered the topsails double reefed to slow down.

Day after day they idled back and forth, dreaming of China-bound ships stuffed with Californian gold, holds bursting with Northwest furs. Day after day they sailed north, then tacked south. Day after day of no sails.

After a week of traveling back and forth in a vacuum Lining wrote that he was "getting pretty tired of it." The tropical paradise was turning into a boring hell.

"On a cruiser," Hunt philosophized, "one constantly alternates between a life of stirring excitement and stupidity. . . . time drags wearily, and if one has not the resource of some mental occupation, it falls, in the course of time, just short of unendurable." There is only so much work on a ship, and the hands resented being kept busy with nonsense tasks. After Mason went aloft to watch for a sail and came down disgusted, he was ordered to turn out the entire hold in a search for a cask of cheese. "The wretched cheese has been the bane of my life," he moaned. The cheese had not been seen since Melbourne, and he was compelled to spend the day in the close, overheated space "rummaging and turning things upside down."

Some of the earliest recruits began to threaten to leave the ship, grumbling that they had signed on for six months and their enlistments were up. If they met a neutral vessel they would board her. Anything would be better than sticking with the *Shenandoah*.

Waddell decided to move north. Perhaps they would have better luck capturing some of the rich merchantmen riding the southwest trades of the Forties on the return run from China to California. But by then his officers and crew were so out of sorts that he could not win.

"What difference does it make where we are?" grumped Lining. "Had I the regulation of things, I would have remained here longer, since it is certainly the track of ships . . . and at least the weather is pleasant, this not being the region for gales."

No sooner had they made their northing (after a week of slatting back and forth through lumpy seas and shifting winds) than the weather went foul. On the morning of May 13, the sea was calm, ruffled only slightly by a light breeze. The ship gurgled along under smoothly bellied sails.

"It suddenly turned very cold," remembered Lining, "and the barometer went lower than it had ever been." The needle dropped to 29.10. A black cloud hurrying toward them from the northeast hugged the surface of the water so close that some "atmospheric convulsion" seemed determined to blot the ship out of existence. The first gust staggered the *Shenandoah*, careening her over until the ends of her lower yards were drenched in spray.

"She started up like a frightened stag," said Waddell, "and bounded off before the awful pressure. . . . squall after squall struck her, flash after flash surrounded her, and thunder rolled in her wake."

The main topsail blew out in shreds and there was no choice but to point the bow downwind and go careening madly off before the building seas while the watch struggled aloft to pull in the flapping canvas.

The officer of the deck immediately ordered the maintop-men aloft to secure the remnants of the sail, and Hunt watched in awe as the shreds of canvas beat the air like gigantic whips trying to drive away anyone who might attempt to repair the disaster. The scene was terrific. Slowly and painfully the sailors toiled up the shrouds, sometimes blown against them and held there with such force that further progress was impossible, then hanging on for their lives as the screaming wind tried to tear them away. One moment the yard was cockbilled toward the heavens, the next plunging down toward the waves. The ship rolled madly in the boiling seas.

"I don't think I ever saw it higher than it was that night," said Mason. Not even during the Christmas gale in the Indian Ocean. The waves towered over the mizzen topsail yard, making a fearful noise and hurling the ship forward at a dizzying rate. Scarcely was the wrecked sail secured and replaced than a sea heavier and more violent than the others roared aboard and flooded the deck to the waist. Axes were called for, the ports knocked out; the *Shenandoah* groaned, then shuddered and shook herself free of the water.

"We had just rid the decks of that sea when another came rolling over us," Mason continued. For the second time in the voyage, the wave picked up a man in a swirl of foam and swept him overboard, where the next washed him back aboard again.

The typhoon continued for twelve hours, driving the raider more than a hundred miles from her course. All the while, thousands of "right whale birds" (gray pigeon-sized seabirds that commonly feed in the same areas as their gigantic namesakes) hovered overhead, piping and calling, "as if speculating upon the position of affairs, and wondering whether we would be able to weather the tempest."

Late in the evening the wind abated. The decrease was followed by a downpour so heavy that the sheer volume of water falling from the sky beat the seas flat. Behind the fast-moving front came colder weather. A few hours later it was twenty-six degrees.

It snowed, rained, and then snowed as it rained. Steep swells broke over the ship. For days everyone was constantly wet, which Lining blamed for a plague of ailments that swept the crew. Mason came down with chilblains. Dabney Scales had neuralgia. Irvine Bulloch stumbled around on rheumatic, swollen knees. Sergeant Canning had the worst of it; the poorly healed gunshot wound to his lung had him hacking and coughing in the cold air.

Three days after the first typhoon they were slammed with another, and they were forced to lie to and blow out of control toward the coast of Japan. Afterward, hundreds of exhausted robins landed in the rigging and fell to the deck (probably a migrating flock driven offshore by the storm.) Plucked and roasted, McNulty noted dryly, the birds made a delightful change from salt horse.

"This is an awful place," groaned Mason, "and I hope we will soon get out of it. The *Shenandoah* seems fated to wind up in out-of-the-way places where it blows a constant gale."

Stalking the Forties was a failure. More than a month had passed since leaving Ascension Island and they had not seen a single ship. Waddell decided to make a run for the coast of Russia. With the help of the charts seized from the Ascension whalers, he was certain he would find Yankees there, hunting whales in the Sea of Okhotsk.

THE *OHOTSKOJE MORE*, or Sea of Ohkotsk, lies behind the Kamchatka Peninsula, a steep thumb of land that dangles down from Siberia, pointing toward Japan, 750 miles away. Between the peninsula and Hokkaido, the Okhotsk is separated from the Pacific by a chain of windswept rocks called the Kuril Islands. Powerful currents surging up from a twenty-six-thousand-foot-deep ocean trench outside the Kurils sweep in through the barrier of islands to form a cyclonic flow that runs north along the inner coast of the peninsula, then turns west toward Sakhalin Island before boiling across an expanse of shallow banks. Every spring, a cloud of nutrients welling up from the depths feeds a bloom of plankton, which in turn nourishes a myriad of krill, the tiny shrimplike creatures that constitute the primary food of baleen whales. Whales, of course, attract whalemen, and that is what Waddell was betting on as he steered the *Shenandoah* toward the Kamachatka Peninsula.

On May 20 the ship was three hundred miles south of Petropavlovsk, forty miles from the entrance to Amphitrite Strait. Due west of their position, at the foot of the Ural Mountains, below the southeast corner of the Siberian plains, green shoots of cotton ordered planted by the czar to replace Russia's blockade-disrupted supply were beginning to poke up through the soil bordering the Aral Sea. But Kamchatka and the Okhotsk were still in the grip of winter, and the closer the *Shenandoah* got to them, the more ice appeared. First small bits, then larger bergs began bobbing in her wake, with now and then the helmsman having to steer around a truly big one. By late afternoon the snow-clad mountains that form the backbone of Kamchatka were towering off the starboard bow.

"They look terribly cold," said Mason, "and make one shiver at the thought of what we are going to find farther north." Only three weeks before, the deck thermometer had read one hundred degrees; now it was hovering in the twenties.

The late hour and swirling currents made Waddell nervous. He ordered that steam be raised to go through the pass, then changed his mind and decided to heave to for the night. It would be better to go through in broad daylight. The next morning he startled everyone by barking at Lieutenant Chew as the watch worked the sails.

"Make haste there, Mr. Chew," he shouted. "I don't want to go on shore here." His officers looked at each other behind his back in wonderment. The weather was calm and clear, the shore still several miles off. The *Shenandoah* was completely safe.

Their commander's skittishness unsettled the junior officers, and before the ship was well into the Sea of Okhotsk they were deriding him regularly, complaining first that he was keeping too far from shore—"We ought to know by this time that whalers fish close along the coast. Won't he ever learn by experience?"—then bashing him again for his overprudence after he reduced canvas to topsails because it was foggy, "as if we would run into anything in broad daylight." Next he stood a watch for Dabney Scales, who was not feeling well. A captain standing watch when there were idle lieutenants was unheard of; it was a slap in the face for Lieutenant Whittle.

"He is crazy," muttered Lining. "And there is no doubt about it."

Catching a prize should have improved the atmosphere. Instead, it made things worse.

THE *ABIGAIL*, under Captain Ebenezer Nye, was thirty-three months out of New Bedford. As much trader as blubber hunter, she had made her way up into the Sea of Okhotsk after a stopover in Yokohama, Japan, where her officers bought silk dresses and lacquer boxes for the voyage home. When a lookout perched in the *Shenandoah*'s rigging spotted her at around noon on May 27, she was coasting along behind a field of jumbled icebergs.

"She was on the other side of the ice," said Lining, "and we made all sail to get around it, which we did about 3 p.m." Immediately upon spotting the *Shenandoah*, Nye ordered more sail and stood directly toward her. Waddell lured her on by running up the Russian ensign, an appropriate disguise to the latitude. Nye responded with the Stars and Stripes.

Whittle dropped the Russian flag and hauled the Confederate up in its place, and a shot from the signal gun brought the *Abigail* around. Dabney Scales and Joshua Minor were sent to board her. When they pulled alongside, Skipper Nye looked them over for a moment, scratched his head, and said "Well, I suppose I'm taken. But who on earth would have thought of seeing one of your Southern privateers up here? I have heard of some of the pranks you fellows have been playing, but I supposed I was out of your reach."

"The fact is," Scales replied facetiously, "we have entered into a treaty with the whales, and are up here by special agreement to disperse their mortal enemies!"

Nye agreed laconically. "All right. I never grumble at anything I can't help, but the whales don't owe me much of a grudge. Lord knows I haven't disturbed them much this voyage." Being captured by an enemy vessel was not enough to rattle a man like Ebenezer Nye, who had once been cast away in a small open boat with six other men and sailed seventeen hundred miles to salvation with only a half dozen biscuits and a beaker of water to sustain them. Besides, he had been captured by a rebel raider once before. His last vessel had been sunk by the *Alabama*, a bit of bad luck for which one of his mates began to upraid him in front of Scales and Minor, saying, "You are more fortunate in picking up Confederate cruisers than whales. I will never go out with you again, for if there is a cruiser out there you will find her."

Nye brushed the mate's comment aside and turned to Scales. "It is cold talking here. Come below and take something to warm your stomach while I will get my papers."

It did not take long to condemn the *Abigail*. Waddell's clerk valued the old hull at only fifteen thousand dollars, the twenty barrels of whale oil in her hold at seventeen hundred more. Nye took it all in stride. He was not worried, he said; he had a new vessel waiting for him in San Francisco. And when his thirty men were sent over to the *Shenandoah*,

Hunt said they too "accepted their change in fortune with general good humor." Even single irons and confinement in the forepeak did not depress them, and they were "about as plucky and sailor-like a set of fellows as fell into our hands during the entire cruise." (What they did not tell Hunt was that they had already sent a load of oil home via another vessel, a rich haul of 330 barrels valued at $156,000, or nearly 2.5 million in today's dollars.) And when the prize crew began emptying out their hold an even better reason for their good cheer became apparent: the *Abigail* was stocked with a bountiful supply of liquor. Nye had brought barrels and barrels of rum, whiskey, gin, and straight alcohol from Massachusetts to trade for furs along the Siberian Peninsula. There were over seven hundred bottles of brandy, cases of schnapps and wine, and a plentiful stock of champagne. It did not take long for the *Shenandoah*'s seamen to succumb to temptation. Before the rebel officers knew what was in the hold, every one of the seamen aboard the *Abigail* was drunk.

"As soon as this was discovered," said Hunt, "the inebriates were shut into the [*Abigail*'s] forecastle, and the more obstreperous placed in irons. But while this discipline was progressing, the rest got wind of the captured treasure and by the time one detachment was secured, another was in condition to receive the same polite attention we had shown their fellows." The news spread like wildfire. A squad of marines sent over to quell the situation threw in with the boozers, and a second squad sent over from the *Shenandoah* to find out what was going on did the same.

"It was the most general and stupendous spree I have ever witnessed!" laughed Hunt. "There were not a dozen sober men on board except the prisoners, and had these not been ironed it might have proved a dearly bought frolic." Lining went over to see what was going on and found Scales and Chew with a pile of Japanese curios they had put aside for themselves. After pilfering a few things for himself, he shoved off, jumping into a boatload of drunks being returned to the *Shenandoah*. On the way, one of the drunkards deliberately jumped overboard and had to be hauled back aboard with a boat hook and lashed into the bottom of the boat. Lynch, the ship's carpenter, grew so unruly he had to be handcuffed to his bunk, and when he broke out a second time, Waddell had him gagged, taken to the propeller well, and triced up.

Scales, Minor, and Blacker worked all night and into the next day, coercing a small handful of still-standing drunks to shuttle enough of the whaler's provisions over to the *Shenandoah* to feed her captives. Three live pigs gave the tipsy stevedores "particular hell." The last thing to be removed, Hunt chuckled, was twenty-five barrels of whiskey, to be used "in case of sickness," he was sure. At about 6 p.m. the *Abigail* was set on fire.

THE NEXT MORNING it was blowing heavily. A blinding snowstorm obscured the smoke from the smoldering whaler. All of the *Shenandoah*'s men were hungover, sick, or drunk; not all of Nye's trading stock had been of the highest quality. Lining scribbled that things were "getting worse and worse." The carpenter was still drunk, the steward a basket case. Hopkins, the cook, was out cold. The binge lasted three days.

Waddell responded by becoming a martinet. After a beaker of whiskey was found in Dabney Scales's room he suspended the lieutenant from duty, and when a search of the cook's quarters turned up a box of liquor, Waddell pitched into his clerk, throwing Blacker out of the cabin, banishing him into steerage, convinced he'd had a hand in secreting the bottles. Next the boatswain's mate was broken and disrated, stripped of his rank. Then for good measure Waddell banned smoking in the engine room, which could not have been better calculated to alienate the lower ranks of men for whom a pipe, even when taken in the fumey, coal-fogged atmosphere of the boiler room, was one of life's few pleasures.

"A charming day overhead," wrote Lining. "Sun bright, sea smooth. But on board all is stormy."

BY THE FIRST OF JUNE the storm had passed, and the weather was still delightful. Dabney Scales was restored to duty. Not a breath of wind was stirring and no further episodes of drunkenness were recorded. Waddell, however, was still behaving erratically, first ordering up steam, then stopping and drifting, going nowhere for the rest of the day. The officers passed the time shooting their pistols at seagulls and discussing their suspicions that their commander did not know what he was doing. Their misgivings deepened when a sail was sighted and he chose not to pursue it.

"We were under short sail at the time," said Mason. "And the captain thought the vessel in question was a brig. And as the Yankees have no vessels of this class, he decided not to give chase, not wishing to speak to a foreigner or be known by one. . . . I have my doubts about the propriety of this, for it is by no means certain that the ship we saw was not an American, and indeed, most of those who saw her insisted upon her being a barque."

The prisoners from the *Abigail* had said there were at least fifteen Yankee whalers in the area, but the farther north the *Shenandoah* ventured, the more Waddell came to rely on the advice of Joshua Minor, who although only a master's mate was the only officer aboard to have served on a whaler, as well as the only one to have made multiple voyages into the Arctic. And it was Minor who first declared the sail was not a Yankee.

"The captain has great confidence in his opinion," declared Mason, "and pays great deference to all he says. Indeed, it is generally thought that our skipper pays rather too much deference to his opinions. . . . My candid opinion is that we lost a prize we might have had with ease." It was the last ship they would see in the Sea of Okhotsk. By evening the weather had begun to change, with high scudding clouds moving in to obscure the sun and the temperature dropping to seventeen degrees. A lookout shouted out that they were bearing down on ice.

AT NOON the next day Smith-Lee made a note in the log of "large quantities of ice passing the ship." More disturbing was the rain, a heavy swirling drizzle that froze as it fell. At 12:30 Smith-Lee added that the rigging was becoming covered with ice.

It was the third day of June, President Jefferson Davis's birthday, and Waddell was down below toasting the occasion with his officers when word came that the barometer was dropping. The wind was backing to the east, the weather deteriorating. A vicious, fast-moving gale was on its way. Waddell and Whittle went topside to see what should be done.

"The captain came on deck and ordered the yards braced aback," said Mason. "But this was a difficult task, for everything was frozen stiff. The braces and blocks were so covered with ice that it was impossible to budge them."

Whittle sent men aloft with clubs to beat the ice from the rigging, but the wind was increasing, the rain was falling harder, and ice was forming faster than the lines could be cleared. With her rigging locked in place, the raider surged ahead, faster and faster, unable to slow down. At four o'clock, a lookout called down that between squalls he could make out a solid sheet of pack ice dead ahead.

"It became imperative to relieve the ship of her perilous position," said Waddell. "Weathering a gale in that sea is secondary to the heavy ice, which a vessel might be forced against and wrecked." Even if the rigging had not been frozen, heaving to with the ice pack so close to leeward would probably still have resulted in her being driven against it and wrecked.

The crew went to work with a will, desperately hacking and bashing at the sails and lines until they were limber enough to drag first one plank-stiff canvas down, then another. It took four hours for a work gang sweating under Smith-Lee to brace up the main and foretopsail yards and another two for Lieutenant Chew's watch to back the mizzen topsail. The maneuvers gave the helmsman enough control in the gale-force winds to steer the ship parallel with the face of the solid ice pack, but not enough to tack away. With the wind growing stronger, Waddell made a desperate decision: he ordered the watch aloft to keep a lookout for an opening into the crowded bergs, a lane through which they might hope to pass in search of open water beyond. It was not until the ice glimmered with the pale Arctic midnight twilight that a lookout cried out that a narrow lead lay ahead. It was a mere thread of open water, dark and glimmering between two towering icebergs. Waddell hesitated, and then ordered the helmsman to take her in.

The full force of the gale broke over the ship just as they entered the opening, the wind howling and tearing at the wet, frightened men as they clung to the ice-slicked yardarms with one hand and flailed at the ice with puny clubs in the other.

The wind suddenly lost its force. Sailing into the lee of the largest iceberg was like stepping through a doorway into a world suddenly at peace, where at a given signal a struggling army had laid down its arms. "In a short time," said Waddell, "[the ship] was lying to under close sail and the floe to windward, which a little time before was our dreaded enemy, was then our best friend, for the fury of the seas was expended on it and not against the sides of the Shenandoah." In other words, the looming iceberg was acting as a breakwater, behind which the ship could lie in smooth water. Waves hurling themselves against its outer face filled the air with spray.

"The wind was bitter cold," said Waddell, describing the refuge. "[And] the braces, blocks, yards, sails, and all other running rigging were so thoroughly coated in ice from a half to two inches thick that it was impossible to use the braces."

The gale lasted nine hours. Although safe from the seas, the ship continued to forge ahead, driven slowly by the wind and current until she was deep in the pack. Within half an hour they were surrounded, blocked in.

When morning came the rain had exhausted itself; dawn came bright and clear. Waddell was elated by the good fortune of bullseyeing his ship into the narrow safety of the lead; his pleasure in his surroundings was of the sort normally reserved for those who have recently survived a brush with death, an appreciation for elements of beauty more elusive under normal circumstances. "Icicles of great length and size hung from every portion of the vessel and her rigging," he exulted. "And the rosy tints of morn prepared us for a scene of enchantment. When the sunlight burst upon that fairy ship she sparkled from deck to truck as if a diadem had been thrown about her, awakening exclamations of enthusiastic delight."

Not everyone was so enchanted. Lining, who had hoisted so many hot rum punches the night before in honor of Jefferson Davis's birthday that he had slept through the whole thing, found the situation terrifying. The *Shenandoah*, he thought, looked like a "glass ship," doomed to become part of the ice-encrusted landscape. What he saw was floe ice—a great field of broken ice covering the ocean for miles and miles. "[We] were completely surrounded, presenting the curious spectacle of a vessel floating in mid ocean without a drop of water to be seen anywhere." It was a desperate situation, said the surgeon, and Cornelius Hunt agreed.

"We were fairly jammed in," said the petty officer. "On every side of us, as far as the eye could reach, extended the field ice, and as the ponderous floes came together, the crushed and mangled debris rose up into huge mounds of crystal blocks, seemingly as immovable and imperishable as the bluffs on shore. Indeed, it was impossible, while gazing off over the scene of wilderness and desolation by which we were surrounded, to conceive the possibility of an avenue of escape." Much of the ice surrounding the ship was fifteen feet thick, some of the larger bergs forty. "Had the weather been rough," worried Lining, "our frail ship would be crushed to pieces in a few moments."

Mats of thick rope were hung over the bow to protect the hull. But as the sun rose and the air grew warmer a new danger presented itself: the icicles in the rigging began to lose their grip and plunge, the dagger-pointed shards making things "dreadfully uncomfortable for those who had to be out on deck."

Miraculously, no one was hurt, and Waddell had the presence of mind to order every available water tank, cask, and receptacle filled with the clear ice to augment the ship's supply of drinking water. As soon as the rigging was clear and the blocks were again serviceable, grapnels were run out on the floes and hooked to large bergs, and the backbreaking labor of warping, or turning the ship around, begun. The sound of ice grinding along the hull was frightening. No one was sure the planks sheathing the hull would hold. It took six hours to work their way out of the ice, using the bow as a wedge to move the bergs.

Fog formed and lifted, followed by flurries of thick snow. Overhead, the sky came and went in blue patches. When they finally broke out into open water at 8:30 in the morning, the crew went so giddy with relief they erupted into an impromptu, no-holds-barred snowball fight that threatened to spread to the poop deck and engulf their captain. Chew quelled the outburst by having the watch shake out the topsails. Waddell went below to consider a new course of action. From notes in the margins of the seized whaling charts and information garnered from the *Abigail* prisoners, it appeared Jonas Island, near the middle of the Sea of Okhotsk, was a likely place to find whalers gathered. Half an hour later he gave the order to point the ship northwestward. Jonas Island was a day and a half away.

THIRTEEN

EIGHT HOURS LATER they were trapped again. Thick fog had rolled in, obscuring the visibility and limiting the world to a wall of gray. Then came heavy snow. Near midnight, a lookout called out that they were bearing down on ice. Lieutenant Scales had the deck and issued orders to turn around, but by the time the sails were backed and the vessel started to come about, more ice was discovered close to windward. Blinded by the weather, they had sailed straight into the ice field's waiting maw. The ship shivered to a halt; the boatswain's pipe whistled; but with only a breath of wind stirring, there was not enough power in the sails to turn her. Getting up steam would take too long. The raider lost all steerageway and the ice closed its jaws.

"We were jammed in again," Hunt remembered. "And as I lay in my berth, I could hear the huge blocks thundering and chaffing against the side of the ship as though it would dash her to pieces. It was an anxious night to all on board. None of us were familiar with Arctic cruising, and consequently were to a great extent incompetent to judge the imminence of the danger."

This time it only took a couple of hours to free the ship, but Waddell had had enough of the Sea of Okhotsk, deciding, "It was evident from the quantity of drift ice in view that the flow was westward, and to continue in that direction would be useless and dangerous."

He called a council of war in his cabin, pressuring his lieutenants to agree, citing Joshua Minor's advice that it would be impossible to push through two hundred miles of ice to Jonas Island to persuade them. The *Shenandoah* had not been built to deal with ice. A majority of the officers consented, but the decision was not met without some grumbling. Sergeant Canning petitioned Waddell to press on, saying his wound was bothering him greatly and if the captain would put him ashore near the Amur River, on the opposite shore of the Sea of Okhotsk, he would attempt to travel overland to one of the major European cities, where he might receive sufficient medical attention to survive.

"He feels he will never get well on board the ship," Lining told Waddell. "And I agree with him perfectly . . . but I doubt the propriety of putting him ashore." Waddell refused, primarily because the prisoners from the *Abigail* had also asked to be put on the beach—whether Okhotsk or Kamchatka they did not care, so certain were they another whaler would find them—but with the temperature near freezing, he did not want it said that he had cast prisoners away in such an inhospitable place. No, he told Surgeon Lining, Sergeant Canning and the prisoners must stay on board. Then he ordered a course set for Amphitrite Strait; they would leave the Okhotsk immediately to go hunting in the Arctic.

Mason, like Canning and the prisoners, was disappointed by the decision and spoke for everyone when he sniffed that they had been three weeks in the Okhotsk with nothing to show for it except "one old sea turtle," which even its owner called "the meanest and least valuable of all the vessels in this area."

"And now we are going to leave without another effort!" he cried. "It is not for me to judge the captain's actions, but I cannot help expressing my opinion very decidedly in this instance and mine is the same as that of most of the other officers. . . . it stands to reason that if we go away after the capture of one miserable old coffin, the meanest ship in the whole sea, we will have failed in the object of our cruise. The authorities at home will be disappointed. The Yankees will laugh at our stupidity and crow over their escape!"

He was wrong on both counts. First—and he had no way of knowing—there no longer were any authorities back home to be disappointed: Jefferson Davis had already been captured and his government stamped out. And far from laughing, several of the Yankees on hand were ready join the raider.

The first was Thomas Manning, the second mate from the *Abigail,* who had chafed Ebenezer Nye for surrendering. On the whole, the *Shenandoah*'s men felt the *Abigail* sailors to be a "good and wholesome lot," admirable for the grace with which they accepted their confinement. But Manning was a weasel, described by Hunt as "a Baltimorean by birth, anything by profession, and a reprobate by nature." A lifelong Democrat, Manning had bragged to one of his shipmates aboard the *Abigail* that he had sold his vote to Lincoln (a Republican) for a drink of whiskey. And more than Manning's vote was for sale: after being brought aboard the *Shenandoah,* he immediately told Waddell that in exchange for a job as an officer, he would be glad to help him find the Arctic whaling fleet. (And his own brother was aboard one of the ships he was willing to finger!)

"It is always unpleasant, though sometimes necessary, to accept the services of the most disreputable of men," said Hunt. "But as this was an opportunity which was not likely to occur again for securing a guide to a prize we sought, his overtures were received, and Thomas S. Manning was enrolled as ship's Corporal, and at once entered upon the discharge of his duties."

Having sold himself to the Confederates—and the other, unsus-

pecting Yankee whale ships down the river—the Yankee Judas immediately set about seducing as many of his fellow seamen from aboard
the *Abigail* as possible into joining him, enticing them with promises of
conditions far superior to those they had suffered on Nye's small, antiquated ship.

"These poor devils," said Mason of the largely Hawaiian crew.
"They have never been on any other ship than a Yankee whaler, where
they are hard worked, maltreated, poorly fed, and worse paid, [and]
seem to think this a sort of paradise." Grog twice a day, coffee four
times, and tea at regular intervals were luxuries the *Abigail*'s men could
hardly imagine. And the chance to work "watch and watch," four hours
on and four hours off, instead of around the clock seemed like a vaca-
tion. What Manning did not tell the *Abigail* sailors was that he intended to help the raider capture ships manned by their friends. (The
whaling community was a relatively small one, and the men from the
Abigail were sure to have known some of the men aboard the other
whalers since childhood or to have served with them aboard other
ships.) "Had they been aware of it," said Hunt, "I do not believe a man
of them would have enlisted under our flag."

But in their ignorance, several of the *Abigail*'s men did join. An
Englishman, a Prussian, and a Portuguese volunteered for Canning's
marines, while nine Hawaiian "Kanakas" signed the *Shenandoah*'s articles as common sailors. Using the names given to them by Yankee captains, Jason California, Aloha Givens, John Mahoa, Cyrus Sailor,
William Bill, John Boy, and Jason French moved their gear into the
Shenandoah's maintop forecastle.

"The remainder stood out resolute against all inducements," Hunt
said admiringly. "The more we learned of the *Abigail*'s crew the better
we liked them, with the exception of Manning, the second mate, who
though he rendered us good service we could not help despising."

In addition to Ebenezer Nye, whom the rebels enjoyed for his constant good humor and entertaining stories, Hunt particularly admired
the *Abigail*'s first mate, "a staunch old sailor, true as steel to his own

government." This did not stop Hunt from manipulating the mate in a way that seems as bad in its own way as Manning's treachery: the *Abigail*'s guileless mate took great pleasure in pointing out on the charts to Hunt the more dangerous areas of the Arctic, giving him the benefits of his experience and insights into the difficulties of cruising in the region. Hunt bragged that he had taken occasion at leisure intervals "to make such inquiries as I could without exciting suspicion. . . . [And] the old fellow never dreamed that I had any other purpose than to satisfy a seaman-like curiosity." After gleaning all he could from the admirable old sailor, he took the information straight to Waddell, who combined it with Manning's services to develop a plan for hunting down the Arctic whalers.

ON JUNE 8, eleven days after burning the *Abigail,* the *Shenandoah* turned her bow southward. It was a delightful warm day, and with all sail set the ship lumbered along at a stately four knots. But the barometer was rising, and the next day's log shows the speed slowing from three knots to two, then one, followed by a penciled "calm." Whales were playing near the ship.

"A good many," Lining noted, including two huge finbacks that came so close they nearly touched the hull. Lolling and spouting, the gargantuan mammals blew great puffs of fishy-smelling breath across the decks, exciting Lieutenant Chew so much he lost his hat overboard when he leaned over the rail for a better look. It was his last cap—all the others had already gone over the side—and everybody laughed when Smith-Lee made a big production out of lowering a boat to fetch it. Embarrassed, Chew lashed out. It was the first time anyone had ever seen him angry.

Tempers were wearing thin. Frustrated by weeks of no prizes turning into months without real success, tired, typhooned, and icebound, their nerves grown taut under the strain of living cheek by jowl with others whose every tic and peculiarity had long ago begun to grate— everyone was grinding down. Throw in a diet of drab, dried, salted, weevily things overcooked or underdone in dirty kettles, eaten shoulder to shoulder at cramped tables with men who had not bathed in weeks, and one can understand how certain parts of the ship were becoming powder kegs. On one of the *Shenandoah*'s last days in the Okhotsk, Joshua Minor—a big, strapping man made rough around the edges by his years aboard whaling ships—lit the match.

"Mr. Minor is caterer of the steerage mess," wrote one of his fellow sailors, "and in that capacity tyrannizes over his mess mates and bullies the smaller men and those he knows to be cowards." As caterer, he was in position to intimidate the smaller, younger men into accepting the more offensive portions of the day's rations and take the best for himself, and often humiliated his victims with needled barbs while doing so. Since he had become Waddell's fair-haired boy, this sadism had gotten worse. Then on one of the *Shenandoah*'s last days in the Sea of Okhotsk, he went too far. Lodge Colton was Minor's roommate and for eight months had borne the brunt of his bruisings silently.

"Mr. Colton," said Midshipman Mason, "a master's mate from Baltimore, is by no means a coward, and the smallest member of the mess. Minor bullies him on all occasions." Finally, Colton had enough. The master's mates were at supper when Minor took a slice at Colton, expecting nothing more than the usual reaction. Everyone was stunned when the diminutive Colton leaped to his feet and challenged the hulking Minor to a fight with swords.

"It was evident Minor was very much startled by the proposal, but he could not with any pretensions to manliness refuse after the insults he had heaped upon the head of the weaker party—so out they both came, naked swords in hand, and put themselves *en garde* after the most approved style."

The duelists circled, sword tip to sword tip, each waiting for the other to make a move.

Nothing happened. Colton feinted halfheartedly. Minor retreated behind a glare. After a few harmless demonstrations of uninspired swordsmanship, someone in the circle of onlookers giggled. It was apparent to everyone that Minor was the less eager of the two to see blood spilled, but no one felt inspired to save either of the combatants from their embarrassment.

"I don't think I ever saw a more absurd spectacle in my life," laughed Mason. "Here were these two fellow with their naked weapons crossed. And one of them was scared and the other afraid!"

The duel sputtered to a halt. Afterward, Minor behaved.

FOURTEEN

H OLD YOUR HANDS out in front of you and
make two fists. Now cock your wrists and
rotate them together until the index knuckles
nearly touch. Hold out the right thumb in a relaxed, slightly curved fashion. What you are looking at is a map of Alaska and Asia above the 50th
parallel. The Arctic Circle runs just above your
nearly touching knuckles, and your outstretched
thumb represents the Aleutian Islands. The
Aleutians are a string of treeless, windswept volcanic islands that stretch twelve hundred miles between southwestern Alaska and Japan, separating
the North Pacific from the Bering Sea. On June
13, 1865, the *Shenandoah* left the Sea of Okhotsk
(just above the break of your left wrist) and turned
left toward the end of your thumb. The log describes the weather as "strong winds with fog"—
typical for the Aleutians, where meteorological
tables promise 154 days of fog every year, and another 23 when the visibility is reduced to less than

half a mile by snow or pounding rain. Even worse, say the tables, is the wind. In winter the rocky outposts are subjected to full-blown gales (defined as winds greater than thirty-four knots, or about forty miles per hour) one day out of three, generated by a more or less permanent weather system called the "Aleutian low" that squats in the middle of the northern ocean in a state of constant cyclogenesis. In other words, half the time you can't see where you're going and the other half you are trying not to blow away. From a bird's-eye view, you would see the fog part now and then to expose gnarled islands being pounded by breaking waves. At regular intervals the tips of smoking volcanoes thrust up through the clouds like conical anthills dotting a fogscape plain.

There are fifty-seven volcanoes in the Aleutian Islands. Twenty-seven of them are active, and they are the living womb of the chain. Geologically speaking, the archipelago is still young and growing, being a submerged mountain range still in the process of creation by the collision of the Pacific and North American plates, which continue to grind into each other along the five-mile-deep Aleutian Trench releasing veins of lava from deep within the planet's core. The islands are the tops of the volcanoes, and when measured from the depths of the trench, the largest—Shishaldin, on Unimak Island—is two thousand feet taller than Mount Everest. The geology is so wild and dynamic that some of the islands come and go, appearing and disappearing in a game of blind man's bluff that has puzzled navigators for centuries. Bogoslof Island, in the eastern part of the chain, first popped its head up out of the water in 1768 and has bobbed up and down ever since, eroding away in the fierce weather, then reappearing with the next eruption. Some early charts show it and some don't. And Kasatochi, a spectacular salt-water-filled crater not far from Adak Island, got its name from an aboriginal word that translates literally as "wasn't there yesterday."

It took the *Shenandoah* five days to grope her way north from the Okhotsk and through the Aleutians into the Bering Sea, through what Waddell described as "thick, black fog and unpredictable currents." So persistently thick was the weather that he never got a navigational fix for the entire time. At the end of the traverse, he was thirty-seven miles off in his calculations and had to tack the ship hurriedly away from the sudden loom of land to avoid wrecking. The land was Copper Island, the first landmark on the northern, or Bering Sea, side of the chain, and he had managed to slip the *Shenandoah* through the barrier of islands without ever seeing them, into a world that was even farther, wilder, and more unpredictable than the volcano-pocked region through which he had just come—and which in 1865 was at the epicenter of one of the most devastating environmental ravagings the world had ever seen.

A hundred years before the *Shenandoah* ghosted by Copper Island, America's demand for whale oil had been met by ships working the waters around Greenland and along the coast of Labrador, where swarms of right whales—so called because their bulbous bodies rendered more easily into large amounts of oil than other, less "greasy" species, making them the right whale to pursue—provided an easy target for the whalers' lances. At the time, the population of right whales was so high that demand was easily met by fishing "onshore," close enough to land to allow a killed whale to be towed in whole for rendering, or if a bit farther out, chopped into chunks and loaded into barrels for delivery. But like all the great whale species, the Atlantic right whale is a slow reproducer, with a birth rate that could not keep up with the success of the whalers.* By the middle of the eighteenth century the stocks of Atlantic right whale were depleted, and the whalers had to look farther afield for the leviathans necessary to lubricate the world's machinery and light its lamps. Since longer voyages meant raw blubber could not be kept on board without spoiling, this led to the invention of the "try-works," the large cast-iron pots mounted in brick furnaces on a ship's deck which allowed on-board processing. Rendering blubber into oil and storing it in casks meant whalers could hunt wherever they wished, and over the course of the next century, the whaling fleet expanded throughout the North and South Atlantic, then around Cape Horn

---

*Today the population of North Atlantic right whales is estimated to be no more than three hundred. In the Pacific, the species is so exceedingly rare that *any* sighting is a major event.

into the waters of the Pacific, up to the Galapagos Islands and Chile, then westward to the great midocean sperm-whaling grounds that lie between 105° and 125° west along the equator. Everywhere they went, it did not take long to thin out the stocks and move on. The first whaler appeared off Hawaii in 1819 and others were soon exploring the coast of Japan. From there it was a short leap to the Sea of Okhotsk and the Gulf of Alaska, known as the Kodiak grounds.

All over the world, populations of sperm whales, right whales, humpbacks, fin whales, and gray whales were wiped out or greatly diminished. Then fashion struck. Around 1840 it became the rage for women to have hourglass figures, accentuated by tightly strapped corsets and bustled hoop skirts, which required flexible staves of strong baleen. Driven by this new market, between 1840 and 1844 the price of whalebone doubled, which was both good news and bad news for the whales, as it took some of the pressure off the decimated stocks of sperm whales (which are toothed) and moved it onto the right whales of the northern regions, whose mouths are packed with baleen. By 1846 the demand for whalebone had pushed the American whaling fleet to its zenith, with more than six hundred vessels in the fleet. With so many lances poised to strike any whale that came up for a breath anywhere in the Pacific, it did not take long for the population of every commercially viable species to be reduced to scarcity. Within a few years, the vast herds of right whales that had so recently populated the waters of the Sea of Okhotsk and the Gulf of Alaska were gone, leaving hundreds of whale ships with nothing to do.

Then in July of 1848, just seventeen years before the *Shenandoah* arrived on the scene, Captain Thomas Welcome Roys of the 275-ton bark *Superior* became the first Yankee whaler to sail north of the Aleutians. At the time, the Bering Sea was unknown, penetrated only by the occasional Russian trader, polar explorers, and a military expedition or two. Roys's crew were so disturbed by venturing into its uncharted waters that they were almost beside themselves with fear. His first officer suffered a nervous breakdown, said Roys, and "I actually believe if they [the crew] had any hope that an open mutiny would have succeeded they would have tried it to get away."

They were right to be afraid. The Bering Sea is a terrifying place, full of shifting shoals, drifting pack ice, and sudden storms. But Roys— a big blue-eyed man with a fiercely red beard and a burning sense of curiosity—was supremely confident, certain that though the venture was dangerous, the reward would be worth the risk. Two years earlier, he had been laid up in the hospital at Petropavlovsk, Kamchatka, after having his ribs smashed by a thrashing right whale, and while convalescing he met a Danish captain who told him of taking an unusual whale near the Aleutians—a large, full-bodied animal whose description matched what Roys knew of the long-decimated "Greenland," or North Atlantic right whales, famous for their yield of oil. Curious, he used his time in Kamchatka to befriend a Russian naval officer who told him of seeing lots of whales during an exploratory cruise to the Arctic. Roys talked the officer into selling him charts of the Bering Sea.

Two years later he went back, having convinced himself that the Danish captain's "polar whale" was but one of a vast number of right whales waiting to be found in the Arctic. To avoid a mutiny, he concealed the *Superior*'s course from his crew. Their first clue as to where Roys had taken them was the appearance of several large umiaks filled with Eskimos paddling toward them out of the fog. Unsure of the Natives' intentions, Roys sailed away. It was not until the next evening when the fog lifted and he could consult the Russian charts that he knew where the Eskimos had come from: the *Superior* was just south of the Diomede Islands, two black, flat-topped pillars of crumbling rock that jut out of the sea in the middle of the Bering Strait. (Make your fist map again and look where your knuckles nearly touch. The slender gap is the fifty-mile-wide Bering Strait. To the left lies the massive headland of East Cape, Siberia; to the right, Cape Prince of Wales, Alaska. Above lies the Arctic Ocean, where few sailors had ever been.) Perhaps more important than his location was what he saw when the mists parted: all around him huge, shiny black bodies rolled to the sur-

face of the water; V-shaped blows marked the horizon in every direction. Everywhere he looked there were whales, in numbers greater than
anyone had ever seen.

Roys himself manned the first boat in the water. The first whale to
feel the bite of his harpoon dove and stayed down for nearly an hour.
When it came up, it was killed, and Roys's officers—still convinced that
Roys had risked their lives for no reason—declared it to be a
humpback.

They were wrong. The whale was not a humpback, which was
known to yield relatively little oil and had marginal baleen. It was an
entirely new species. When they towed the whale back to the *Superior*
and began "cutting in," they found the baleen to be an astonishing fourteen feet long, superior to even that of the highly desirable but nearly
extinct right whale. And when the blubber was tried out, it yielded 120
barrels, three times as much as any other species of whale.

Within a month the *Superior* penetrated 250 miles into the Arctic
Ocean. By working around the clock in the Arctic twilight they landed
a dozen whales, filling 1,600 barrels with prime oil. Unable to take on
another gallon of oil or pound of baleen, Roys steered back through the
strait (to the infinite relief of his still-tremulous men) and set a course
for Honolulu. In one daring swoop, he had discovered a new species—
Balaena mysticetus, the bowhead whale—and revitalized a moribund
industry.

Word of Roys's discovery exploded out from Hawaii into the cabin
of every whaling ship in the world, setting off an oil rush that was in
many ways the equivalent of the gold rush then coming to a head in
California. In the spring of 1849, fifty ships felt their way gingerly
through the Aleutian Islands and into the Bering Sea. Their success
was spectacular. In that first year, 571 bowheads were killed, and when
the fleet returned to Hawaii in September, the average catch per ship
was over 1,300 barrels, with the largest haul coming aboard the *William
Hamilton,* which wallowed into port loaded down with a mind-
boggling *4,000* barrels. In six months, with the rest of the world's whale
stocks depleted, the captains who had been willing to dare the dangers

of uncharted waters had taken as much oil as many expected to see in ten years. The new bowheads averaged 150 barrels apiece, three times as much as a full-grown sperm whale and five times as much as any gray or humpback. One giant yielded an unbelievable 375 barrels. Half a dozen such monsters could fill a ship.

More, reported the pioneer captains, the bowheads were slow swimmers and "quite tame," rarely putting up the kind of fight for which sperm whales and right whales were known. Right whales often slashed boats in half with their pectoral fins (as had happened to Roys when his ribs were broken) or smashed them into kindling with their tails. Sperm whales had sunk full-sized ships. The bowheads, on the other hand, rarely fought back. And dead, they floated, which made towing a carcass back to the ship much less arduous. The baleen from a single large whale could weigh three thousand pounds, enough to pay nearly all the expenses of outfitting a trip.

The next year the number of ships in the Arctic tripled and two thousand bowheads were taken. In 1852 twenty-six hundred died. From there, the catch rate declined precipitately, partly for reasons of thick ice and bad weather, but also because like its right whale cousin, the slow-moving bowhead could not reproduce as fast as it was being slaughtered. By the time the *Shenandoah* ricocheted off Copper Island into the Bering Sea, with the Yankee turncoat Tom Manning pointing the way, the oil from nearly nine thousand whales had been shipped back to New England. The population had been cut in half.

For the whales—and the Eskimo people who relied on the lumbering mammals for sustenance—Roys's discovery was a disaster. But for the businessmen of Hawaii, the influx of ships calling for supplies on their way to the Arctic created a boom, while under the influence of the blockade of Southern ports another new industry was in full bloom: by 1865, most of America's sugar, which prior to the war had come from the cane fields of Louisiana, was being grown and processed in Hawaii. Between sugar and oil, the number of American-owned businesses multiplied exponentially, adding weight to a growing effort by the islands' merchant class to persuade the independent kingdom's monarchy of the wisdom of becoming an American territory. (During his travels in Hawaii in 1866, Mark Twain wrote that while the average yield in Louisiana had been fifteen hundred pounds of sugar per acre, in Hawaii it was ten thousand. The cost of customs duties to import the sugar into the United States added much impetus to the planters' efforts.)

But even as sugar was waxing, whaling was on the wane. After a decade and a half of unregulated harvest, the bowhead population was on the ropes. In the last year of the Civil War, 455 were taken, down from a high of 2,500 two years after Roys's discovery. It is no surprise that among creatures as adaptive and intelligent as whales, those remaining were turning cagey. The survivors quickly learned that their only hope of avoiding the lance was to move into the ice at the first splash of an oar. To keep up with the whales' changing tactics, the more daring captains began pushing their ships deep into the ice pack, searching out leads of open water amid the vast plains of drifting bergs.

It was a dangerous business, this reaching farther and deeper into uncharted waters in pursuit of an ever diminishing number of whales. Unpredictable currents, violent gales, and ugly surf combined with ship-crushing ice to make every voyage a game of chance. One ship was lost out of every twenty that cruised. In the spring of 1865 there were eighty-odd ships listed in the North Pacific whaling fleet, and by June the *Shenandoah* had already sunk six of them—the *Edward* at Tristan da Cunha, the *Hector, Pearl, Edward Cary,* and *Harvest* at Ascension Island, and the *Abigail* three weeks before entering the Bering Sea. Of the remaining, ten were hiding behind Jonas Island in the Sea of Okhotsk, and fifty-eight were working north of the Aleutian Islands in the Bering and Arctic seas. For these, the already risky business of chasing whales among the ice floes was about to get much more dangerous. Within a week, the *Shenandoah* was going to sink nearly half of them.

FIFTEEN

WEDNESDAY, June 21, was the longest day of the year. At 62° north, the sun merely dips below the horizon for a few minutes, then rises again shortly after midnight. The day before had been horrible, full of rain and wind, but the solstice brought fog and calm. During a brief increase in the visibility, Bulloch got a fix on the ship's position that placed the raider fifteen miles off the Siberian shore, below the snow-covered slopes of Cape Navarin. Shortly afterward, Lieutenant Grimball made the following deadpan entry in the log: "At 1:30 made Cape Navarin bearing west northwest; At 3:50 sail reported in the west. Braced up spanker, hauled up courses, and stood off in chase. 4 to 6 p.m.—Chase proved to be a rock."

After catching the rock, a chagrined Waddell ordered the ship's heading altered eastward. Three miles later the keel sliced through the meridian exactly opposite the globe from Greenwich,

England, marking the point at which the *Shenandoah* had sailed halfway around the world.

"On this day we crossed the one hundred and eightieth meridian of longitude," wrote Surgeon Lining. "Having gone half way around the globe from our starting point [in London]. And like Mr. Phineas Fogg in his celebrated voyage around the world in eighty days, we had gained a whole day in time, having traveled eastward always." But unlike the character in Jules Verne's novel, the navigators aboard the cruiser were aware they had crossed the date line, traversing the imaginary point that separates east from west, where today flips over into yesterday and North America slides into Asia.* In other words, the twenty-first of June was forty-eight hours long—or would have been had not a lookout peering into the fog suddenly pointed ahead and cried, "Leans-o!"

Everyone stiffened. "Fat-leans," as whalers called the offal left over from cutting in a whale, meant the fleet was near.

More seamen and a midshipman scuttled into the bow, all pointing and crying out at the strips of flayed meat and bits of organs that were beginning to appear. A section of giant pink lung bobbed on the swell like some strange, repulsive lily. The long white coil of an immense gut writhed in their wake.

The sailing master stepped to the rail to check the current. In the western Bering Sea, the prevailing current flows northeast along the coast of Russia to Cape Navarin. The stream of guts and hacked meat ends floating toward them from out of the fog meant that the whalers were behind them. Waddell ordered the ship brought around. Half an hour later, the *Shenandoah* slipped across the date line and back into yesterday.

---

*In 1865 the International Date Line was still considered to be the 0°/180° meridian, which passes through the eastern edge of Siberia. It has since been jiggered around to accommodate geopolitical realities in the Arctic, bending to the right to pass between Russia's Big Diomede Island and America's Little Diomede at 169° west, then making a dogleg back to the left all the way to 172° east at the far end of the Aleutian Islands in order to keep Attu Island in the same day as the rest of America.

THEY SMELLED the first whaler at 10 a.m. Pungent smoke rising from the *William Thompson*'s try-pots and the stench of decomposing whale led the raider straight to the largest whaling ship ever to sail out of New Bedford. The ship was lashed alongside a half-flensed whale, with no chance to escape. A second sail was in sight a few miles off to starboard. Lieutenant Grimball strapped on his sidearm and sword and went over with a prize crew and orders to seize the ship, then followed along behind the *Shenandoah* while the raider pursued the second vessel. Lining went along, hoping to replace some of his depleted stocks of medicine.

An hour later the raider caught up with the second ship. The *Euphrates* hove to without suspicion when Waddell raised a British ensign. Just as a boarding party under the command of Smith-Lee pulled away, a lookout in the raider's rigging spotted a third ship on the horizon. Waddell sent a gun crew to the forward cannon, ordered steam raised, then paced impatiently as Smith-Lee hustled the officers and crew of the *Euphrates* into their own boats for transfer to the raider and set the whaler on fire, bringing off a sextant and three chronometers as booty. Smoke was already billowing from the *Euphrates* by the time the boarding party and prisoners were brought on board. Worried that the flames might serve as a warning to the third vessel, Waddell hurried the boats aboard and telegraphed the engine room for "full speed ahead."

It took until 7 p.m. to overhaul the *Robert Towns*. Waddell did not believe it when she raised the British flag. He answered with a Russian ensign, and a shot from the forward gun brought the *Robert Towns* around.

"What ship is that?" bawled her skipper in a Yankee accent.

"The *Petropavolvka*," came the drawled reply. McNulty chuckled that it was "easy to imagine how this unpronounceable name sounded from such an un-Russian source," and Mason added that he too doubted whether the whaler believed it, what with one ship already burning and sailors suspiciously hard at work hoisting cargo from the hold of the other.

It did not take long to learn that though the whaler's captain was from Nantucket, the flag he flew was authentic: the ship's register proved the *Robert Towns* was Australian. Unable to detain a neutral, Waddell had no choice but to let him go. With one ship in flames on the horizon and another obviously being looted, it did not take long for the *Robert Towns*'s captain to put two and two together and realize the oddly accented Russian was probably the same "pirate" that had been so much in the news when he left home. As soon as the *Shenandoah* steamed away, he headed north to alert the fleet.

Back at the *William Thompson,* Smith-Lee had loaded the whaler's boats with seven barrels of liquor, a gallon of gin, one of brandy, three kegs of rum, and ten pigs. But in spite of the delectable plunder, when he and Lining pulled alongside the returning *Shenandoah* they greeted their fellow officers with long faces. Unable to find the medicines he wanted, Lining had scooped up an armload of newspapers, and the news, although a couple of months old, was grim: Charleston had been captured—"This I was expecting, as I did not think we could hold it against Sherman's army"—and Richmond and Petersburg evacuated. "But when I heard that General Lee had surrendered with the whole of the Army of Northern Virginia," admitted the surgeon, "I was knocked flat aback." Official letters from both Grant and Lee published in the California papers made the news hard to disbelieve, "but if it proves true it will be terrible." Maybe the Yankees were just publishing official lies. Could Lee really have surrendered with twenty thousand men? Mason worried that the accounts were difficult to believe, "but the accounts are so minute that there must be some truth in it."

It took the glum rebels until 3:30 in the morning to loot the *William Thompson* and fire her. The *Euphrates* was already a solid sheet of flame. Fog was moving in when the rebels steamed away.

They ran into ice an hour after leaving their blazing prizes. Judging it too dangerous to proceed in the fog, Waddell ordered the engines stopped. Near noon, after a flurry of heavy snow, a light breeze rose from the northeast, stirring the fog through the masts and rigging before parting it. When the fog lifted, it revealed a calm sunny day. But even better than the weather were the nine ships in sight. The two nearest flew foreign flags, but beyond them to starboard was the *Milo,* of New Bedford, a staunch, slow-sailing vessel built overly stout and strong for dealing with the ice. The *Milo* was following slowly behind one of its own boats, which had just fastened to a large whale and was being towed rapidly toward the ice. Smoke was rising from the try-pots of another half dozen ships dotted here and there throughout the ice pack.

"Upon the whole it was a scene of stirring activity," wrote Cornelius Hunt. "The sun was shining with more than its accustomed radiance as we advanced toward them, and as its rays reflected from the glittering fields of ice, the effect was indescribably beautiful. . . . Seals in vast numbers were swimming in the water, or composedly floating on the drifting ice, and notwithstanding their cold bed, seemed to enjoy vastly the rays of the sun that for so small a portion of the year makes its heat felt in these high latitudes." When Captain Jonathan C. Hawes of the *Milo*—"a fine looking old veteran, standing over six feet two, and straight as an arrow"—came over the side and handed his papers to Lieutenant Whittle, his outlook was a good deal less sunny than Hunt's.

"Good God, man!" he thundered after being escorted below to be interviewed by Waddell. "Don't you know the war is over?" He was surprised to find the *Shenandoah* in the northern latitudes. The last he had heard, the raiders were in Australia, and he had presumed the black-hulled ship coming toward him was a ship known to be engaged in laying a telegraph cable between Alaska and Siberia.*

"I asked for documentary evidence," said Waddell, "but he had none, and said he only 'believed' the war was over." This was not enough, Waddell said, but upon learning that Hawes's wife and daughter were on board, the Confederate skipper offered him a deal: With

---

*Actually, the cable was never laid. The ship mentioned was merely in the region performing survey work in preparation for laying the cable. The trans-Siberian telegraph cable project was canceled when the company backing it was beaten to the punch by a transatlantic cable that tied the business interests of North America and Europe together more effectively.

the crews of three captured ships already on board and several more on the immediate horizon, the *Shenandoah* would soon be overflowing with prisoners. If Hawes would agree to ship the captives and sign a pledge to sit out the rest of the war and proceed directly to San Francisco, his ship would be bonded instead of burned. Sensibly, Hawes agreed, and signed an IOU saying he owed the Confederate government forty-eight thousand dollars. (Of course, the bond was never paid, and two years later when he published his memoirs, Cornelius Hunt could not resist throwing a tongue-in-cheek dig at the Yankees, saying, "I shall be pardoned, I trust, for reminding the parties interested that this and a number of similar vouchers taken by us during our cruise have not yet been paid. . . . The above amounts, therefore, may be sent to me, care of my publisher, who is hereby authorized to receipt for the same.")

But before the prisoners could be shifted aboard the *Milo*, there was other business to attend to. Sharp eyes aboard the other whalers had made out what was going on aboard Hawes's ship, and boats were being recalled, whales cut loose, and sails hoisted in preparation for a dash to safety. To prevent the *Milo* from escaping while he chased the scattering flock, Waddell put a prize crew aboard her with orders to send her officers and men over to the *Shenandoah* and do it quickly.

"A breeze had sprung up," said the Confederate master, "and the vessels were taking alarm. I knew that the work before me required promptitude and management or the rascals would have a good joke on me." The two nearest, a ship and a bark, appeared to have been in communication and devised a plan that might ensure that at least one of them would escape. The ship-rigged vessel broke for the ice, hoping to make it into an open lead where the *Shenandoah* might not be able to follow if the pack shifted, while the bark, more nimble and fleet of foot than its companion, headed toward the coast of Siberia, where it could claim to be in neutral waters if it got within a league of shore.

Ordering the lookout aloft to keep a sharp eye on the latter, Waddell gave his attention to the first, running the *Shenandoah* close to and parallel with the edge of the ice pack to bring the guns to bear. The first shot whistled by just forward of the fleeing whaler's figurehead. The second tore a hole in her mainsail.

"Being by this time convinced not only that she was within easy range but that we were capable of riddling her in a very brief period," said Hunt, "she gave up, went about, and steered toward us."

The "pretty looking ship" turned out to be the *Sophia Thornton,* also of New Bedford, valued along with her cargo of oil at seventy thousand dollars and carrying a crew of thirty-five. Dabney Scales was sent to seize her, with instructions to join the *Milo* as it followed the *Shenandoah* while the raider pursued the escaping bark. The northeaster had increased to a stiff breeze and the fleeing Yankee was "going to windward quick." As soon as the captain and officers of the *Sophia Thornton* were aboard and confined, Waddell ordered the officer of the watch to hoist all sail and give him full steam. With the engine roaring out sixty revolutions per minute, the raider was soon doing eleven knots. It still took two hours to catch the *Jireh Swift.*

A round from one of the thirty-two-pound Whitworth rifles fired into the water beneath her stern brought her around. Fifty years later, a crewman aboard the *Milo* reported that as soon as the raider was within hearing distance, the *Swift's* Captain Williams, who "was not in his best mood" turned to the "privateer" and shouted, "Lo there, you are a bunch of cowards! . . . come on my quarterdeck and fight me! If you thrash me, burn my vessel, but if I thrash you let me go in peace!"

"Captain Williams made an obstinate effort to save his bark," said Waddell dryly, "but saw the folly of exposing his crew to a destructive fire and yielded to his misfortune with a manly and becoming dignity." When Lieutenant Smith-Lee rowed over to the whaler with a boarding party, he found its skipper and men with their personal effects already packed, ready to leave the *Jireh Swift* and come to the *Shenandoah* in their own boats.

While Waddell was interviewing Captain Williams, Tom Manning piped up that he "knew for a fact that he had fifteen thousand dollars in gold on board," claiming Williams had received it as the proceeds from a recent sale of oil. The *Jireh Swift's* skipper scoffed and swore there was no such amount on his vessel. "And as we had already discovered that our newly enlisted ship's Corporal was a most accomplished liar," said Hunt, "we did not enter into a very close examination." Another sail was already in sight, and rather than waste time, Waddell took Williams at his word. Twenty minutes later the bark was wrapped in flames, but before the *Shenandoah* could catch up with the other vessel it escaped into the ice. The ice pack was shifting, the current shoving large masses of it into spinning gyres that coalesced into moving barriers. The Yankee preferred taking his chances among the colliding bergs to bucking the odds against the approaching raider. The tactic spared the rest of the fleet as well.

"Several of the vessels which we had first seen engaged in trying out blubber," said Hunt, "we now discovered were surrounded by such extensive fields of ice that we dared not venture after them." With their experiences in the Sea of Okhotsk still fresh in their minds, the men and officers aboard the raider remained more than a little wary of taking such a risk again, "and for once, these hardy [whalers] had occasion to thank as their preservers these icy barriers that had so often proved their destroyers." Stymied, the raider turned back to the *Milo* and *Sophia Thornton*, eager to dispose of the prisoners and retrieve the prize crews so they could continue pursuing the fleet before word of their presence spread.

To expedite this, said Hunt, "Captain Waddell now determined to give the prisoners permission to take whatever they desired from the *Sophia Thornton* in the way of provisions and other necessaries to make them comfortable on their passage to San Francisco." The order was received with "general satisfaction" (after all, it was not every day the underpaid whalers got a chance to loot the property of the owners and companies that so grossly exploited their situation), but there was an accompanying order that was not greeted with much enthusiasm: Waddell said they had to burn the *Sophia Thornton* after they had taken everything they wanted.

"This," said Hunt, "they reluctantly promised to do. But fearing in

case a favorable breeze should spring up the temptation to run away
would prove too strong for their virtue, we cut away the spars and gave
them to understand that they would be within range of our eight-inch
shells, which would certainly be dropping down among them if our instructions were not implicitly obeyed." For the prisoners, this was a deal
they could not refuse, and while the carpenters worked at bringing
down the *Sophia Thornton*'s masts, Waddell quizzed the three captive
captains regarding what they knew about the war. The difference in
their opinions, he said, was distinct. The masters of both the *Milo* and
the *Thornton* were adamant that the war was over, and took the opportunity to remind Waddell that the actions he was engaging in were now
by definition piracy. Captain Williams of the *Jireh Swift* disagreed, stating he did not believe the war was over, but that the South would
nonetheless eventually yield. Williams also told Waddell he thought
the Confederacy had erred in not sending a cruiser to the Arctic earlier
in the war, "for the destruction of that northern whaling fleet, from
which New England gathered her wealth, would have more seriously
affected the Northern mind than a dozen battles in Virginia."

Williams's comment, said Waddell,

indicated a just idea of the Yankee character and its policy in the
war; they made money by it, and for this reason they waged it.
Politicians fed on fat contracts and immense government expendi-
tures, enriching the agents through whose hands the money
passed. A high tariff taxed the people without their seeing it, while
the manufacturers realized fortunes. The newspapers of the large
cities, filled with the details of battles, greatly increased their circu-
lation, and their proprietors grew correspondingly wealthy. The
government stimulated business by issuing paper and creating a
debt that it intended the South is eventually to pay. It is thus that
the war is waged and continued, and it is only to be stopped on the
mercenary principle of showing that it would no longer pay to keep
it up!

The *Jireh Swift's* captain, felt the Confederate commander, "spoke the genuine philosophy and morality of his countrymen," and thus embittered, Waddell dismissed everything the other two captains had to say, buttressing his belief that the war could not be over with the fact that three of the new prisoners had asked to sign on with the *Shenandoah,* to be of service to the Confederacy. This he took as proof of his argument, because who in his right mind would join a losing— or already lost—cause?

The three captains, the *Jireh Swift's* crew, and the men and officers of the *Abigail* were shuttled over to the *Milo.* Upon leaving, Hunt said, many of the *Abigail's* crew grew sentimental, "several of them warmly shaking hands with us at parting, and expressing the hope that we might meet again under different and more pleasing circumstances. It was a sentiment in which we could heartily concur, and I may say that American whalers are officered by some of the noblest, most high-minded and generous men among the great brotherhood of seamen."

Smith-Lee went aboard the *Sophia Thornton* a last time to retrieve a chest of "slops," spare clothes to be given out to the men whose own was inadequate to the Arctic, and a case of coffee for the officers' mess. As the *Shenandoah* glided away, heading toward the Arctic Circle, the crews of the *William Thompson, Euphrates, Sophia Thornton, Jireh Swift,* and *Abigail* could be seen shuttling back and forth between the disabled vessel and the *Milo,* transferring the provisions they would need for the voyage to San Francisco. Around midnight a bright tongue of flame was seen rising from the *Sophia Thornton,* and the Confederates knew the prisoners had, as demanded, "performed their distasteful task."

"A more unpleasant duty," said Hunt, "I trust will never be assigned to any of them. It is hard enough to see the oaken cradle in which one has rocked for so many weeks and months destroyed by the incendiary torch, but when necessity compels a sailor to light with his own hand the fire that is to consume the ship he has learned to love, he has good grounds for complaint against the fates, for the ungenerous usage to which they have subjected him."

What none of the rebels knew was that at least two of the unfortunate whalemen were even then thumbing their noses at the fates and
taking matters into their own hands. While others were moving supplies aboard the *Milo,* Captain Ebenzer Nye and his first mate from the
Abigail were loading food, water, sails, and oars into one of the *Sophia
Thornton*'s whaleboats. As soon as the *Shenandoah* was hull down below
the horizon, Nye and his mate slipped away, heading for Cape Bering,
nearly two hundred miles away, where they knew they could find a large
group of whalers. The crusty old shellback who had entertained the
Shenandoah's crew with his yarns was proving to have exactly the sort of
mettle for which they so admired him: not only was the notion of sailing a small open boat through hundreds of miles of open ice-studded
water extremely risky, but Nye and his mate had signed paroles agree-
ing not to take any action against the *Shenandoah* or the Confederacy.
If they were caught, it would be rough; they might even be hanged.
They pushed away from the *Milo* and raised sail, intent on warning
their fellow whalers.

Others were also intent on spreading word of the *Shenandoah*'s presence in the Arctic. The *Robert Towns,* the Australian ship which
Waddell had hove to shortly after burning the *Euphrates,* was well under way toward Cape Bering, following the same impulse that steered
Captain Nye. One of the foreign-flagged vessels Waddell had ignored
when first approaching the *Milo* was the *Gustav* of Le Havre, and during the entire fracas her French captain had lain quietly watching from
less than two miles away. The *Gustav* was painted a dull, flat gray, and
what no one aboard the *Shenandoah* noticed was that tied alongside her
on the opposite side was the *William Gifford,* another Yankee ship from
New Bedford. It was a stroke of luck that the *William Gifford* was also
painted the same shade of gray as the *Gustav,* a colorless camouflage
that blended so well with those of its consort that from a distance the
pair looked like a single ship. During all of the chasing, looting, and
burning, Captain Vaulpre had maneuvered to keep his ship between the
raider and the *William Gifford,* playing a remarkably skillful game of
hide-and-seek. As soon as the Confederate sailed away, the two ships

parted. The *Gifford* made a break for open water to the south. Vaulpré went north to warn the rest of the fleet.

Two days later the bark *Mercury* of New Bedford was weathering a fresh gale off Cape Bering when a lookout spotted a lone boat approaching from the east. It was Captain Nye, who after having threaded his way through two hundred miles of shifting ice in a small open boat in less than forty-eight hours had arrived to spread the warning.

"Captain Nye stated that [the raider] was within a few miles of us and if we went any farther east we would be in danger. . . . We hauled our wind and warned the *Florida,* the *Corinthian,* and the *Peru* and we all put to westward hoping to keep out of sight." That same day the *Gustav* met up with the *Minerva,* Vaulpre warning the bark's captain that the *Shenandoah* was nearby and burning ships. Edward Penniman, master of the *Minerva,* panicked; all of his whaleboats were out of sight chasing whales and he had no way to recall them. Then he remembered an old cannon stored belowdecks and thought he might call his boats back by firing it.

"We got it up on deck and lashed it down on the gangway," said Penniman. "Mrs. Penniman [his wife] had by this time gone down to breakfast and didn't know what we were doing. . . . When the gun went off it rose right up in the air and, coming down on deck, made a great hole in the planking. Everybody was scared out of their wits, while the concussion was so great that it broke all the glass in the skylight to the cabin," showering Mrs. Penniman and her breakfast with the shards.

Not everyone was as responsive to the news as Captain Penniman. After cleaning up the mess and reassuring his wife, Captain Penniman had run across the *Governor Troup,* under Captain E. R. Ashley, who did not believe him and said the warning from Captain Vaulpré of the *Gustav* was just "a damn French trick to best us in whaling." The next day Penniman was off the west end of St. Lawrence Island when the masthead lookout spotted a ship bearing down on them at full speed. It was Ashley, hollering, "Get out of here, Penniman. That was no French trick! I saw six ships burning!" The *Shenandoah* had fallen upon the unarmed fleet like a falcon on a flock of ducks, scattering them in a total rout. The *Robert Towns* warned the bark *Martha,* which gathered up the *Louisiana, Cornelius Howland, Eliza Adams,* and *Oliver Crocker* for a dash to the presumed safety of Kotzebue Sound. On the way, the *Louisiana* ran aground and was wrecked. Trying to get into the protection of the ice pack, the *Gratitude* hit an iceberg and sank, making her the second ship the raider destroyed without lighting a single match. Still, the carnage was not enough to satisfy everyone aboard the *Shenandoah,* where the discontent built up over months of voyaging still had a hold. Even young Mason, who early on had had many complimentary things to say about his captain, bitched that "out of the nine sails in sight, we captured but three [the *Milo, Sophia Thornton,* and *Jireh Swift*]. Rather a poor day's work, I think. . . . of course, the Captain ought to know best, but my humble opinion is that if we had gone properly to work, we would have taken at least six."

He need not have worried. There was plenty more to come. Early on the morning of the twenty-third, less than two hours after slipping away from the burning *Sophia Thornton,* they spotted their next victim. At 6:30 the log notes a sail sighted. By 8:00 a.m. they had run it down. It proved to be the brig *Susan Abigail,* on a trading and whaling voyage out of San Francisco. The *Shenandoah* was the first ship the *Susan Abigail* had seen in a month. Her hold was filled to bursting with barrels of cheap liquor, old guns, gunpowder, tobacco, calico, and "Yankee notions" her captain intended to trade with the Eskimos for furs.

"It was a money-making trade I should judge," said Hunt. "From what I learned, for an old gun and some ammunition, fifteen or twenty sables were freely given in exchange, and a good knife would purchase almost anything." With more than two thousand gallons of booze in his hold, it was clear that more than being a whaler, the captain of the *Susan Abigail* was a "thorough speculator," one of the flimflam artists who for years had been enriching themselves by cheating Eskimos out of their precious furs and whalebone in exchange for cheap trinkets. It was common to grease the deals with copious amounts of rotgut liquor.

When the *Susan Abigail*'s captain stormed aboard, he was dressed head to toe in a magnificent fur coat, "and begged very hard that his ship might not be burned," said Hunt, "as that was to be his last expedition to this part of the world and he expected to clear about thirty thousand dollars."

Waddell ignored him. The *Susan Abigail* was burned, but not before several of her crew joined the raider, bringing the *Shenandoah*'s complement up to a full 125 men and making her one of the few war vessels in history to be staffed almost entirely with recruits from the enemy. The boarding party got another shock when they found newspapers on board her dated two weeks later than those retrieved from the *William Thompson*. These carried more up-to-date reports of Grant's capture of the Confederate capital at Richmond and Lee's surrender at Appomattox. They also carried articles reporting the flight of Confederate president Jefferson Davis to Danville, Virginia, along with a proclamation issued by the fleeing leader urging the South to fight on.

"The proclamation issued by President Davis announced that the war would be carried on with renewed vigor," said Waddell, who took it as encouragement to continue his depradations. In part, Jefferson Davis's proclamation read:

> We have now entered upon a new phase of the struggle. Relieved from the necessity of guarding certain points, our army will be free to move from point to point, to strike the enemy in detail from his base. If, by the stress of numbers, we should be compelled to a temporary withdrawal from [Virginia's] limits or those of any other border state, we will return until the battled and exhausted enemy shall abandon in despair his endless and impossible task of making slaves of a people resolved to be free.

In other words, Davis—although apparently oblivious of the irony inherent in referring to the "impossible task of making slaves of a people resolved to be free" to inspire resistance from a society fighting to preserve slavery—was calling on Southern forces to begin a guerrilla war, to resort to the hit-and-run tactics of an insurgency, which described the raider's mission against the whaling fleet perfectly.

"It must be borne in mind," Hunt added years later, "that we had as yet received no tidings of the cessation of hostilities between the United States and the Confederacy. So far as we knew, our armies, though repulsed at many points and sadly depleted in numbers, were still making a gallant stand against the Northern hordes. . . . consequently our hearts were buoyed up with the thought that we were still aiding the great cause to which we had devoted our lives.

"I questioned the captain of the *Susan Abigail* upon the general opinion in San Francisco about the military condition of American affairs and he said: 'Opinion is divided as to the ultimate result of the war; for the present the North has the advantage, but how it will end no one can form a correct opinion. As to the newspapers, they could not be relied upon.' " None among the Confederates was willing to openly consider that the end of the war might be at hand.

But one thing was certain, added the *Susan Abigail*'s captain: "You've murdered the President." A newspaper dated April 17 carried a full account of Lincoln's assassination. And when the *Susan Abigail* left San Francisco, all the flags in the city were flying at half-mast.

"The news occasioned a general feeling of astonishment and indignation throughout the *Shenandoah*," said a stunned Cornelius Hunt. "That one who sympathized with the Southern cause should have deliberately planned and executed an act that would strike with horror every honorable man, whatever his partisan sentiments might be, and thus redound to the discredit of the Government for whose success he professed to be laboring, seemed passing strange. . . . undoubtedly, designing men would endeavor to fasten upon the Southern people at large, and especially upon their leaders, the odium of that hideous crime . . . but only the Southern people know how cruelly unjust is such an accusation."

Not quite believing the newspapers and finding no consensus among the Yankee captains, Waddell decided to carry on. It was a decision that could have serious consequences. If the war was indeed over, every action they had taken against Northern shipping since April (including burning the four ships at Ascension Island) could arguably be

considered piracy, for which no nation in the grip of a burning desire
for revenge over the assassination of its president could be expected to
show any mercy. All in all, they had already destroyed or captured
twenty-seven ships. Yet Waddell's decision must be considered in context: It had been years since he or any of his officers had set foot on
Southern soil, and when they had left, a Confederate victory had
seemed imminent. At the time, there had yet to be a single significant
Yankee victory, and rebel troops were camped within a day's march of
Washington. True, there had had been a significant shift in the balance
of the war during the time the officers waited in Britain for their ship
to be readied, but most of the South's worst defeats had taken place
since the raider left England. And though they knew something of the
horrific losses incurred by the Confederacy, no one on board had any
visceral understanding of how badly things had deteriorated. None had
any personal experience of the empty bellies, mass graves, or chaos that
was engulfing the South. In spite of the reverses, it was easier to believe
that their comrades back home were still fighting. So they confined the
Susan Abigail's men in the raider's forepeak and carried on.

Painting depicting the Confederate cruiser in the Arctic ice, circa June 1865 (above) and under full sail (below) in a nineteenth-century photographic repro- duction of an artwork. Note telescoping smokestack, which allowed the raider to alter her profile—a fine capability for a vessel wishing to operate in disguise.

(U.S. NAVAL HISTORICAL CENTER PHOTOGRAPH.)

SIXTEEN

THE HULK of the *Sophia Thornton* was still smoldering when they passed her, standing northeast in light airs. The weather was cool and misty. Whittle kept some of the crew busy slaughtering hogs taken from their latest victim. The rest labored under Mason, sorting and stowing the newest haul of supplies. At 6 p.m. a sail was sighted, but the chase lasted only until a fog rolled in and they were obliged to abandon it.

"There was heavy floe ice in sight," said Hunt, "which necessitated the keeping of a bright lookout for fear of running into it." Ice had been visible off to starboard all day long, extending as far north and south as the eye could see. By midnight the fog lifted, but even at that late hour the sky was still pale blue.

"No one can conceive until they have experienced it the strange effect produced upon a native of the Temperate Zones by the endless day of the polar regions," said Hunt. "There is something so supernatural and fantastic in the sight of the sun traveling perpetually round the horizon, just dipping beneath it at one point for a brief space . . . that until you become in a measure accustomed to it, to sleep is almost an impossibility. But trying as is the long day, the long night is infinitely worse, according to the testimony of all who have experienced it."

By the next morning the fog was back and of such unusual density that the ship was forced to heave to, sounding its foghorn at regular intervals. If another ship answered, it might give them a target. If they dared steer for it, that is.

"Indeed," said Hunt, "to see a ship's length in any direction was utterly impossible, and with huge fields of ice drifting near us, and crashing into each other with a report like thunder, our situation was anything but desirable." They lay most of the day, being swept helplessly north and east by the current, listening to the ice grind against itself with a sound like some giant creature gnawing at a stack of bones. What Hunt does not mention in his memoir is that some of the men cracked from the strain, and he, apparently, was among them; the log notes that he and Waddell's secretary, Blacker, were placed under arrest for fighting. When the fog cleared—which it does in that region with the same rapidity with which it develops—St. Lawrence Island was visible from the masthead, a few miles off on the port beam. Low and flat on each end, the ninety-mile-long island humps up in the middle, silhouetting itself against the horizon like a rising whale.

"The island is inhabited by a somewhat numerous tribe of Esquimaux," wrote Hunt, "who carry on a considerable trade in furs with whalers and other vessels that visit these seas. They subsist almost entirely upon the flesh of seals and walrus, which is generally eaten raw. How they can exist in a climate where for two months in the year the mercury freezes in the thermometer tube is a mystery I leave others to explain."

Floe ice—"seemingly as impenetrable a barrier to sailing in that direction as a similar extent of solid rock"—prevented the *Shenandoah* from approaching. To avoid the ice, Waddell steered north under steam. Along the way, the raider overhauled one vessel that displayed Hawaiian colors and a second they correctly took to be French: it was the *Gustav,* under Captain Vaulpré, come to warn the whalers he knew to be in the vicinity of St. Lawrence Island. But Vaulpré was too late. Without an engine, there was little he could do in the calm weather but watch helplessly as the *Shenandoah* steamed by toward a vessel near the end of the island. (This must have been doubly frustrating for the Frenchman, who was trying to repay a long-standing personal favor. During the Crimean War, his own ship had been saved from a stalking Russian by a warning from an American whaler.)

It took only two hours for the *Shenandoah* to skirt the edge of the ice pack and nab the *General Williams* of New London. "I had the pleasure of boarding her with Smith-Lee," said Midshipman Mason. "Her captain was a miserable old whine of a Yankee. He cried like a baby when we told him his ship was to be burnt."

"He took it very hard," agreed Hunt. "And was quite disposed to make a personal matter of it." When the captain of the *General Williams* came aboard with his papers, he demanded of Waddell "what injury he had ever done us, that we should hunt him like a wild animal and destroy his property," whining all the while that he had "never done us no harm."

"He was a dirty old dog," sneered Waddell. "Certainly a Jew, the second of his kind I had seen." (He was referring, one presumes, to the captain of the *Susan,* the leaky old coal scow sunk seven months before in the Atlantic.)

"Of course, we had no feelings of personal animosity to gratify," Hunt reassured the whaler's master. "Our blows were aimed only at his government, though they might fall heavily upon private individuals. But this was far from satisfying him, and I believe to this day he is half inclined to the opinion that the Shenandoah went up to the arctic expressly to look after his ship, through some spite conceived against himself by the government of the Southern Confederacy!"

The thirty-four men making up the rest of the *General Williams*'s crew took their capture with more complacency, loading their personal

effects into the whaler's boats for transfer over to the raider without arguing. Lieutenant Smith-Lee brought back five chronometers. He also
grabbed the captain's sextant, three hogs, and four hundred dollars, and
while the prisoners and hogs were being transported to the raider and
the ship was being prepared for burning, four skin boats loaded with
Eskimos were spotted pulling out from St. Lawrence Island. The
Eskimos made their way through the ice floes and asked by signs and
gestures to come aboard.

"Their boats were ingeniously constructed affairs," said Hunt. "The
frame is something like that of a whale boat, over which is stretched a
walrus hide, which renders them completely impervious to water." In
addition to making the craft much lighter than similar-sized wooden
vessels, the skin-and-frame construction makes the umiak more flexible, and thus better suited for dragging in and out of the water or man-
handling across thick broken ice.

"Few and simple as their implements are," Hunt continued, "these
nomadic savages succeed in capturing a good many whales. They first
blow a walrus hide, previously prepared for the purpose, full of air and
to this they fasten one end of their harpoon line. Watching their opportunity, they dart the harpoon into the whale, and thus attach to him a
great buoy, which materially interfers with his diving propensities.
Another and another is attached to him in the same way, until the poor
animal can no longer get below the surface and is in the end fairly worried to death."

The Eskimos—or Yup'iks, as the indigenous people of St.
Lawrence Island are more rightly called, "Esquimaux" being a corruption of an early French word meaning "eaters of raw meat," which was
applied rather haphazardly to all the various peoples of the polar regions—were by then having a good many fewer opportunities to take
whales than Hunt envisioned. By the time the *Shenandoah* arrived on
the scene the depletion of the bowhead and right whale stocks had
reached such an extent that it was becoming extremely difficult for the
islanders to catch one. The bulk of the animals had so changed their
habits under the pressure of the commercial hunt that they no longer

followed the migration patterns known and understood by the Yup'ik for millennia. After a decade and a half of unregulated killing, the remaining whales, rather than being the sedate, relatively easy-to-catch creatures the Yup'ik had relied on for centuries, had grown wary, fleeing into the broken ice pack at the first sound of a paddle. Every season, the hunters were required to go farther and farther from their homes, deeper into the shifting ice, to feed their villages.

At the turn of the nineteenth century, St. Lawrence Island had an estimated population of around four thousand people. By the outbreak of the Civil War, that number was in decline. And in another twelve years, after achieving the near extirpation of the bowhead and right whales upon which the Natives depended, the Yankees would turn to decimating the Arctic's walrus herds for what small amount of oil those animals could render, subjecting the entire region to a famine so extreme that entire villages were wiped out. The Yup'ik clambering aboard the Confederate cruiser were probably not, as Lining noted, "a fat, healthy looking lot;" but being more round faced and full cheeked than the average Westerner, and with their frames, however emaciated, hidden beneath the bulky, knee-length *kuspuks* and parkas of traditional dress, they may have appeared so, even to someone trained as a doctor. (However, nutrition was not Lining's strong point. His doctoral thesis was on gunshot wounds to the face.) The depth of the Yup'iks' hunger might be better measured from the bottom of a bucket of grease and scraps one of the cooks brought up from the galley. The visitors snatched and gobbled at the waste with both hands, prompting one wag to comment that "nothing seemed to please the savage more for dessert than the stub end of a tallow candle."

Lining, as usual, noticed the women ("much fairer than the men"), but he seems not to have noted the implications of the Yup'iks' eagerness to trade valuable ivory and furs for dabs of tobacco or food, delighting instead in an exchange he made of two small plugs of tobacco for a fine "dog skin" (more likely a wolf). Dabney Scales and Francis Chew wound up with a pair of finely worked mukluks, or seal-skin boots, and a fur parka each. None of the diarists mention the Eskimos' reaction to seeing so much good cordage, wood, and iron—all precious in a place as remote as St. Lawrence Island—destroyed when the *General Williams* went up in flames. It must have perplexed the Natives greatly when some of the crewmen from the *Shenandoah* jumped down into the whaler's perfectly good boats and knocked holes in their bottoms. The Eskimos drifted nearby in their umiaks, watching silently as the conflagration consumed the *General Williams,* and the *Shenandoah* pulled away.

CORNELIUS HUNT was restored to duty. Manning, as a reward for his part in leading the raider to the whalers, was promoted to acting master's mate, a position from which he was allowed to take control of the ship when it became necessary to work westward through several extensive fields of ice.

"He did it remarkably well," said Lining. Manning's years of working aboard Arctic whalers were paying off; he knew exactly where to look, and as the sun lowered itself toward the northwestern horizon, bathing the water in pink and gold light, three sails were sighted becalmed on the far side of a thick field of broken ice. Waddell was concerned that the plumes of smoke still rising from the *General Williams, Sophia Thornton,* and *Susan Abigail* would alarm the waiting ships. If the wind rose, they could easily scatter into open leads and escape. He nodded for Manning to take her straight through the ice instead of trying to find a way around it.

It took until one o'clock in the morning to wend the 225-foot ship back and forth through the iceberg, working first along an opening to the west, then back to the northeast, idling through tight turns and shifting passages. At times they were blocked off entirely and there was no choice but to nudge up to an ice floe, call for more throttle, and push ahead. The whalers, sitting slack sailed and helpless, could do nothing but watch the black-hulled raider advance.

The first to go was the *Nimrod,* a barque from New Bedford. Next were the *William C. Nye* and the *Catherine.* In the space of two hours, all were torched. When he saw the steamer stop and send off a board-ing party, Captain Clark of the *Nimrod* must have shaken his head at the irony: two years earlier, a ship under his command in the Atlantic had been captured by the *Alabama*, and Smith-Lee, who was the first over the rail to seize the *Nimrod*, had also been in charge of that prize crew. "We meet again," grinned the Confederate lieutenant.

"So we do," sighed his prisoner.

With a hundred prisoners already on board from the previous day's catch, Waddell had a serious problem: bringing the crews of the three barques on board would augment the number of prisoners to nearly 250, "a much larger delegation of Yankees than we cared to have on board the *Shenandoah* at a time, with nothing to do but plot mischief." Should they be willing to absorb the casualties incurred in overpower-ing Sergeant Canning's armed marines, that many prisoners might rise up and take the ship. After a little consideration, Waddell decided the solution was to place the newest lot into the whalers' longboats and take them in tow. While this was being sorted out—food and water were passed to the boats, the tow lines were rigged—a lookout shouted that five more sails were in sight, becalmed in a pocket of open water to the east.

"After setting fire to the [first three] prizes, we steamed after them," said Hunt. "And it was a singular scene upon which we now looked. Behind us were three blazing ships, wildly drifting amid gigantic frag-ments of ice; close astern were the twelve whale-boats with their living freight; and ahead of us the five other vessels, now evidently aware of their danger, but seeing no avenue of escape."

Winding through the ice floes at six knots was the best the raider could do, but with Manning's expertise the raider finally made her way to the little fleet. The first was the *Benjamin Cummings*. Like the three already captured, the *Benjamin Cummings* was a barque from New Bedford, but before the raider could come alongside, the prisoners in the boats began to shout, "Avoid her!" There was smallpox on board. Taking her captive would expose them all to infection.

"We consequently gave her a wide berth," explained Hunt, "and turned our attention to the next in order." The *General Pike,* also of New Bedford, had lost her master (no one knows of what cause) and was in the hands of its first mate, Hebron Crowell, who when he came on board the *Shenandoah* with the ship's register asked Waddell as a "special favor" to ransom her. "He said 'if you ransom the Pike, her owner will think me so fortunate in saving her that it will give me a claim on them for command.' " It was an easy wish to grant. The raider needed a way to lighten her load of prisoners, and for his signature on a bond of thirty thousand dollars, the *General Pike*'s mate was willing to take them.

Waddell may have advanced the career of the *General Pike*'s acting master, but there was no gratitude in Crowell's heart for the Confederate's leniency. After the vessel arrived in California, the August 3 edition of a San Francisco newspaper carried an extensive extract from the *General Pike*'s log which quoted him as saying: "Waddell, the pirate chief, said he should put about one hundred and sixty men on board of me, but instead of that the brute, as he is, put two hundred and twenty-two men on board, making with my own crew, two hundred and fifty-two all told, crowded into this small ship. . . . as I was leaving the pirate chief to return to my own ship, he said that if I did not have provisions enough on board to reach San Francisco I must cook Kanakas (Hawaiians) as I had plenty of them"—a bit of flippancy that would result in bold headlines screaming that the raider's victims had been advised to resort to cannibalism.* All of the officers of the captured ships told the newspapers that in spite of Waddell's promise that they would be allowed to keep their personal property, once they were on board the *Shenandoah* "Captain Waddell robbed them of everything, or allowed his officers to do it—showing plunder and robbery to be their object."

---

*Some of the discrepancies in the number of prisoners reported to be on board the *General Pike* can be accounted for by the fact that two days after leaving for San Francisco the ship put into Plover Bay to take on freshwater and while there encountered a vessel bound for Honolulu. The *Richmond* agreed to take fifty or more of the "Kanakas" with them. None of the newspaper accounts mention whether this left the *General Pike* short of rations or not!

Nonetheless, said Hunt, "It required but a few minutes to arrange the preliminaries, and ere long our prisoners were paroled and en route for the vessel that was to take them home." With so many men on board the bonded vessel, the prisoners were allowed to take only a single bag of clothes. No sea chests or trunks were allowed. There was not even room for their bedding. And three more ships were within easy reach.

Next in line was the *Gypsy,* and it fell to Hunt, as the only officer off duty, to accompany the prize crew on board of her. "The Captain, who met us at the side, was terribly frightened. He was pale as a ghost, and could scarcely return an articulate answer to any question addressed to him. He evidently imagined he was to be burned with his ship, or at best run up the yard-arm, and could scarce believe it when I assured him that no personal injury or indignity was intended him." Below-decks, the *Gypsy* was a study in luxury. A fine library with two hundred volumes adorned the bulkhead behind a beautiful writing desk. The furniture would have done credit to an English drawing room.

"He also had several cases of choice wines and liquors, which I destroyed to prevent the sailors from getting at them," said Hunt after setting aside a bottle or two of the finest as a treat for himself. It took very little time to transfer the captives to the *General Pike.* A few trinkets and furs were "appropriated" and the torch was applied.

While the flames licked at the *Gypsy's* sails, the *Shenandoah* moved on to the next prize. The *Isabella,* lying two miles away, was in the second year of her voyage, with ten thousand dollars' worth of oil in her barrels. As he watched the *Shenandoah* approach, her captain, Hudson Winslow of Freetown, Massachusetts, had plenty of time to formulate an argument with which to convince Waddell that his ship should not be burned. He failed. The raider's master fell back on the same position he had taken with the other captains—namely, that there was no evidence the war was over beyond a few articles in various lying Yankee newspapers. Little was taken from the *Isabella* other than her nautical instruments, but after sending her officers and crew along to the *General Pike,* Waddell ordered the whaler warped alongside, where the weary Confederates labored until nearly midnight pumping her supply of freshwater into the *Shenandoah*'s tanks.

Since the solstice, the raider had sunk or bonded eleven ships, eight of them within the last forty-eight hours. One caught a puff of wind and escaped.* No one seemed to care about the getaway; satisfied with his work, Waddell ordered the raider steamed a short distance from the last burning prize and the engine stopped. The off-duty watch went below to their bunks. Everyone was exhausted. They did not get much rest. A few hours later the boatswain's pipe whistled. An east wind was rising and ten more sails were in sight.

"I felt no doubt of their nationality," said Waddell, "but to attempt the capture of any of them while the wind blew would mean the loss of the greater part of them." Far better, he thought, to move the raider into open water from where they could stalk the fleet until the weather grew calm again. Without engines, the helpless whalers would be easy pickings. They let the boiler fires go down, lowered the smokestack, and commenced beating northward under sail. Waddell ordered the sails luffed, spilling the wind to slow down.

"We continued on in the rear of the whalers," he explained, "retarding her progress as much as possible, so as to arouse no suspicions among the Yankee crowd." From a distance, under sail and without the silhouette of its smokestack, the *Shenandoah* might be taken for a large, slowly cruising whaler. To further the bluff Whittle had the carpenter and a crewman rig a "crow's nest" of wood and canvas in the rigging, simulating the type of masthead lookout used aboard the whalers. According to Mason, this gave the ship quite an "oily" appearance, but because she was a "sharp clipper," they gained steadily on their victims anyway. To slow down even more, the watch double-reefed the topsails and tacked away.

They stalked the fleet all day. The weather was foggy and cold, and the barometer was slowly dropping. At four in the afternoon it began

---

*Presumably this was the *Governor Troup*, which went fleeing west toward the coast of Siberia, where it encountered Captain Penniman aboard the *Minerva* (page 212).

to rise. Watching the mercury creep up in its tube, Waddell predicted a return of better weather, accompanied by the hoped-for calm. At 6:30 the next morning the breeze was softening. The Diomede Islands were visible twelve miles away. A lone sail was spotted drifting slowly to the south of the *Shenandoah*. To the northwest was a cluster of several more.

"This was one of the pleasantest days we experienced from the time we entered the Okhotsk Sea until we finally got clear of those icy regions," said Cornelius Hunt. It was clear, with warm temperatures under a partly cloudy sky. "At eight o'clock, we commenced what proved to be our last day's warfare against the commerce of the United States, by starting in chase, under steam, of the sail we sighted a little way to the southward."

The sail proved to be the *Waverly*, of New Bedford, riding low under the weight of five hundred barrels of oil. "We soon gobbled up this poor fellow," said Mason, and burned her, taking on thirty-three prisoners while the prize crew broke open the barrels of whale oil and prepared to torch her.

"Her officers and crew were at once sent on board the Shenandoah, after which she was set on fire, and we steered off to westward until twelve o'clock, then shaped our course to the northward, passing through an extensive field of ice." At half past one, the raider neared ten ships gathered at the entrance of the Bering Strait. The wind had died completely while they were setting fire to the *Waverly*.

"For the purpose of deceiving them," said Hunt, "we hoisted the United States flag, though there was not a breath of wind at the time and not a shadow of a chance for any of them to escape. It seemed as though the Fates had interposed to render our last achievement the most imposing and brilliant of the cruise, if not the war." As she plowed nearer the becalmed fleet, every one of them answered the *Shenandoah*'s signal with American colors. Most were at anchor, gathered around a New Bedford whaler with the name *Brunswick* on its transom. A Union flag hung upside down from the *Brunswick*'s rigging. At three o'clock that morning, the Yankee's inattentive second mate had driven the vessel hard into a cake of ice, crushing in the bow. Now she was slowly sinking, and the upside-down flag was a signal of distress. Only her oil casks were holding her up.

"Under the circumstance," explained Hunt, "it is the custom of whalers to collect all the vessels of the fleet within signaling distance, and if the craft is found so badly injured that it is impossible to repair her, an auction is improvised and she is sold to the highest bidder."

A sinking ship is worth nothing, but the *Brunswick*'s Captain Potter was offering his oil for sale at twenty cents a gallon. He also asked the gathered captains to serve as expert witnesses, to back his statement that the damage had been irreparable and his losses unavoidable when it came time to collect the insurance. From the Arctic, it was too far to the nearest port where he could make repairs. Ruel Cunningham, master of the *James Maury*, had agreed to buy Potter's whalebone, but the rest were eager to fill their own casks and declined the opportunity to buy his oil. So when Potter saw the black-hulled steamer coming toward the gathered fleet, his spirits rose on the hope that he might be able to charter the stranger to carry his oil to either Honolulu or San Francisco, where it could be sold for enough to take some of the sting out of the disastrous voyage. He immediately dispatched one of his boats to ask.

"Seeing our vessel standing in with the United States flag at her peak," Hunt chuckled, "a boat came off from the disabled Brunswick to ascertain if our Captain could lend him a carpenter or two and render any other little assistance that might be required." The rebels were busy lowering their own boats and arming the prize crews when Potter's boat approached. Lieutenant Whittle could barely keep a straight face when he leaned over the rail and answered, "We are quite busy now, but stand by. In a little time we will attend to you."

As soon as the raider's boats were manned and in the water, Waddell ordered the steamer turned broadside to bring her guns to bear. When all was ready, the five boats and their prize crews started out as one. The Union flag came down and the Confederate fluttered up. At Waddell's signal, the gunner aimed, jerked a lanyard, and fired the last shot of the American Civil War.

Hunt sounded gleeful as he remembered how "all now was consternation. On every deck we could see excited groups gathering, gazing anxiously at the perfidious stranger, and then glancing wistfully aloft where their sails hung idly in the still air. But look where they would, there was no avenue of escape. The wind, so long their faithful coadjutor, had turned traitor, and left them like stranded whales to the mercy of their enemy."

Two of the whalers opted not to rely on mercy. First the *Nile* of New London chopped its anchor cable and began to hoist every scrap of sail, begging salvation from any stray breeze. With three armed men under his command, sailmaker Alcott had no trouble catching her.

"I'll shoot if you come alongside," bellowed the *Nile*'s master.

"Shoot and be damned," Alcott replied. A thrown grappling hook grabbed the whaler's rail, and the Confederates scrambled aboard brandishing their arms. The master of the *Nile* sat down and cried.

Not so with the *Favorite*, a bark under the command of a crusty seventy-year-old Yankee named Young. "As soon as it dawned upon her grim old Captain that a wolf in sheep's clothing had strayed into their fold," laughed Hunt, "he mustered his men on deck, armed them with muskets, got up an old bomb gun used to discharge harpoons into whales, and stood resolutely on the defensive, a cutlass in one hand and an old-fashioned revolver in the other." Captain Young bellowed, "Boat ahoy!" as soon as the boat came in hailing distance.

"Ahoy!" came the response.

"Who are you and what do you want?"

From the tiller of the approaching boat Dabney Scales replied: "We come to inform you that your vessel is a prize to the Confederate steamer *Shenandoah!*"

"I'll be damned if she is, at least just yet, and now keep off or I'll fire into you!"

Captain Young squinted along his bomb gun, sighting in on the approaching boat. His men paced, handling their muskets in a "decidedly business-like fashion" to make it clear they were backing their captain's threat.

At Scales's order the prize crew backed their oars, came about, and rowed back to the cruiser, where he consulted with Waddell on how to handle the situation. Scales wanted to fight it out, but Waddell, in a burst of admiration for the grizzled old whaler's courage, refused. It would be better to show overwhelming force.

"Load the forward rifle gun," he ordered. "Steam alongside until they bear." Young stood by his bomb gun, his crew ranged along the deck. As soon as the *Shenandoah* was near enough a rebel shouted, "Haul down your flag!"

"Haul it down yourself, god damn you!" Young yelled back. "If you think it will be good for your constitution!"

"If you don't haul it down we'll blow you out of the water in five minutes."

"Blow away, my buck, but I may be eternally blasted if I haul down that flag for any cussed Confederate pirate that ever floated!"

In a voice loud enough to be heard aboard the *Favorite*, Lieutenant Whittle gave the order to aim the rifle guns. From his own quarterdeck, Waddell watched in amusement as Young's crew, who understood what a broadside would do to a whaler, lowered the *Favorite*'s boats and abandoned him. Young snatched up an old-fashioned cutlass and waved it.

"Shoot away, and you had better shoot at me!"

"He was obviously drunk or crazy," shrugged Lining, dismissing Young's resistance. "So we were loathe to shoot him." Lieutenant Whittle loaded a boat with Sergeant Canning and three marines. When they pulled alongside, Young aimed, growled, pulled the bomb gun's trigger, and heard a *snap!* One of his own crew had removed the detonator.

Young collapsed, surrendering to the prize crew quietly. He said nothing during the row over to the *Shenandoah* except to turn once to Whittle and mutter, "You are darned lucky not to be shot, for if my officers and men had stuck by me I would have shot you sure!"

"When he came on board," said Hunt, "it was evident he had been seeking spirituous consolation. Indeed, to be plain about it, he was at least three sheets in the wind. But by general consent he was voted to be the bravest and most resolute man we captured during our cruise."

Waddell scoffed at this, harrumphing that "he was unable to take care of himself for drunkenness. . . . All the captains and mates were more or less under the influence of liquor, with some of them swearing their sympathy with the South, while others spoke incoherently of cruisers, fire, and insurance. . . . As a whole, I found the whaling captains and mates of New England to be a drunken and brutal class of men."

While the struggle for the *Favorite* was going on, the rest of the prize crews were busy shuttling back and forth between the remaining eight whalers and the *Shenandoah*, bringing their officers and registers on board. On one they found the master to be even deeper in booze than the rest: early in her voyage, the *James Maury* had lost her skipper to an appendicitis attack, and his widow, who was aboard with their three children, had had her husband's body preserved in a barrel of whiskey. He was literally pickled.

"His widow was very much frightened when the boarding officer stepped on deck," said Waddell, "and besought him with tears in her eyes not to destroy the ship that had been her husband's home." He hurried to reassure her that no harm would come to her, "that I knew she was an owner in the vessel, and that the men of the South never made war on helpless women and children. Though an example to the contrary had been set them by their Northern enemy, we preferred the nobler instincts of humanity." He ransomed the *James Maury* for thirty-seven thousand dollars, designating it to as a transport to ferry the growing number of prisoners to safety, as he did the *Nile*, whose master signed an IOU to the Confederacy for forty-one thousand dollars.

By five o'clock the whole fleet had been taken. The *Hillman, Nassau,*

Brunswick, and *Isaac Howland* had their bulkheads knocked in, skylights smashed out, and hatches thrown open. On the *Martha,* whale oil was splashed about as she was readied for burning. The *Covington* and *Congress* received the same. One by one, all were torched.

"We hauled off to a little distance and anchored with a kedge to watch," said Hunt. "It was a scene never to be forgotten by any one who beheld it."

The glare from the burning vessels lit the sky, glowing pink off the icebergs all around them. So intense were the flames that the heat set the air in motion, billowing the vessels' sails and sending them careening wildly into each other. Soon all were a mass of flames. Burning spars and rigging crashed to the decks. Barrels of oil erupted. Storerooms of baleen ignited, overlaying the conflagration with a fetid stench. In describing the picture, Waddell spoke of "the indescribable grandeur, the water covered with black smoke commingling with fiery sparks, and discharges on board which resembled distant artillery."

A few hundred yards off, from where the *Shenandoah* was lying to, red light from the flames brought each detail of the two ransomed vessels into relief; Hunt said, "We fancied we could see the varied expressions of anger, disappointment, fear, or wonder that marked the faces of the multitude on those decks as their eyes rested on this last great holocaust."

The pillar of smoke and flames could be seen for miles. In eleven hours, the *Shenandoah* had destroyed nine vessels and ransomed two, loading them down with 336 prisoners. Nine of the captured whalemen—"all intelligent soldiers, men who had been educated in the use of the Enfield rifle"—immediately signed on with the rebels. Before the *Shenandoah* arrived, a total of fifty-eight whalers had been working the water north of the Aleutian Islands and in the Arctic Ocean. When the smoke and flames dissipated, the raider had destroyed nearly half of them (including two who sank themselves trying to escape and another five sunk in the South Atlantic and at Ascension Island). All told, in the nine months since leaving Madeira Island, Waddell had captured thirty-eight ships and taken more than a thousand prisoners.

SEVENTEEN

A T 11 P.M. on June 28, after the final orgy of smoke and flames near the Diomede Islands, Waddell ordered the kedge anchor raised for an attempt to head north, where, Manning assured him, another fleet of whalers lay waiting. At one o'clock in the morning they steamed across the Arctic Circle. By ten the next morning they had passed through the Bering Strait. It was the warmest, clearest day they had seen since coming through the Aleutians, the sea smooth and unrippled as a sheet of glass. The snow-covered bluffs of Asia loomed to the left and the extreme frontier of North America to the right. Ahead lay the Arctic Ocean—"a desolate prospect," according to Hunt. "As far as the eye could reach extended one vast unbroken sea of ice, where two weeks before had been comparatively open water." Within a few miles, the ice had become an impenetrable barrier.

"To attempt to penetrate such barriers would have been sheer madness!" added Hunt. "The undertaking would have been attended with the gravest peril, even with the auxiliary of a vessel expressly fortified and strengthened for the rough encounter."

After brief consideration, Waddell decided to make no further effort. If the ice shifted, the danger of being trapped was too great. He decided to turn back, to the approval of everyone but Mason, whose lust for fire and destruction had been well lit by the carnage of the previous week. "We might have gone around [the ice]," complained the midshipman, "but we turned around and steamed to the south, so that in reality we were in the Arctic Ocean proper not more than eight or ten hours, and captured nothing." He was sorry, he said, "to see the old ship go back so soon, for I wanted to see the work well done after such a good beginning. It was certain that more than twenty vessels had gone up ahead of us . . . but the captain would neither wait for a clear day nor try to get around, but came about instead."

The midshipman may have thought his captain had lost his nerve, but in reality Waddell was laboring under other considerations. The *Milo,* the *General Pike,* and the *James Maury* would certainly be beating their way south with their loads of prisoners as quickly as possible, and should they encounter a Union warship, all the enemy cruiser would have to do to bottle the Confederates up in the Arctic would be rush north into the narrow opening of the Bering Strait. And somewhere in the back of his mind, behind his gruff insistence that the war was not over, Waddell must have been nursing a niggling worry that the repeated claims of the Yankee masters and the newspaper articles might be right, that the South had surrendered, and that he, his ship, and his crew were now no better than common pirates.

If so, he kept his doubts to himself, leveraging his belief with the argument that if the war was over, why would nine men from among the captured whalers have joined the *Shenandoah?* No, he said, "the time had arrived to take the steamer out of these constricted waters into more open seas, because if intelligence had reached any of the enemy's cruisers which were part of the Pacific squadron or China stations . . . or other vessels received warning of danger from the drift of wrecks or the illumination of the sky above the bonfires, or through the agency of foreign whalers, it would not have been difficult to blockade or force the *Shenandoah* into action." To avoid this, he claimed, was his duty. He headed south, delighting everyone but Mason.

A day later even the midshipman was regretting they had not left sooner. The sunny weather turned foggy. Scattered icebergs began to appear. The first cakes were small and crumbling; then came others the size of whales. At one o'clock on the morning of July 1, while going along under topgallant sails at six knots, Mason said he heard the lookout cry out, "Ice ahead!"

"In five minutes, before the men could get to the braces, we were into it and struck several blows on the stem."

The impact was so great that several of the officers were thrown from their bunks, "and for a time," said Hunt, "the impression was general that we had struck upon a rock and sustained serious if not fatal injury."

"I don't know when I have ever been so scared!" said Lining after throwing on his clothes and running up on deck. The ship was surrounded by a field of heavy ice. Worse, after striking so hard that she stopped in her tracks, the sails had backed, and she was beginning to surge backward. Before anything could be done the ship struck stern first against another berg, throwing the rudder to one side and snapping the heavy tiller chain with a *crack!*

"At first some of the men thought the ship was stove," said Mason, and were gathering their gear in expectation of an order to abandon ship. Even the unflappable Lieutenant Whittle, who the midshipman maintained had a "wholesome terror of ice," came unglued and was "very much excited and making a tremendous noise."

But as soon as it was ascertained that the rudder was intact and no water was flooding in, calm was restored. All hands were called to furl the sails. Boats were lowered to put work parties on the ice, where lines fastened to grapnels driven into the bergs were used to heave the ship around. Steam was raised and the propeller was lowered, observed

Hunt, and "when daylight returned, a cheerless spectacle was revealed to us. Ahead on both bows were great fields of ice extending to the utmost verge of vision, and for a while it seemed as though we were to experience another jam. But ere long, another stretch of water opened into which we steamed, more because it was the only space of open water than because it promised an avenue of escape."

It took five hours to work into clear water. Waddell ordered extra rum for all hands. This time, even Mason had had enough, and was glad to see the Arctic falling away astern as they turned south again. They were done with the North. But the North was not done with them.

"TWO DAYS before the steamer left the Bering Sea," wrote Waddell, "a black fog closed upon us and shut from our view the sky and all objects fifty yards distant." The course was due south, straight for the pass through the Aleutian Islands the whalers referred to as "one seventy-two" for its position on the 172nd meridian. "When the dead reckoning gave the steamer a position near Amukta Pass, through which I intended she would enter the North Pacific, the fog continued thick and gloomy, but she dashed along on her course, trusting to the accuracy of judgment and a hope that the fog would lift so that land could be seen from four to five miles distant should she fail to strike the center of the passage."

The raider charged along at six knots, blind but unable to slow down with a stiff northwest wind pushing them. For a full day the fog was so thick it was impossible to get a fix. On the second, it thinned long enough to get three sun sights, but no two of them agreed and all differed from the dead reckoning. Waddell paced the deck all night. Amukta Pass was a narrow target, the approach lined with rocks.

"It would have been a culpable mistake to stop steaming or run in a circle because the weather was foggy, in a sea and near islands where currents are irregular in direction and force, for the drift of the ship would perhaps prove more fatal than running on a direct course from our last observations." He decided that running for the pass, aiming for the middle, made more sense. "It only required a little nerve."

By some accounts, Waddell's "little nerve" kept him awake for three days. Watching the penciled line of the ship's estimated position stretch across the chart toward the maw of the pass was torture; he grew more and more tense as it progressed. Even a degree or two of error could mean being wrecked. But whether by luck or by genius, his navigation was impeccable.

"When I expected the ship to be about the center of the pass, much to my relief land was seen on either beam." After running blind for three days, frantically calculating and adjusting the ship's heading for the current's set and drift, they had run directly and perfectly into the center of the pass. Halfway through, the fog cleared entirely. They popped out the other side in bright sun. Behind them, one of the Aleutian chain's volcanoes poked its head above the fog bank, spouting smoke and flames.

Waddell was so exhausted he had to be helped to his bunk. He had been standing for three days, and his feet were so swollen it was necessary to cut his boots off. But it was the greatest experience of his life, he said after recovering, to know the ship and all those aboard were safe.

"Again in the North Pacific Ocean, with fine weather, and the Aleutian Islands astern, I felt an unbounded sensation of freedom on the surface of that vast expanse of water. . . . And when looking in that direction where we had seen such hard and dangerous service, I voluntarily breathed away dull care. And why not? I no longer felt trammeled by iceberg, floe, and land; no longer to hear the masthead lookout cry 'ice ahead!' We had run out of a gloomy vapor into a bright, cheerful, sparkling ocean and as soon as a hot sun thawed the frosty timbers and rigging of the craft she would be more than a match for anything she might meet under canvas."

Cornelius Hunt agreed, saying that he was "free to confess that I had had enough of Arctic cruising, and if I never look again upon those icy seas and barren shores, fit residences only for Esquimaux, seals, and polar bears, it will not occasion me one moment of regret. . . . The principal part of the duty assigned us had been discharged in the destruction and dispersing of the New England whaling fleet and it was with feelings of profound relief that we at last saw these frozen seas, with their many perils seen and unseen, where for weeks we had been battling with ice, or groping blindly in impenetrable fogs, fading in the distance."

It was the Fourth of July. By the evening of the fifth, the Aleutians, the volcano, and the frozen world Hunt referred to as "a region of terrors" were well behind them.

FOR THE NEXT THREE WEEKS the ship lazed along on a southerly course toward the latitude of southern California. Hunt sighed that "never was the advent of balmy air and soft breezed hailed with more genuine delight. Heavy woolen clothing began to be no longer an indispensable concomitant of discomfort, and a watch on deck, instead of an irksome duty, had become a pleasant pastime."

The crew was kept busy cleaning and painting, scrubbing away the battered, weather-beaten look of the Arctic. For a month after leaving the Bering Sea they saw no sails, but this was fine with everyone, with the exception perhaps of Lining, who seemed manic depressive, exulting one day that they were "homeward bound again!" and complaining the next that for not trying harder to intercept more enemy shipping, the "Shenanigan" and its Captain were "like a dog which has stolen a bone and jogs off with its tail between its legs." Between bouts of "the blues" he fretted about encountering an enemy warship, worrying that "we are already making preparations lest we have to fight, making shot plugs and etc. How I do hope we never have any need for them." Waddell let it out that his intention was to place the *Shenandoah* in the path of steamers plying between California and Panama or the Orient, but he does not seem to have been trying very hard to make an encounter happen.

"The ship had by that time lost the cold, cheerless prospect which circumstances had imposed on her in the higher latitudes," he wrote. Her decks were once more a place of respite, where "Jack" took shelter from the scorching sun under the shade of her bulwarks alongside the raider's latest haul of live hogs. "The connection is singular," mused the indolent crew's captain. "But I have seen Jack use a hog for his pillow, by scratching a hog to sleep in order to use him as a pillow afterwards. A sailor bathes all over every morning and that is cleanliness; but he is nonetheless a dirty fellow."

After the hardships of the Arctic, he seemed to be done in, taking it uncharacteristically easy on his men. But while pondering the character deficiencies of his hog-hugging deckhands, he was also hatching an audacious plan. From the newspapers taken from the captured whalers he had learned that the commander of the Federal naval station at Mare Island in San Francisco had recently been replaced by an old shipmate, Commander Charles McDougal of the U.S. Navy. Before resigning his commission to join the Confederate navy, Waddell had served aboard the USS *Saginaw* with McDougal and did not think much of him. He was, said Waddell, rather "too fond of his ease. . . . any officer aboard the *Shenandoah* was more than a match for him in activity and will." So instead of waiting for a mail steamer or cargo vessel rich with California gold to stumble into their path, why not go to the source? Why not capture San Francisco itself? A second newspaper article had supplied the valuable intelligence that the only vessel protecting the harbor was an old ironclad too slow and cumbersome to be of any use in the war, useful only as a mobile battery to defend the installation. McDougal, thought Waddell, was so lazy that the ironclad would be only lightly guarded and therefore "would not be in our way." It should be a simple matter to steam into the harbor under cover of darkness, ram the Yankee broadside, and during the ensuing confusion throw Sergeant Canning and his marines on board, where they could slam and lock all the hatches, trapping the Yankee crew belowdecks before they knew what was happening. With the ironclad's crew confined, the rebels could turn the guns of both the *Shenandoah* and the Yankee vessel on the city, making its residents the helpless prisoners of the Confederacy. In a scheme worthy of Drake, the entire Bay Area could be held for ransom. The newspapers had also reported that the month's deposits of gold rush bullion and silver to the San Francisco mint amounted to $2,227,000, and the *Sierra Nevada,* which had just arrived from Portland and Victoria, was loaded down with another $274,000.

Waddell kept his plan to himself. There was no need to share it with his officers until one more thing was in place. Because the newspaper accounts were now almost three months out of date, it would be prudent to obtain fresh intelligence before invading San Francisco. For that, they needed to overhaul an outbound ship. He ordered the *Shenandoah's* head turned south, hoping to intercept a vessel bound for Panama.

ON OR ABOUT THAT SAME DATE that Waddell began formulating his plan, newspaper headlines in San Francisco were screaming "THE PIRATE SHENANDOAH! SHE STEERS IN THE TRACK OF THE WHALERS! GREAT HAVOC EXPECTED!" Word of the raider had come from Honolulu, where a three-week-old edition of the *Honolulu Advertiser* had carried nearly identical headlines after the Hawaiian trading schooner *Pfiel* (probably the *Pelin* of this story, page 160) had arrived from the South Pacific with word of having been overhauled by a suspicious warship, "a propeller under sail, flying the English flag," that had inquired rather too deeply into the disposition of the Yankee whaling fleet. The collector of customs for San Francisco immediately wrote to Union secretary of the navy Gideon Welles with the news. The day after the letter was posted, the *Milo* sailed through the Golden Gate, loaded down with the crews of the *Shenandoah's* first victims in the Arctic. That same day, the merchants and insurance underwriters of the city immediately began circulating a petition requesting that Commander McDougal telegraph the Naval Department for permission to charter and arm the steamer *Colorado* to pursue the raider, since there was no effective U.S. war vessel closer than Acapulco. No reply came from the Naval Department to McDougal's telegram, and the following week San Francisco's *Alta California* ran an editorial arguing that "there are many here who look with distrust, not to say contempt, upon the whole project [of chartering the *Colorado*] as they believe, with a show of reason, that Waddell had long ere this left the Arctic regions entirely and made off for a new scene of plunder."

Others were afraid the new scene of plunder was likely to be California. The treasure ship *Golden City* had just left the harbor carrying $1.46 million worth of gold rush bullion for New York and England. Two weeks earlier the San Francisco mint had announced that it had pressed $19 million worth of gold and silver coins for the fiscal year.

Then the *General Pike* and the *Nile* arrived with their loads of Arctic refugees. At about the same time, the *James Maury* showed up in Honolulu. The newspapers broke out with cries of " 'THE ENGLISH PIRATE 'SHENANDOAH' STILL AT HER INFAMOUS WORK—EIGHT MORE SHIPS CAPTURED—SEVEN BURNED—TWO HUNDRED AND FIFTY TWO MEN ROBBED OF EVERYTHING, ADVISED TO RESORT TO CANNIBALISM!' "

California went hysterical. Editorials began calling for citizens to take matters into their own hands, to form a maritime posse, arguing that "the local authorities, though the whole shipping of this port be destroyed, would take weeks to awaken to their senses. . . . Circumstances at present call for action on our part to suppress this wholesale robbery and wanton destruction. Let private enterprise, with whatever government aid may be obtained, send out an expedition to put [an end] to this marauder. If this be done, Waddell might soon be added to the collection of beasts in the Willow Museum, and thus gratify many residents of the Pacific."

Nothing happened. Like so many public movements, there were more speech makers than shakers or movers. The *Colorado* left on a freight run to Panama. Finally, a message from Commander McDougal at Mare Island reached the admiral of the Pacific squadron, who was attending a court-martial in Acapulco. Admiral Pearson immediately dispatched the USS *Saranac* to search for the raider, but she went the wrong way; McDougal informed the committee of San Francisco businessmen that the warship was bound for the Bering Sea, never guessing that the *Shenandoah* was already south of the city, drifting along in light airs, scanning the horizon for a fresh-from-San Francisco ship to quiz for information. Shortly after noon on August 2, the rebels spotted what they were looking for.

"Sail ho!" came the cry from the lookout. Waddell ordered steam raised. It took five hours to overtake the vessel, which proved to be the bark *Barracouta* of Liverpool, thirteen days out from San Francisco. Irvine Bulloch was dispatched with a boat and men to question her.

"In the course of half an hour the boat returned," said Hunt, "bringing intelligence of the gravest possible moment." The English master of the vessel, who was sympathetic to the Confederates and had no reason to lie, had convinced Irvine Bulloch that the war was over. He had given Bulloch newspapers from California and Germany that confirmed it. "Our gallant generals, one after another, had been forced to surrender the armies they had so often led to victory," said Hunt. "State after state had been overrun and occupied by the countless myriads of our enemies. Star by star the galaxy of our flag had faded." With news from so many non-Yankee sources, it was no longer possible to deny that the Southern Confederacy had ceased to exist.

As soon as the English vessel was on its way, Waddell summoned the entire ship's company aft. Standing above them on the poop deck, he formally announced the disturbing news, reassuring them that "no man among you has any reason to blush for the service in which you have been engaged. Our cruise has been projected and prosecuted in good faith . . . but now there is nothing more to be done but to secure our personal safety by the readiest and most efficacious means at hand." At the end of the speech, Dabney Scales made the final entry of the CSS *Shenandoah's* war in the log. His hand trembled lightly as he wrote:

Having received by the bark Barracouta the sad intelligence of the overthrow of the Confederate government, all attempts to destroy the shipping or property of the United States will cease from this date. In accordance with which the first lieutenant, William C. Whittle, jr., received the order from the commander to strike below the battery and disarm the ship and crew.

Without a country, said Hunt, "we no longer had the right to sail the sea. We were liable to capture by the ship of any civilized nation, for we had no longer a flag to give a semblance of legality to our proceedings." Or as Whittle put it, they were "bereft of country, bereft of Government, bereft of ground for hope or aspiration."

The same large tackles used to hoist the heavy cannons aboard from the *Laurel* at the start of the cruise were broken out and put to work dismounting the battery. Everyone worked silently, exchanging little more than the necessary orders as the heavy cannons were swung into the hold and the gun ports were closed up. Sergeant Canning's marines were disarmed. The last step was to fire off all the pistols and send them along with the cutlasses down into the spirit room, leaving the ship "as harmless as an old woman without fingernails or teeth."

"It was the blackest of all the black days of my life," mourned Lining. "For from that day forward I knew I must look to beginning life over again, starting where I cannot tell, how I cannot say. But I had learned for a certainty that I had no country." Hunt compared the experience to every man aboard suddenly hearing of the death of a dear relative.

For Waddell, the weight of having violated all standards of chivalrous warfare felt heaviest of all. As master, the responsibility for having preyed on his victims well after the cessation of hostilities was his and his alone (though all would likely hang together), as was now the responsibility for the disposition of the vessel and the safety of its crew. For a moment he slid toward self-pity. "My life has been checkered, and I am tutored to disappointment," he groaned before bucking himself up by saying the issue had "cast a deep stillness over the ship's company and would have occupied all my reflection had not a responsibility of the highest order rested upon me in the course I should pursue, which involved not only my personal honor, but the honor of the flag entrusted to me, which had thus far been triumphant."

To the men, the significance of the headlines blazoned across the newspapers Bulloch brought back from the *Barracouta* was plain. As Lieutenant Whittle said, the word "pirate" screamed over and over again made it clear that theirs was "a situation desperate to a degree to which history furnishes no parallel. Piracy is a crime not against one nation but against all. A pirate is an enemy of mankind, and as such amenable to trial and punishment under the laws of nations, by the courts of any country into whose hands he may fall."

"Indeed," added Hunt, considering their recent work in the Arctic, "it required no prophet to foretell what construction the people of the North would put upon our actions. We well knew the inveterate hatred with which they regarded the people of the seceded States. From the first they had stigmatized our cruisers as pirates, even when we were recognized as belligerents by the leading powers of the world, and they would not be likely to let slip such an opportunity as our last escapade furnished them with to glut their vengeance with our blood, should we fall into their hands." In all likelihood, falling into those hands would mean the rope. Perhaps the young cabin boys and blacks would be spared, but the bulk of the men—and all of the officers— would hang.

Waddell paced the poop, huddling alone with his thoughts. His officers took turns telling each other what they thought they must do.

"It is strange how much difference of opinion there is about the course which we should pursue," said Mason.

Two important questions arise: First, are we bound to give up the ship? Or would Captain Waddell be justified in destroying her? Second, if we must give up the Shenandoah, into what port would it be most advisable to do so?

Let us take question number one; one fellow says "we know the war is over, of course and there is nothing more to be done, therefore, let us blow up our ship and go ashore in a foreign land. Why shouldn't we blow her up? From all we can learn there has been no formal treaty of peace, but simply an annihilation of our government; now here is the Shenandoah, the last remnant of the old Confederacy. Why can we not destroy her?"

Another says "our government is destroyed, all the property belonging to it is now the lawful prize of the enemy. We should therefore go into the nearest United States port and deliver up our ship and our persons, abiding the consequences."

Again, a third advocates a medium course. Take the ship into an English or French port, give up our vessel, which is public property, but our persons not belonging to government, we are not bound to surrender them.

"After a brief consultation," said Hunt, "the crew presented a petition signed by nearly all of their number requesting our captain to proceed at once to Sydney, Australia, the nearest English port, and there abandon the ship to her Majesty's authorities and let each man look out for his own personal safety." Lining agreed, saying that "it is the opinion of the majority of the officers that we ought to take her to Australia, turn her over to the government, and we ourselves leave for England." Everyone was delighted when Waddell laid a course for Sydney—"or almost every body, for some still think we ought to go to England." It was a question, he knew, that divided the ship. But he was too depressed to think about it. He went to his cabin and cried.

FOR A FULL TWENTY-FOUR HOURS the ship wallowed sluggishly in light airs, barely making headway as work gangs obliterated the last details of any warlike appearance. Work proceeded slowly. Everyone was glum, unsure of what to do.

"We certainly were a blue looking set," said Mason. "Wandering about the ship with the most doleful countenances or sitting in knots about the deck talking over the dreadful news."

Then Waddell made a decision that shocked everyone.

"Our captain had at first decided to go to Sydney where he proposed to give up the ship to the Yankee consul," said Mason. "The course was altered to southwest and we all expected fully to fetch up in Australia. But not so—this morning the captain changed his mind, hauled up to the south and east, and intends going around the Horn to Liverpool!" Liverpool was seventeen thousand miles away!

Hunt, adamant that any attempt to sail halfway around the world would end up in capture, turned vicious, exclaiming that "for a full twenty-four hours the vessel was actually headed for Sydney! But events proved he really had no intentions of ever going there, and at the end of the time I have mentioned, he altered the course of the ship without announcing the fact to anyone. . . . I speak from my own personal knowledge when I say he promised his crew to run the Shenandoah into Sydney, and then, without their cognizance, steered for another and more distant port, thus subjecting them to what they considered unnecessary peril, for the sake of securing a considerable sum of money which he knew to be lodged in the hands of one of our secret agents at Liverpool." (How, from the middle of the ocean on the opposite side of the planet, he could have known of this supposed secret fund Hunt never explained.)

Lining explained that Waddell had changed course suddenly at the end of the graveyard watch, the commander saying it was "nonsense to think of carrying us to Australia and turning us loose penniless—but does he not think that the same thing must occur at Liverpool, besides the risk of getting there?"

Smith-Lee approached Waddell and asked him to go to Sydney. Bulloch begged him to go. "But it was no use," said the surgeon. "He had made up his mind to go to Liverpool and he said he would be God damned if he did not take her there!"

Mason rose to Waddell's defense, saying later, "Our captain's position was indeed a most difficult and embarrassing one, and I do not envy him, but he must decide this matter on his own responsibility, without calling any council." Then he hedged, claiming he was sorry to say it, but it was "a melancholy fact that our captain is not the firmest or most decided man alive, for he vacillates, never being positive about anything, always afraid of doing either too much or too little."

Waddell grew defensive.

I first thought a port in the South Atlantic would answer all my purposes, but upon reflection saw the propriety of avoiding those ports and determined to run the ship for a European port, which involved a distance of 17,000 miles—a long gantlet to run and escape, but why should I not succeed in baffling observation or pursuit? There was everything to gain and only imaginary dangers. After all, the ship up to that time had traversed over 40,000 miles without accident. I felt assured a search would be made for her in the Pacific and that to run the ship south was of importance to all concerned.

Some nervous persons expressed a desire that the steamer should be taken to Australia or New Zealand, or *any* near port, rather than attempt to reach Europe. But I considered it due the honor of all concerned that to avoid anything like a show of dread under the severe trial imposed on me was my duty as a man and an officer in whose hands was placed the honor of my country's flag and the welfare of 132 men.

Whether Liverpool or Australia, one thing was certain: in twenty-four hours they had gone from being a bona fide military force to being criminals on the run. And they had to get out of there. They were lying becalmed, smack in the middle of one of the busiest shipping lanes in the Pacific, making so little progress that the *Barracouta*, from which they had parted company a full day ago, was still in sight. The black gang went to work raising steam.

"If the worst comes," wrote Mason in his diary, "I think I could hang as gracefully as any other man, though I must confess the idea is unpleasant, and when I think of it, I feel a sort of choking sensation."

Twenty-four hours later they were still going nowhere. After ordering steam, Waddell had recanted, saying fuel was running low. They had not coaled since leaving Melbourne and ought to save what was left for making a run for it if—or rather when—the outline of a Union gunboat showed on the horizon. Then he reversed course again, saying coal could be saved by not running the water maker. "Put the men on half rations of water and we will run south until we get out of these doldrums." Then for the first time in the voyage, he made a move which could best be described as leadership, by appealing directly to the men.

"About one p.m. he called all hands aft and made a very pretty little speech," said Lining, "saying that it was true that the South had been conquered, that we were in such a position as a ship had never been placed before, but that our cruise would go down in history. He then told them that he would carry them into *the first English port*, promising them that he would stick by them and asked only that they stand by him. . . . He would carry them into the *nearest* English port, but at the same time saying that if he thought proper to go elsewhere they must continue to obey him as they had always done."

It was a shrewd move on Waddell's part. By aligning himself with the men, while at the same time presenting himself as a strong leader and therefore their best chance at salvation, he offset both the possibility of the dissenting officers turning against him, and the chance of the men themselves mutinying, as many of the officers feared they would. After all, the polyglot of British, German, Hawaiian, Irish, Swedish, Malay, Russian, and a half dozen other nationalities in the forepeak— much less the dozen or so Yankees—owed no real allegiance to the Confederacy or its officers, whose commissions, without a government to back them, were not worth the paper they were printed on. But the "little speech" was so well done that many of the seamen, who Hunt described as "the sweepings of the waterfront," and several of the officers were moved to tears, amid cries of "Hear, hear" and "We will stand by you, Captain." ("I did not exactly cry," wrote Mason later. "But I am afraid I did the Captain injustice in my last remarks about him. I am sure of it. I was too hard on the old gent.")

In the ten months since the *Sea King* had become the *Shenandoah*, it was the first time Waddell had shown any knack for leadership or diplomacy—both of which would be taxed in the days ahead.

EIGHTEEN

I T WAS HOT. The sultry hot of the tropics, when the air is still and scorches the lungs. Belowdecks things grew clammy. In the forepeak, the men's hammocks and straw mattresses crawled with vermin. Everything smelled of sweat and dirty socks. The reek of coal smoke hovered around the ship. With only seven days' worth of coal on board, the raider was too lightly ballasted and wallowed across the endless swells toward the equator.

"The hilarity which had so long been observable throughout the ship was now gone," said Cornelius Hunt, "and there were only anxious faces to be seen in the ward room and forecastle. The lookouts, it was true, still mounted aloft, but it was not to scan the seas for ships that might be captured, but to maintain a faithful watch and ward over any suspicious sail that might make its appearance above the horizon." For as long as it took to reach safe harbor, they must stay out of sight of other vessels, far from the traffic lanes and away from shore.

"All hands are still terribly depressed," added Mason. "For the last day or two I have had no appetite for reading, writing, eating, sleeping, or anything else." Lining felt so bad he diagnosed himself as sick. When wind came, it was intermittent and hard on the nose.

"All day long you hear nothing but the old cry royal clewlines! Flying jib downhaul! Royal sheets and flying jib halyards!" complained Mason as watch after watch fought to capture every puff of wind. The ship drifted steadily off course to the east, rolling, wallowing, and corkscrewing across a sloppy sea of mixed swells. The sails flapped, the rigging slack, in light to nonexistent airs.

"I am heartily sick of the sound of blocks and ropes; of being knocked about when lying or sitting. And when walking, it is always on an inclined plane which is continually changing its position. I never want to hear a bosun's whistle again; it is about the only 'music' we have except perhaps some wretched accordion, horribly performed on by some amateur artist; of all musical—or rather discordant—instruments, can anything be more unmusical, more detestable than an accordion? I think the man who invented such an abortion should have been hung for murder in the first degree. No rain and an eight knot breeze."

The slow progress wore everyone's temper thin. Waddell grew suspicious of his officers—when he caught Bulloch and Lining talking aft of the propeller house he called them "a couple of croakers"—and the officers began distrusting each other, Lining saying that a long talk with Bulloch and Whittle had convinced him that a rumor that Waddell was taking them to the Cape of Good Hope or some other place before England was true, or at least "Whittle talked in such a way as to mislead us and make us believe so."

The contrary weather stayed and stayed. When Waddell finally snapped and ordered steam raised in a desperate measure to motor south against the inhibiting headwinds, the lowering rods for the propeller broke, prompting Lining to note that "not only the wind, but also steam seems to wish to prevent our going southward. . . . some seem to see the hand of God in it, warning us, as it were, that there is danger in that direction."

As they clawed closer to the equator, a heavy current set against them, and it was not until two weeks after learning the war was over that the *Shenandoah* lumbered across "the line," into the southeast trades, where Waddell's innate caution reasserted itself and cost him much of the leadership currency earned by his inspiring speech. Mason began complaining that though they were averaging 180 to 200 miles a day, "he won't hold on to his canvas during the night or we would do much better," and Lining noted that a common subject of discussion among the officers was what sail the ship would be under were someone else in command of her.

Assistant Surgeon McNulty began to drink.

FROM THE SOUTHERN TIP of California, all the way to the equator, the *Shenandoah* managed to avoid encountering other vessels. Once she was through the doldrums and into the Southern Hemisphere, beyond the fringe of the southeast trades, a west wind set in, blowing strong. They were cracking along, averaging ten knots, when the lookout shouted down that a vessel with all sail set was standing on very nearly the same course as they.

"Our glasses soon revealed the fact that she was English and not a man-of-war," said Cornelius Hunt. "Consequently there was nothing to apprehend from her, and as she seemed to bear a singular family likeness to our own good ship, we resolved to have a nearer view of her.

"At the time we were under top-gallant sails, but before many minutes the topmen were aloft loosing the royals which were soon sheeted home and hoisted away." It is a maxim among sailors that any time two vessels are within sight of each there will be a race, and the Englishman, too, began to crowd sail on.

"For a time it was doubtful how the contest would end," continued Hunt. "Both had a heavy press of sail and were dancing along at the rate of twelve or thirteen knots. But the *Shenandoah* was too much by the head and at last it became apparent that the stranger was slowly leaving us. Observing this, we signaled her to learn who she was and the bunting soon informed us that it was the sister ship to our own, built by the same firm on the Clyde. In brief, one was almost a counterpart of the other."

When asked their own identity, the Confederates did not reply. It was the first time the *Shenandoah* had been outsailed by another vessel. Waddell attributed the defeat to the worn condition of the copper on the *Shenandoah*'s bottom, and this worried him; should they encounter a Federal cruiser, it would require all possible fleetness to outrun it.

Although ignorant of the details, he had good reason to be concerned. The USS *Saranac*, which Admiral Pearson had dispatched to the Bering Sea almost simultaneously with the *Shenandoah*'s encounter with the *Barracouta*, had turned around after reaching British Columbia and was coming after them. Two more Union cruisers were sent toward Hawaii, with orders to search the sea lanes along the trade winds. The USS *Iroquois*, which had followed the raider into the Pacific from the Atlantic, had rendezvoused with the USS *Wyoming* off the Cape of Good Hope on August 8. Along the coast of South America, the USS *Wateree* and the USS *Saint Mary's* were in position to enforce a proclamation from U.S. president Johnson that excluded Waddell and his officers from a general amnesty granted all other Confederates, and the ten-gun *Suwanee* was on its way to join them. All in all, though the holes in the net were wide, the *Shenandoah* was surrounded as soon as it entered the South Pacific.

Worse, it was no longer just the Feds that were after them. In a kiss-and-make-up effort to placate the United States over its part in the *Sea King* skullduggery, Lord Palmerston's government was composing a circular to be sent to its colonies around the world saying the *Shenandoah* was to be detained in any British port she might enter. "You will detain the vessel by force if necessary," it ordered. "And at all events, you will prohibit any supplies of any description to the vessel, so as to give her no facilities whatever for going to sea."

Further, wrote Foreign Minister Russell, the *Shenandoah*, "after having been duly appraised that the confederate flag has ceased to be recognized by any nation as the flag of a belligerent, has continued her captures and depredations on the high seas"; therefore, all commanders of Her Majesty's ships of war were ordered to "forcibly seize her upon the high seas." It was time, suggested a letter from the British Foreign Department to the U.S. consul in Victoria, for the English and Americans (read Yankees) to remember that they had "a common origin, language and religion" and that English and American vessels had not so long ago fought together against Chinese pirates when British vessels were attacked on the China coast. "Every opportunity," the letter suggested, "which might create good will between the two governments ought to be pursued."

Which meant the *Shenandoah* was on its own. And under the pressure of flight, whatever unity may have remained aboard the troubled ship after Captain Waddell's rousing speech was starting to come apart.

"Big row," wrote Lining in his journal on Thursday, August 24. "Scales overslept this morning and did not come to quarters. The Captain sent for him and told him that though he was now only master of the ship [meaning Waddell no longer had a valid military commission and therefore had no right to punish him] he *would* relieve him of all duty—that Scales might consider himself as a 'passenger at large' aboard this vessel until he got into port."

Mason scoffed, "His august majesty accused Scales of willfully violating the rules of the ship, of giving the crew an example of insubordination and etc., etc. Poor Scales could not but plead guilty in part, while at the same time assuring the Captain that he turned in at four o'clock this morning without the slightest idea or premeditated intent of oversleeping."

Lining continued: "Not content to kick up the bees, [Waddell] must go and kick over the hive, by doing the most impolite thing he could possibly do." He appointed Blacker, his clerk, to take Lieutenant Scales's watch, elevating him over the heads of other, more qualified officers.

"This was excessively maladroit," judged Mason. Affronted, Scales made a show of "thanking" Waddell for the passage he had so kindly given him, but at the same time told him he would prefer to move into the forepeak and work for his passage as a common sailor before incurring such an obligation. A few hours later Waddell called Mason aft and told him that he had given Blacker the watch, and if Mason or Midshipman Brown had any objections he would be pleased to relieve them from duty as well.

"I replied that under the circumstances, so long as Mr. Blacker and myself did not come in the same watch, I would sacrifice my feelings for what he considered the good of the ship." Blacker, Mason felt, was a consummate braggart, always mouthing off behind Waddell's back about how *he* would run the ship, with a "disgusting braggadocio" that "provokes me exceedingly."

Lining was incredulous. "It was utterly ridiculous to attach so much importance to so small an offense!" Cornelius Hunt, who had been at dagger's point with Blacker since they had both been placed under arrest for fighting shortly after burning the *Sophia Thornton* in the Bering Sea, refused to do duty under the captain's clerk. "And he *also* was told to consider himself a passenger!"

Mason explained: "Mr. Hunt was guilty of the enormous offense of remonstrating with the captain," then went on to say that Blacker went to Waddell when he got wind of the uproar and asked to be kept out of it, to which the captain replied that "he could do without him, too—that he was able to keep the watch himself, and so on.

"The captain's clerk is only a civil officer and not supposed to know anything about seamanship. It was the most preposterous thing to think about giving him the quarter deck, especially when the first lieutenant, sailing master, and two mates were all available to do duty."

Waddell, however, stuck to his word and took the dogwatch until Bulloch went aft and asked to take over, explaining that he did not think it was right for the men to see their captain keeping watch with so many officers on board.

The gale of offended egos did not blow over easily. When Cornelius Hunt tried to come up for duty the next morning, Waddell, still miffed, informed him that his services "could be dispensed with." Twenty-four hours later Smith-Lee, whom Waddell had always treated as a favorite, was "fired" for smoking on duty. It was the first time Robert E. Lee's nephew had been in any sort of trouble since joining the navy.

"Losing our nice trade winds," groaned Lining. "The wind is hauling north."

THINGS JUST KEPT GOING WRONG. Two deckhands had their hands crushed when the yardarm slipped. Then a representative from the forecastle approached Lining and Grimball to report that the men were growing disillusioned: with the defeat of the South, they knew they had lost any chance at prize money, but now a rumor was going around that no matter where they made harbor they would receive only a shilling for every pound owned them in wages. An investigation fingered Cornelius Hunt as the source of the rumor. Whittle gave him a stern talking-to and confined him to quarters.

Remarkably, as the ship approached Cape Horn the weather stayed settled, with none of the furious blows for which the Roaring Forties are known. This had pros and cons. The advantage was that the already weary crew did not have to shoulder the burden of working the ship in heavy weather. The problem, however, was increased visibility. Under normal conditions fog and rain would lend concealment, but under clear, sunny skies the cloud of their sails would be visible for miles. Extra lookouts went aloft, with orders to look sharp. Several westbound vessels were spotted in time for evasive action.

One thing on their side was the state of the moon. It was waning, and the approach to Cape Horn—the bottleneck of the Southern Hemisphere, where all traffic between the Atlantic and the Pacific must pass—was made on September 16 in total darkness. With the wind out of the northwest, the ship had been running at fifteen knots for several hours before making the turn east, well south of the Horn, out of sight of the normal traffic lanes. No sooner had she made the turn than she got slammed.

"We were just congratulating ourselves upon our fortunate passage round this dreaded Cape," said Hunt, "when we encountered a gale which was absolutely terrific, forcing us to lay-to under close reefed main-topsail and fore storm trysail, with a tarpaulin in the fore rigging to ride it out. The sea ran mountains high, dashing spray far up into the rigging, and more than one huge wave made a clean breach over us, leaving such a quantity of water on our decks as to engender at times grave fear for our safety."

"Everything was upside down in the steerage," said Mason.

A beaker of water capsized, which flooded all our rooms; tables, chairs, sofas, trunks, and chests were playing "hide and seek" all night, accompanied by the rattling of the crockery. . . . sometimes there would be a heavy lee roll, followed by a perfect avalanche of furniture. I would hold on like grim death in my bunk and think the ship would certainly turn over. So uncomfortable was I in bed that it was actually a relief when four o'clock came and I turned out for the morning watch; I gained little by the change however, for it was scarcely more comfortable on deck than below, though I had plenty of work to look out for, such as unbending and bending storm sails, getting up preventer braces, and etc. Still, I got wet to the skin almost as soon as I got on deck and remained so for five hours. The part of the ship where I was obliged to stand was the waist where she shipped the most water and it seemed as if I was fated to catch every sea that came over the rail.

I must say that twelve months experience at sea has destroyed all the romance of a sailor's life for me; the constant confinement within the narrow limits of the ship; the total deprivation of the society of women, which has so softening an influence on all men; the many other privations, among which the miserable diet is not the least important—all these produce a sum total which can only be properly appreciated by those who have experienced them. What must this life, so unbearable to me, be to a common sailor, who has ten times the privations an officer would have?

On the Atlantic side the storm was blowing hard on the nose, out of the northeast, forcing the ship far south of its course into a region packed with Antarctic icebergs.

"Did you ever see darkness so black that it seemed tangible or seemed impenetrable to light?" asked Waddell. "Where the senses dwell upon such an environment the eye feels oppressed by the black weight and a feeling of suffocation is produced?

"These, the outer struggles of our vessel, were in accord with the dark and gloomy thoughts that now filled our minds. . . . The struggles of our ship were but typical of the struggles that filled our breasts upon learning that we were alone on the friendless deep, without a home or country, our little crew all that were left of the thousands who had sworn to defend that country or die with her, and there were moments when we would have deemed it a friendly gale which buried both our sorrowful hearts and the beautiful *Shenandoah* in those dark waters."

For the next few days—and especially at night—icebergs were a greater danger than Federal cruisers. In one day they had close calls with no fewer than fourteen bergs, said Hunt, one of which he measured with his sextant as being no less than 320 feet high. "It bore a striking resemblance to a church with a lofted pointed spire," he wrote, "but as we neared it and it gradually turned, it assumed the appearance of a mere shapeless block of polar ice, in parts white and sparkling in the sun's rays like crystal, and in others deep blue and seemingly as imperishable as solid rock."

"It would be dreadful to run into one of those things out here after escaping so well in the Arctic," muttered Lining.

Six months had passed since any of them had set foot on land.

RUSTING, weather-beaten, and divided, the *Shenandoah* crept northeast until free of the icebergs. The next storm began in the officers' mess, at a point in the South Atlantic where a course could be laid either north for Liverpool or east for Cape Town. A difference of opinion arose as to whether Waddell had stated he was taking the ship back

to England or had only committed himself to "the next British port"—
and Waddell felt no need to explain himself.

"The opinion of the mess was much divided," sighed Lining. The
wardroom had split into two factions: the Longitudes, or those favor-
ing a run east to Cape Town, versus the Latitudes, who thought a run
north to England the best alternative. "Opinions as to where we *ought*
to go were running very high," high enough for Grimball to leap to his
feet and shout that he would rather be captured and kept in prison for
twenty years than go sneaking into Cape Town, which prompted
Engineer O'Brien to bang his fist on the table and yell back that if they
went for the North Atlantic, he hoped they *would* be captured. ("I can't
see any difference between *sneaking* into Cape Town and *sneaking* into
Liverpool," harrumphed Lining. "Between these two opinions, the rest
of us sit as if between two mill stones, bound to suffer any way we go.)
Mason, who preferred Liverpool, nearly came to blows with Blacker.

The wardroom stewed until September 27, when the temperature
rose to fifty degrees, and the wind, which had been setting hard from
the north, suddenly shifted southwest, ideal for a run to Liverpool.
When Waddell came on deck and gave the helmsman his course, it became apparent to everyone where they were going. The decision nearly
ignited a mutiny.

Breedlove Smith, the paymaster, had had some legal training and
was selected by the Longitudes, who favored a retreat to Cape Town, to
draw up a petition. Early that morning, Waddell was just finishing his
coffee when he received the following message from the wardroom:

To Captain James I. Waddell, master of the steamship Shenandoah

*Sir: In consideration of the present unparalleled state of affairs, we have
taken the liberty of respectfully laying this communication before you, to
convey to yourself the anxiety and regret with which we regard the prospect
of a passage in this ship, under the altered circumstances in which she
is placed, to a country so distant as England. We desire before proceeding
further to remind you that it is only this very alteration of our condition
which has influenced us in forming these our opinions. So long as we had*

a country and Government to support and sustain it was done cheerfully and with alacrity; so long as there was an object to be gained that object was sought for by none more eagerly than ourselves; so long as this ship was engaged in cruising none cooperated more zealously than ourselves. Now, we respectfully submit, all these motives for exertion are gone. Our country and Government have by the sad fortunes of war ceased to exist; our cruise, as such, has long since come to conclusion; our battery and small arms struck below; we are entirely without means of defense—in point of fact, without even the right to defend ourselves if attacked—and are consequently at the mercy of any passing cruiser. Under these circumstances, as an idea that it would be for the best interest of all parties concerned to land us at the nearest and most convenient port, and thus relieve us from our anomalous position, has forced itself upon us with such force and convincing power that we have deemed it a duty to ourselves as being parties interested to the last degree in this question to lay before you, not for your guidance, but for your impartial consideration, the reasons which have appeared to us so cogent. [Author's note: In other words, we did our part. If you want to go to England, go ahead, but let *us* off before we are captured!]

We regard with a proper horror any prospect of capture or imprisonment at this late day, with no Government where would be any show of authority sufficiently great to secure for us any of the amenities usually granted to prisoners of war. It is a well-known fact that during the war, and with threats of retaliation sounding in their ears, the United States authorities frequently, almost generally, treated our prisoners with great rigor and severity. How much more will be the case now that the war has concluded in the manner that it has! Our risk of capture in going from our present position to Cape Town would be comparatively small [not knowing of course that the USS Iroquois and Wyoming had been stationed off the Cape of Good Hope since August 8]. *At best we would have to run the gantlet some 2,000 miles, whereas in going to England we would be exposed and the risks certainly doubled for about three times that distance. This appears so clear and to us so forcible it is needless to dwell upon it.*

Next, we respectfully urge that if the welfare of officers and men is to be consulted, no more certain manner of ascertaining what would be the

general welfare or good of the whole can be found than to take each indi-
vidual wish or desire and by combining them to sum up and find the ag-
gregate. [Let's vote on it!] *In a matter so entirely personal as the welfare*
of either officers or men we respectfully submit that the person himself is
the best judge of what is most to his individual advantage, and a sufficient
number of individual advantages will compose the general advantage of
the ship. [We've got the votes!]

As to the disposition of the ship herself, that is a subject entirely dis-
tinct, and one with which we are far less concerned, from the fact that we
consider it out of our province; but where our persons are concerned, when
capture and imprisonment are a possible alternative to their passage to
England, then we are indeed concerned, and deem it a duty we owe to our-
selves and to those belonging to or dependent on us at least to bring to your
notice these our ideas and opinions as to our individual interests and ad-
vantage, and to request your consideration thereof. [Screw the ship; that's
your problem. But what about our families? Now it's every man for
himself!]

What do we gain by proceeding with this ship to England that we do
not gain by proceeding there in some neutral vessel from a neutral port?
What do we avoid by going to Cape Town with this ship? All risks of cap-
ture, be they great or small. In a word, we have in our humble judgment,
everything to gain by the latter course—and nothing to lose—and just the
contrary by the former. We leave entirely to yourself all questions as to the
condition and ability of the ship herself to accomplish the voyage and con-
tend with the terrible weather we must expect in the North Atlantic and
off the English coast. We see that she is already quite light, and would, if
chased by a United States cruiser, hardly be able to carry on the requisite
amount of canvas to enable us to escape, etc. Still we leave all that with
perfect confidence entirely to your judgment. [It is already winter in the
Northern Hemisphere, and riding out a winter storm or trying to
outrun the Feds unballasted could result in capsize. It's up to you, but
we don't think she is seaworthy.]

In conclusion, we feel sure that you will do us the justice to attribute to
this letter its proper motive, viz, a sense of duty, and not an intention of

casting any disrespect upon yourself. We distinctly disclaim any intention
or desire to trammel your judgment or interfere with your functions.
We have the honor to be, very respectfully, your obedient servants.

Francis T. Chew
Irvine S. Bulloch
Charles Lining
Matthew O'Brien
William Breedlove Smith
O. A. Brown

Waddell made no response. That afternoon, the steerage officers
sent in one of their own, drafted by the captain's clerk Blacker, who unlike Breedlove Smith had had no legal training but *had* gained a repu-
tation aboard as something of a "sea lawyer," a disparaging term usually
reserved for know-it-all troublemakers who preferred bitching to actually solving problems. Blacker's letter began with the usual salutation of
utmost respect, and a request that it be received in the same spirit which
dictated it, then got down to brass tacks, with little of Breedlove
Smith's flowing legalese, beginning "Sir":

The ship has now arrived at a position where we feel the urgent necessity
of impressing you with our feelings as to the destination. On a previous oc-
casion you declared your intention of proceeding to the nearest English
port. We are now near one, viz, Cape Town, which for many reasons holds
out more inducements than any other port to make us wish to be
taken there.

It is right that we should here state our reasons for preferring this port
to the chances of proceeding to Europe. Cape Town is a harbor of constant
resort by the homeward-bound Indiamen and other means of prosecuting
our journey to Europe are afforded by the mail steamers and the Calcutta
steamers. From the universal sympathy that was always shown to all en-
gaged in our cause during the late war, we entertain no doubt that pas-
sages would be allowed or offered us in these vessels, and even were the
reverse the case, we could always work our passages in the aforesaid ships.

Again, Cape Town is now so near that the passage there would only occupy ten or fourteen days, whereas to go to England would take fully forty at the least. Our chances of capture are also lessened, for even were an American ship of war lying in port the English authorities would never give up our persons, whatever they might do with the ship.

Now. On the other hand, proceeding through the North Atlantic, we run two risks, both of them very grave indeed in their nature. The first is capture, and as this ship has gained for herself great notoriety, we may very readily conclude that ships are already on the lookout for us on the usual route, and no other one can we adopt in consequence of the scarcity of our fuel.

We can not reasonably expect any good treatment if we fall into the hands of the U.S. Government. Their treatment of prisoners already has shown how we will be dealt with, and as there are several paroled prisoners on board it will go doubly hard with them.

The next risk lies in the state of the ship herself. She is already so light that even the small quantity of fuel consumed during the last few days in condensing has made a perceptible difference in her stability. Now, to enable us to shorten our voyage or avoid capture by taking an unusual route, recourse must be had to steam (or otherwise stick to the traffic lanes of the trades or risk having no, or contrary, winds) thereby placing the ship in a most dangerous condition, which can not be remedied, and which will render the ship totally unfit and unable to contend with the furious weather that constantly prevails on the British coasts from November to April. Here the lives of all on board will be placed in more jeopardy than their liberties, and we entreat you to seriously weigh over these considerations.

In conclusion, we would request that should you determine not to enter either of the harbors at the Cape you would give us the opportunity of landing at some of the bays to the northward, which we would infinitely prefer to the chances of capture or shipwreck.

"This was the worst, most pusillanimous part of the whole affair," wrote Midshipman Mason.

The document was signed by all of the steerage officers, except Master's Mate Cornelius Hunt, and two of the forward officers, the sailmaker and carpenter. It was to the same purpose as the document from the wardroom, but much more dictatorial, and contained several assertions for which they had no guarantee whatsoever (such as the availability of passage from Cape Town to Europe aboard foreign vessels). In both of them the probabilities of capture were mentioned with wholesome terror and the possible rigor of the treatment we would receive from the Yankees dwelt upon at length and painted in the liveliest colours.

One feature in both of these communications I must mention, which although apparently of small importance, I for one consider a vital point: They laid aside all grade and titles, addressing the captain of the "steamship Shenandoah" (rather than C.S.S. *Shenandoah*) and signed themselves as simply "John Smith," "Moses Adams," etc., thus seeming to assume a position of "independence"—which is as mild an expression as I can use!

Even Sergeant Canning, whose health had begun to deteriorate rapidly after the storm at Cape Horn, signed Blacker's letter, and when Blacker handed it to Waddell personally, the captain blew, towering his full six feet plus over his smaller clerk and screaming, "*I* will be captain of this ship, sir, or die on this deck!" Then he summoned Lieutenants Whittle, Grimball, Lee, Chew, and Scales to his cabin.

"I had intended to carry the ship into Cape Town," he told them. "But since getting on this side of Cape Horn have changed my intention to try to go into some European port. But after having received petitions signed by so many officers requesting to go to Cape Town, I will leave it for your consideration and be guided by your decisions." Then he excused himself.

"The petitions were read and discussed pretty angrily," said Surgeon Lining, who later asked Lieutenant Chew about the proceedings. "No one's opinion was changed and three out of the five were for going to Liverpool, that is Grimball, Lee, and Scales." Lieutenant Whittle, who was one of the paroled prisoners Blacker had referred to in his letter for whom capture would go doubly hard, was in favor of making a run for Cape Town, but still retained enough respect for Waddell and his own now defunct position as a Confederate officer to think the decision was one to be made by the vessel's master.* Whittle recused himself, saying that as executive officer, it would be unseemly for him to go against the wishes of his commander. Only Lieutenant Chew voted to go to Cape Town.

The meeting, fumed Lining, was

the smartest thing the captain had ever done on board this ship. He *knew* before he called them into his cabin the opinion of every officer, because this thing had been openly, loudly, and angrily discussed, time and time again, in the ward room, where every word could be heard in his cabin. He *knew* he would have a majority of the council on his side! He left out Bulloch, who had always heretofore been called in to councils—not to mention other officers who were present at important consultations (e.g. the consultation in Melbourne as to what answer should be returned to Mr. Francis's demand to have the ship searched). In this way, certain that it would be decided as he wished, he threw all responsibility on the shoulders of the council, saying cooly "Gentleman, I will be guided by you." Before he stated this so boldly, he should have remembered the past, when he called upon *all* of the officers to decide whether the ship could be taken to sea or not (at the start of the voyage, off Madeira), he being the one—and the only one—who thought she should instead go into some near port to look for a crew. Had any of the officers other than the watch officers then said other than they did, never, I honestly believe, would this ship ever have made any part of a cruise!

---

*See the note on page 22 regarding Whittle's capture early in the war.

"The great mistake of the Captain," reflected Mason, "was in not putting down his foot in the first place when we saw the *Barracouta* [and received news the war was over].

"Instead, he first squares away for Australia, then the next day heaves up again for Liverpool, then calls up all the men and tells them he is going to the nearest 'English port.' This showed vacillation in the first place and equivocation in the second."

Mason considered himself a Liverpool man, and he, Grimball, Lee, Scales, and Assistant Surgeon McNulty were the only five officers not to sign either petition. Instead, he joined his name with theirs to a short message of support, saying: "It will be a source of gratification for us to know that in connection with those documents you have received, you have also this one, which expresses our unqualified approbation of the course you have determined upon. Be the fortunes of war and shipwreck in our passage (which appear to have excited so much uneasiness in some) what they may, we consider either England or France the only proper destination for the *Shenandoah*."

Then the crew—many of whom were British and wanted to get home—surprised everyone by introducing a petition of their own. Seventy put their mark to a letter stating their "complete reliance and trust in whatever it should please you to do under any circumstances."

With the support of five officers and a majority of the men, Waddell held course for Liverpool.

FEELINGS RAN HIGH. The next day at breakfast, said Mason, "everyone looked as black as midnight and I scarcely dared speak to any of the Cape Town crowd. Even Smith, who is always so cool and hard to ruffle, could not conceal his disappointment . . . having used all his plausible arguments to bring over those who were wavering or who had not the decision of character enough to form an opinion of their own, to fail totally was not only a disappointment but a wound to his pride that touched him to the quick. Being myself a Liverpoolite to the backbone, I was of course pleased with the decision, and although it is anything but a Christian spirit, I must acknowledge that I cannot help feeling immense satisfaction at their signal defeat. As [Grimball] says, 'we hogged them after all.' "

The next day Waddell made a peace overture when the northbound *Shenandoah* sailed across the exact point where the ship had been southbound eleven months before in December, heading into the Roaring Forties. Since leaving London they had sailed nearly forty-eight thousand miles and become the first and only Confederate vessel to circumnavigate the globe.

"The captain brought out a bottle of champagne, which had been kept by him until now, and at supper time he sent it out to the ward room with a nice little message about having been 'round the world, etc." Three of the Cape Town supporters got up and walked out.

"I was surprised and sorry to see the spirit was so strong that three out of five at the table went away," wondered Mason. Only Chew and Lining remained. It was, he said, a display of "contemptible spirit."

Lining remarked only that "some of the officers did not drink but left the table, and whether it was because they did not wish to drink at such an unreasonable hour, or that they did not wish to drink to the event, I do not know. But I do think their point might have been strained under the circumstances, as I think the gesture was kindly and politely meant."

The doctor had other things to worry about besides boorish behavior on the part of his fellow officers: water rations had been cut again, this time to little more than half a gallon per day, not enough for the men who were working twelve hours a day in the broiling sun, or the officers, many of whom, like Lining, were already suffering the headaches and lethargy that come with dehydration. (The officers at least still had coffee; the ordinary sailors had to make do with watered rum.) And after months on a diet of dried and salted food, some of the crew were beginning to show signs of scurvy. Complaints of loose teeth, bleeding gums, and unhealing sores were common. ("I have a wholesome terror of the horrible disease," worried Mason, "much more than

I expected . . . but it is not probable I will have it." The officers had access to what was left of the fresh food.)

The deprivation was hardest on Sergeant Canning, whose chest
wound had driven him into his bunk, where he lay moaning, attended
by his servant Weeks.

"He is very sick," wrote Lining on the second of October. "I hardly
think he will live to reach England. I did want to go through this cruise
without losing a single man, but I am afraid I shall not." Mason spent
his spare time reading to Canning from a French Bible and trying to
console him.

On October 4 the ship sailed across the Tropic of Capricorn, entering the Torrid Zone. That night there was a lunar eclipse.

A YEAR TO THE DAY after leaving London the ship picked up the
southeast trades. "Today is the anniversary of our sailing from England
in the Laurel to meet this ship," remembered Lining. "Only a year ago!
Why, it seems as if I had been gone out of England for some indefinite
period and I look back on it as a kind of dream. If I ever get back, what
changes will I find? Who will be dead, who married, and how many will
remember me? One more man came on with scurvy this morning. I
hope it will not spread too much." William Bill, an older "Kanaka," had
fallen ill from the effects of scurvy, overwork, and syphilis.

DISEASED, dehydrated, and squabbling, the rebels beat north, avoiding traffic where they could, staying always out of sight of land. On
October 11, for the fourth time in the voyage, they crossed the equator. That event, like the circumnavigation, went uncelebrated by all but
McNulty, who went on a drunken spree. McNulty had already been
removed from his duties as assistant surgeon because of chronic
drunkenness, and on more than one occasion had been confined to
quarters, but this time he got so soaked that he stormed into the mess

and confronted Blacker, calling him a "damned old English-Irish Orangeman."

"The most inveterate hatred exists between the two," explained Mason. "Blacker and McNulty, being both Irish, the former an Orangeman and the latter an independent, the insult was of a religious, profane, and political nature at the same time."

"Blacker did right in reporting him," said Lining. Lieutenant Whittle sent McNulty below to his room, with orders not to come back without permission. McNulty staggered off, then returned with a pistol. He brandished the gun at Whittle.

"Stand back, sir!"

Whittle stepped forward and wrenched it from his hand. McNulty collapsed, sobbing.

"McNulty is a confirmed old drunkard," scoffed Mason as McNulty was placed under arrest. "And will probably never reform if he lives a thousand years."

"Our ship is fast becoming a perfect Hell afloat," observed Lining, "and only wants a few more ward room quarrels to become entirely so."

That afternoon Blacker got into a fistfight with Manning.

On October 13 it rained. For that day and the next, everyone had plenty to drink and the luxury of water with which to wash. The farther north the cruiser reached, the more traffic they encountered, all of it merchantmen with whom they exchanged no signals. At three o'clock in the afternoon of the nineteenth all hands gathered to observe an annular eclipse, "one of the most beautiful sights it has ever been my good fortune to witness," according to Lining.* "The ring became perfect about 4:10 p.m. . . . with a perfectly uninterrupted view of it, although before and after it was covered with clouds." Three of the Hawaiians broke out in song, accompanied by a foot-stomping hula. "The singing was very sweet," said the surgeon, but the accompanying dance he pronounced "execrable."

---

*During an annular eclipse the silhouette of the moon obscures the center of the sun, leaving a ring of light showing around the moon.

The next day one of the engineers challenged Hunt and Blacker to a fight, "together or separately." Both scampered to their rooms.

SERGEANT CANNING started coughing blood. Lining had his cot brought up on deck, where he hoped the fresh air might do him good. On October 22, the syphilitic William Bill went into convulsions, lost his pulse, and turned cold. Then—tough old sailor that he was—he coughed once or twice and revived.

TWO WEEKS after crossing the equator the *Shenandoah* sailed out of the northern edge of the trade winds, coasting into a shallow breeze. An hour before sunset she was fanning along with barely enough wind to belly the sails. From aloft, a lookout cried, "Sail ho!"

The lookout's voice brought everyone to his feet. Two points off the starboard bow, far enough away that neither her rig nor her direction of travel could be made out, lay a suspicious-looking craft, its hull below the horizon. Waddell sent the quartermaster—known to have the sharpest eyes in the crew—up to the masthead to describe her.

"If there were a Federal cruiser to be found anywhere, she would be in that region, where most vessels bound for Europe could be intercepted," explained the captain. Between the twin bulges of Africa and South America, where the ocean currents and natural highways of the trade winds combine to squeeze all shipping into narrow traffic lanes, was an ideal position for a Union gunboat to wait. The quartermaster shouted down that she was a brig, with her mainsail hauled up, and a goodly distance between her masts. Between the masts was what appeared to be a funnel.

"She appeared to be a steamer," said Waddell, and the furled mainsail indicated the stranger was "loafing," going nowhere, keeping just enough speed up to maintain steerageway—exactly what a warship would do if she was hanging out in the area inspecting passing ships, bent on ambushing an outlaw raider.

The strange brig was standing on a course almost identical to that of the *Shenandoah*. Everyone looked aloft at the raider's canvas. On parallel courses, it would not take long for the *Shenandoah* to overtake her. A half hour of daylight remained, and the breeze was driving the raider closer.

"I could make no changes in the course of the ship or the quantity of sail she was carrying," said Waddell, "because such evolution would have aroused the stranger's suspicion. And whatever she might be, she had seen the *Shenandoah* and was waiting to speak to her.

"There seemed little chance of escaping communication. The danger was we would approach too near during light. The stranger's hull could already be seen from the deck [which meant she could see the *Shenandoah*] and darkness came on more slowly than I had ever before observed it. The situation was one of anxious suspense; our security, if any remained, depended on a strict adherence to the course; deviation would be fatal; boldness must accomplish the deception. We forged ahead; it would be madness to stop her."

For a year the Confederates had reveled in their vessel's speed; now they damned her. The propeller was lowered to increase drag; a bight of heavy line was run off the stern to slow her down. What wind could be spilled from the sails without observation was spilled while the religious among the crew filled the air with prayers. Before the converging vessels could close the distance, the sun went down, leaving behind a brilliant western sky. A few minutes later it was dark.

"What a relief!" said Waddell. "She could not have been four miles off."

The *Shenandoah* was turned south, and steam was ordered (an operation which took two hours). At nine o'clock the moon rose. Waddell ordered the sails furled to reduce the chance of moonglow on the white canvas giving them away. "The coal was good Cardiff," said Waddell, "and the smoke a white vapor which could not be seen more than two hundred yards. Now that the engine was working, the steamer headed east and we had all the advantage to be expected. It was the first time she had been under steam since crossing the line on the Pacific side.

Indeed, the fires had not been not lighted for a distance of over 13,000 miles."

The Confederates steamed east, looking over their shoulders for fifteen miles, then turned and began running north through the darkness. By daylight, they were a hundred miles away.

NINETEEN

DURING A VOYAGE of more than a year in which she had sunk, burned, captured, or contributed to the destruction of forty ships and taken more than a thousand prisoners, the *Shenandoah* had neither suffered nor caused a single human casualty beyond the few accidental injuries normal to the operation of a sailing ship. The day after escaping the Union cruiser, that changed. (Years later, Waddell was told the ship was the USS *Saranac*.)

"At 5:05 p.m.," wrote Surgeon Lining in his records, "William Bill, a native of Maui, one of the Sandwich Islands, died. He died so easily and suddenly that those who were with him thought that he was asleep, so I was not called until after he was dead.

"Poor fellow! He had been suffering from venereal for a long time and was covered with ulcers, all about the throat and chest. It must have attacked his internal organs as well, as he had all the symptoms of sub-acute inflammation of the brain and chest. I have had very little hope that he would live for some time now, but he went off more suddenly than I expected. He is the first one of our ship's company whom death has carried off and I can only hope he will be the last, though I can hardly expect it."

The next morning at half past nine a mild westerly was blowing. Waddell ordered the watch to heave to. "This was the first time I had seen a burial at sea," wrote Mason. "And I was rather astonished at my own insensibility. There was something about the means of the man's death and the way in which everything was managed that did not give one the feeling of awe usual on such occassions."

"It was very badly managed," said Lining; "the body was just thrown into the sea from the poop."

Mason was more descriptive, explaining how as soon as Bill was dead his body was prepared, sewn up in canvas with two eight-inch shot, and laid out on the side of the poop deck, and a watch was put over him until morning, when he was buried. All hands were called aft as quietly as possible to avoid disturbing Sergeant Canning, who was still resting on deck.

The flag was put at half-mast. All hands stood quietly with their heads uncovered while Lieutenant Whittle read the service and the remains of the Kanaka were consigned to the deep.

Two days later it was Canning's turn. Following William Bill's burial, the ship had been plagued with a series of short squalls and an outburst of fisticuffs and brawls that left some "awful looking eyes" and "a good many swollen heads." On October 30 Canning died.

"He was much worse this morning and I did not think he could live more than one or two days," said Lining. "But death came sooner than I anticipated."

"It so chanced that he was alone," wrote Hunt, "with the exception of his attendant, an old negro. For an hour or more he had been lying quietly on his berth, apparently suffering little pain, when suddenly he reached forth his hand and grasped that of his sable companion.

"Good-bye, Old Weeks," said Canning. "I am going. Take care of yourself."

A moment later, at 5:45 p.m. on a rainy, disagreeable day, the mysterious George P. Canning was dead.

"His disease was 'phthisis,' " wrote Lining in his records, "a wasting disease of the lung brought on by a gunshot wound which, he said, was received at the Battle of Shiloh while serving on General Polk's staff."

Lining, like all aboard the *Shenandoah,* was puzzled by the mysterious Canning, saying,

> There is something in the history of this man that none of us know—his being on General Polk's staff—his coming over to Europe with a wife, a Southerner by birth, whom no one has ever seen since, nor has anyone ever heard him speak of her—his going out to Australia, not having her with him—his great reticence on all subjects related to his past life, never even mentioning any of his family, or who they were or where they lived—no mention being made in any of his journals to anybody or anything relating to his past life. We don't know where any of his relatives live, nor who they are—In fact we know nothing about him—and now after having overhauled all his things, nothing can be found which will give a clue to where any of his people are, or who he has been.

"Canning asked me twice to look out for his things," said Mason.

> To pack them up and send them to his friends in case he should die, saying that I would find the address in his note book. He told me this about two months ago, but the last time he spoke of it, about two days before his death, he commenced to write an address in his journal but stopped, and upon examining his journal, papers, and etc. I find nothing that gives any clue to his family and friends or their whereabouts. Strange to say he was always remarkably reserved on the subject of his family. I spoke of his wife one day and he immediately turned the conversation on some other topic. The

only thing he ever told me was that his friends lived in France and I have heard him speak of his brother in Australia. I fear I shall find it difficult to fulfill my promise; at all events I will pack up his things and keep them carefully until we arrive in England, when I will write to St. Germain on a venture and also advertise in the English and French papers.

"He was an ungrateful man," concluded Lining. "Never thinking that anyone did him a favor by doing anything for him, but rather that all things should be done for him, no matter what it will cost others. He quarreled with everyone who had much to do with him and was generally very abusive in his epithets. But, poor fellow, he has gone to his last long rest. Let his faults be buried with him."

And buried he was, a mere four days after William Bill. As an officer, he was consigned to the deep with slightly more dignity, his body sewn into his own hammock with two thirty-two-pound shot at his feet, and Dr. McNulty, who along with Canning was one of the few Catholics on board, performing the reading.

"A more solemnly impressive scene can hardly be imagined," said Hunt in describing Canning's funeral. "At the well-known signal the whole ship's company assembled on deck, not with the gay alacrity that characterizes their movements when responding to any other summons, but with slow steps and serious faces that were in keeping with the occasion."

Canning's shrouded form was laid on a smooth plank, one end of which rested on the taffrail. The other end was supported by two sailors. Dr. McNulty stood nearby, a prayer book open in his hand to the Roman Catholic burial service.

"All remained uncovered [hats off] while the surgeon, with impressive voice and manner, recited the solemn formula, and as he repeated the words, 'We therefore commit his body to the deep, looking for the general resurrection in the last day, when the earth and sea shall give up their dead,' the inner end of the plank was lifted, and with a sullen plunge the body disappeared forever from our view.

"It must have seemed hard to die with no loved one near to minister to his last necessities," Hunt continued. "But such, however, is often the case with sailors—the Ocean, so long their home, in the end proves the mausoleum that takes their bodies to its keeping, and the last 'goodbye' is whispered in the ear of some rough but sympathetic shipmate."

True to an old saying that a sick man will not die aboard a ship until he "smells land," both William Bill and George Canning lived until the voyage was almost over. Canning went into the water less than six hundred miles from England.

THE MORNING after Canning's funeral was calm. Barely a ripple of wind stirred the water, leaving the ship slack-sailed and unmoving. The lookouts perched in the crosstrees watched the slow rays of the sun bend over the horizon and sweep across the sea. When daylight came, they counted eleven sails around them. During the night, before the wind had failed, they had moved well into the stream of traffic traveling the sea lanes to the English Channel. All eleven ships were far enough away to be unable to identify the *Shenandoah*, but a long, slow day passed with everyone on board holding his breath, praying no wind would rise. Like themselves, the strangers were motionless, but any errant breeze could start them moving and increase the chance of an encounter. And there was no telling which of the drifting vessels might be a Union gunboat. As soon as darkness fell, Waddell ordered the sails furled and steam raised.

"Discretion is always the better part of valor," he admitted, "and I considered it prudent to avail myself of the darkness." With the last scrapings from the coal bunkers they stole away.

WEDNESDAY, November 1, 1865. From the journal of Surgeon Charles Lining: "A fine wind sprang up last night from the south, promising to push us into port in a short time, but today just about mid-day it again shifted to the north, with some prospect of a blow and little prospect of our making a quick passage. Saw another brig and started to run away from her, but she looked so peaceful we hauled up to our course again."

The weather was growing cold. It was winter in the North Atlantic, and running unballasted, with the last of their coal shoveled into a small heap before the boilers, the hull pitched and rolled wildly in every swell. Carrying full sail was out of the question; without a weight of coal carried low in her hold to counterbalance a sudden strong wind, a genuine noreaster ripping down from the Arctic at fifty, seventy, or even a hundred knots could be disastrous. It might capsize her.

The wind shifted, eased, backed, and threatened but did not blow. The stokers fed the boilers carefully, rationing the flames one shovel at a time.

On the second, two more sails were sighted, inbound on converging courses. With no alternative but to steam on, the *Shenandoah* passed them easily. The next day Lining wrote that his ship was "fast nearing port and still going along under steam. . . . Several sail in sight, one outbound. As we get nearer, I get more restless—Last night I was awake during the whole of the mid-watch thinking of what I will do when I get ashore."

"I never longed so much for something nice to eat!" exclaimed Mason. "Not that I attach much importance to such matters, but it is now so long since we have had anything to eat but salt horse and salt pork that everyone hawkens after a good feed of fresh grub."

Lining was savoring hunger of another sort, gloating, "Won't I drink to the health of my 'sweet friends!' God Willing, wherever they may be or be doing, I will see some of them soon!"

On November 4, according to Hunt, "Our reckoning showed us to be near land and all eyes were anxiously scanning the horizon for a glimpse of old England. We knew not what reception was in store for us, for momentous changes had taken place since we set forth on that adventurous pilgrimage around the world, but we were weary of suspense and all were desirous of making port, and learning the worst as soon as possible.

"Night, however, closed around us with nothing but the heaving sea with which we had been so long familiar in sight, and the following morning a dense fog was hanging over the water, effectually concealing everything from view at a ship's length distance."

They steamed ahead slowly, sails furled, with nothing but the chronometers, a suspect compass, and a patent log towed astern to plot a course into St. George's Channel. When the fog lifted, the green shores of Ireland were visible in the distance off the port bow and abeam—"the first land we had seen since we lost sight of the snow-clad bluffs of North America, one hundred and thirty-two days before."

The *Shenandoah* entered St. George's Channel on the morning of November 5, 122 days after passing through the Aleutian Islands. "We had sailed a distance of twenty-three thousand miles without sighting land," commented a satisfied Waddell. "Mr. Bulloch made an excellent landfall; he had not been able to rate the chronometers since leaving Melbourne and could only conjecture their accuracy." Considering this, he said, "the navigation was very beautiful." (Beautiful hardly describes it. To have navigated halfway around the world without ever sighting land or having availed themselves of the opportunity to check their position or the accuracy of the ship's chronometer with another vessel was a feat almost without parallel.)

Land was in sight nearly the whole day. More and more vessels were seen, but by now they were safe in British waters and the fear of Federal gunboats began to fade. Lining grew excited when a passenger vessel swung close by and the passengers lined the deck to wave. "Many of them were ladies!" he blurted. "The first petticoats I have seen for many a day!"

Like everyone else, he started packing, sorting out "shore clothes" put aside many months before. Letters home were written, hair was trimmed, and beards were shaved. Drawing out his ledgers, the paymaster calculated the best way to pay off the men. Officers took a pay cut—Lining received $77.26 of the $547.19 owed him—and Waddell called the rest of the crew aft, explaining, "When we began this cruise, I was given $22,000; eighteen thousand was used for expenses incurred to repair the ship at Melbourne. When I come to consider the large amount due each of you, there is not enough to go around. Therefore, I will divide what is left equally and on arrival in Liverpool seek a source for the rest of your money. Perhaps one of the Southerners who were so helpful before our grand adventure began will now aid in paying off."

A certificate of the exact amount due was promised each man, after which everyone was given the equivalent of five British pounds in either gold or English and American coin. "None seemed dissatisfied," said Lining, "except some who were drunk."

He was wrong. Dissatisfaction was sweeping the crew, a reaction Hunt, among others, saw as natural to the circumstances. "Their prospects were not brilliant," he acknowledged. "None but a very credulous man would feel much confidence in the feasibility of collecting a debt due him from a defunct government."

That night a report went around that some of the more disgruntled sailors intended to storm aft and take over, "to see if they cannot get something to make up their due."

"This is all bosh!" snorted a disbelieving Lining. "The men are too near England to attempt such a thing. Besides, they know the officers too well to try it."

Near midnight, after becoming confused in the welter of unfamiliar buoys and navigation lights leading into the river Mersey and passing to starboard of a light which should have been taken to port, Waddell ordered a rocket fired to request a pilot. Shortly after midnight a small cutter pulled alongside and the pilot climbed aboard. As he came over the side, Whittle greeted him.

"Good morning," the pilot responded. "What ship is this?"

"The late Confederate steamer *Shenandoah.*"

"The deuce it is! Where have you fellows come from?"

"The Arctic Ocean."

"Have you stopped at any port since you left there?"

"No, nor been in sight of land, either. What news from the war in America?"

"It has been over so long people have got through talking about it. Jeff Davis is in Fortress Monroe, and the Yankees have had a lot of cruisers out looking for you. Haven't you seen any of them?"

"Not unless a suspicious-looking craft we sighted off the Western Islands was one of them."

"He was kind of a know-nothing," sniffed Lining. "And the captain asked him if he thought he could carry us over the bar at this tide."

"I don't think I can," replied the pilot.

Waddell mulled this a moment, taking in the pilot's confirmation that the South had been routed, then mumbled, "I don't care much whether she strikes or not. Go ahead and try."

The pilot shrugged and ordered full speed ahead. Waddell went below to his cabin. Four hours later they struck, sliding up onto the mud and sand of the bar at midtide. The pilot asked for coffee, saying, "High tide's in three hours. She'll float off."

An hour later Lieutenant Whittle made the rounds with disturbing news. "Arm yourself," he told each of the officers. "I have seen indications to make me apprehensive that there is a plot afoot among the crew to secure what valuables there are on board and decamp."

Sitting aground, it would be possible for the crew to make a rush for the quarterdeck, overpower the officers, and load the boats with what valuables they could. For common sailors to row ashore and disappear into the hustle and bustle of a waterfront like Liverpool's would pose no difficulty.

"The officers profited by the suggestion," said Hunt, keeping their arms within reach and maintaining a vigilant watch. With arms so prominently displayed, the crew remained in their assigned positions, "perhaps because they perceived that their plans were discovered and that we were ready for any emergency, and possibly because sober second thought had led them to abandon a rashly-formed determination."

At seven, shortly after daylight, the *Shenandoah* floated free. As the steamer plowed up the river, a thick morning fog obscured the city. "And we were not sorry," said Hunt. "For we did not care to have the gaping crowd on shore witness the humiliation that was soon to befall us." Lieutenant Whittle had the Confederate flag broken out and raised.

Under Waddell's direction the pilot pulled the steamer into a position behind Her Majesty's ship of the line *Donegal* and dropped the anchor. Half an hour later a lieutenant from the *Donegal* came aboard accompanied by a contingent of marines. After confirming the identity of the Confederate vessel, he made a short speech officially informing Waddell the war was over.

The crew was mustered aft. Waddell and his officers assembled on the poop. Whittle stood, arms crossed, staring at the flag, and cried. At a signal to the quartermaster, the only Confederate flag ever to sail around the world was quietly lowered. The raider had carried the flag for six months after the overthrow of the Confederacy, on a voyage that covered fifty-eight thousand miles and resulted in the capture of thirty-eight Yankee ships. It had flown over every sea except the Antarctic Ocean. The ship's anchors had been on her bows for eight months. The last shot fired in defense of the South had been fired from her deck on June 22, twenty-four thousand miles away in the Arctic Ocean.

As for the success or failure of the journey, Waddell concluded, "I claim for her officers and men a triumph over their enemies and over every obstacle. And for myself I claim having done my duty."

For better or worse, the *Sea King* was home.

TWENTY

———

THE *SHENANDOAH*'S WAR was over, but not
the drama. Before retiring for the night,
Waddell sat down and composed a letter to Lord
Russell outlining the "singular position in which I
find myself." While he wrote, he listened to the
tread of British sentries pacing back and forth
overhead, keeping watch on the ship and men who
had once been his command but were now Her
Majesty's prisoners.

Positioning himself for defense, he wrote:

> The absence of all precedence on the subject
> will, I trust, induce your Lordship to pardon
> a hasty reference to a few facts connected
> with the cruise lately made by this ship.
>
> My orders directed me to visit certain
> seas in preference to others; in obedience
> thereto, I found myself in May, June, and
> July of this year in the Okhotsk Sea and

Arctic Ocean—both places, if not quite isolated, still so far removed from the ordinary channels of commerce that months would elapse before any news could reach there as to the progress or termination of the American war. In consequence of this awkward circumstance, I was engaged in the Arctic Ocean in acts of war as late as the 28th day of June, in ignorance of the serious reverses sustained by our arms in the field and the obliteration of the government under whose authority I had been acting.

He went on to describe the encounter with the *Barracouta*, saying,

Your Lordship can imagine my surprise at the receipt of such intelligence, and I would have given it little consideration if an Englishman's opinion did not confirm the war news. . . . I desisted instantly from further acts of war, and determined to suspend further action until I had communicated with a European port, where I could learn if the intelligence was true. It would not have been intelligent in me to convey this vessel to an American port for surrender simply because the master of the *Barracouta* had said "the war is ended." I was in an embarrassing position; I diligently examined all the law books at my command, searching for a precedent for my guidance in the future control, management and disposition of the vessel. I could find none. History is, I believe, without a parallel.

Finding the authority questionable under which I considered this vessel a ship-of-war, I immediately discontinued cruising and shaped my course for the Atlantic Ocean.

As to the ship's disposal, I do not consider that I have any right to destroy her, or any further right to command her. On the contrary, I think that as all the property of the Confederate Government has reverted by the fortune of war to the government of the United States of North America, that therefore this vessel, inasmuch as it was the property of the Confederate States, should accompany the other property already reverted. I therefore sought this port as a suitable one wherein to "learn the news," and, if I am without a government, to surrender the ship, with her battery, small-arms, machinery, stores, tackle, and apparel complete to Her Majesty's government for such disposition as in its wisdom should be deemed proper.

Captain Paynter, the commander of the *Donegal,* agreed to forward the letter immediately to Lord Clarendon at the Foreign Ministry and telegraph for instructions.* In the interim, Paynter ordered the British gunboat *Goshawk,* under Lieutenant Alfred Cheek, brought up and lashed alongside the *Shenandoah,* with orders not to allow the cruiser to weigh anchor, light fires in her boilers, or hoist out any property which might now be considered that of the U.S. government. Along with the *Goshawk*'s marines came representatives of Her Majesty's Customs House. A shore battery was trained on the river to support the *Donegal* and *Goshawk* if the *Shenandoah* tried to leave. All this was done, claimed Waddell, at the instigation of Charles Francis Adams, the American minister to Britain, and was "intended to be an offense to a defeated but unconquered enemy; to men who had succeeded in disposing of the Shenandoah in a way not congenial to the Yankee Nation." (He was wrong. The move was made at the order of the Admiralty Board, with no suggestion from Charles Francis Adams.)

"It was ridiculous," scoffed Lining. "As if we had not just come off such a sea voyage as to wish to go to sea again!" All that the officers and men aboard the *Shenandoah* wanted to do was party, get off the ship and blow off a little steam. Sympathizers on shore had sent out

---

*Lord Palmerston died one month before the *Shenandoah* arrived in Liverpool. Earl Russell then became England's new prime minister. Lord Clarendon replaced Russell as head of the Foreign Office.

two boatloads of fresh provisions, including two casks of beer, and there was still a great deal of wine, whiskey, and rum remaining from the haul taken from the *Abigail.* There was nothing to do but wait for a response from Earl Russell and the British government to Waddell's letter, said Hunt, "which would advise us whether we were to be held as prisoners by the British, turned over to the United States authorities, or set at liberty.

"There was enough in the uncertainty involving our fate to depress the most buoyant spirits. But sailors seldom quite despond. They generally discover some bright spot in the darkest horizon, and are prompt to take courage if their situation is anything but desperate."

He was right. By nightfall one of the midshipmen had organized a half dozen junior officers and invaded the steerage mess, taking the position that far from having done anything to be ashamed of, they should be proud of their accomplishments and celebrate by kicking out all the stops, which was "just the kind of proposition to strike favorably a sailor's ear!"

"Ere long, a frolic was inaugurated that gradually extended through almost the entire ship's company. A stranger dropping down among them would have been justified in thinking, from the boisterous hilarity, that we had returned in triumph from some grand expedition and were celebrating our victories. And had he been told that the noisy, rollicking company were waiting to learn whether they were to be set free or handed over to implacable enemies to be tried for their lives, he would have considered the informer either insane or endeavoring to practice upon his credulity." The customhouse officers went aft to join the party, and one got so drunk he passed out in the scuppers. The party soon spread throughout the ship, and in the wardroom, the higher ranks laughed, drank, and sang, rejoicing in full bellies and fresh provisions.

But the next morning—hungover, dry mouthed and stomachs roiling—they realized again the gravity of their situation. The day passed without any response from Earl Russell or Lord Clarendon to

Waddell's letter. By evening, said Hunt, "the gravest apprehensions were beginning to be entertained, with little else talked about among the officers than the prevailing opinion that the British authorities, fearing that they would be held responsible for the depredations we had committed, would turn us over as a sort of peace offering to appease the wrath of the United States." It was tacitly agreed that a time had come when it was "every man for himself."

At nine o'clock Hunt went on deck, miserable and depressed. A drizzling rain was falling. "In brief, it was the kind of night to make one melancholy under any circumstances and I firmly resolved that the Shenandoah and I should part company that night at all hazards. I had a constitutional objection to ornamenting the yard-arm of a Yankee man-of-war, but by the appearance of things, I stood a remarkably fair chance of obtaining that elevated position. But how was I to effect my escape? We were at anchor in the stream, our decks closely guarded by the marines from the Donegal, and no boat was allowed to approach us, under severe penalties.

"But the attempt had to be made. At worst I could but fail. Approaching the marine who was pacing backwards and forwards near where the accommodations ladder was suspended over the side, I opened a careless conversation with him. Watching my opportunity, I slipped into his hands a bottle of the venerable old whiskey we had captured in the Okhotsk Sea. The fellow gave me an intelligent glance, pocketed his bourbon, and marched sedately forward, while I dove down to the ward room and in a few moments metamorphosed into as genuine an old shell back as ever broke biscuit in a forecastle."

When Hunt slipped back on deck the sentry glanced at the immense sea boots, oilskin jacket, and sou'wester the petty officer was wearing, and turned his attention to some pressing matter on the other side of the ship. Hunt slid down the accommodation ladder, signaling frantically to a passing boat. The boatman hesitated, and then approached. Hunt jumped in. At the Liverpool landing, he gave the boatman two pounds, leaving himself with eight pounds as the sole proceeds of the thirteen months he had spent aboard the *Shenandoah*.

At roll call the next morning the crew was lighter by eight or ten men. Lieutenant Cheek of the *Goshawk* took the news lightly, saying he didn't mind if the lads made a run on shore "as long as I don't know about it."

Cheek's attitude reflected that of the British government and the populace at large: they were stuck with the *Shenandoah*, greatly inconvenienced by the diplomatic complications it created, and just wished the whole thing would go away. Charles Francis Adams had been assailing the British government for months with demands that it recognize its responsibility in the creation of Confederate raiders such as the *Alabama*, *Florida*, and *Shenandoah*, and demanding millions of dollars in reparations. The Foreign Office rejected Adams's claims out of hand, stating it had never had any legal control over the vessels nor broken any laws that might oblige it to incur such liability. Now, to have the outlaw suddenly appear on its doorstep was an embarrassment, an unwelcome reminder that at the beginning of the war British policy had, whether stated outright or not, been one of meddling support for the Confederacy. And it was proving damned inconvenient to have backed the losing horse. By the end of the Civil War the United States had the largest, best-trained, and best-equipped army and navy in the world, and there was widespread fear among England's aristocracy that the new superpower would use its vast strength to punish the British for having attempted to influence the outcome of the war. With the collapse of the South, Her Majesty's government found itself in the uncomfortable position of needing to placate the tempestuous giant while simultaneously maintaining a steadfast denial of any culpability for its earlier policies. On the same day Lord Clarendon received Waddell's letter, he also received a message from Charles Francis Adams requesting that the *Shenandoah* be turned over to the American government and suggesting that charges of piracy and vio-

lation of Britain's Foreign Enlistment Act be brought against Waddell
and some of the officers and members of the raider's crew. The first
thing Lord Clarendon did was call his lawyers. Both Adams's and
Waddell's letters were forwarded to the Crown law offices for
consideration.

By the second evening of detention the sailors aboard the
Shenandoah were going crazy. It had been nine months since any of
them had set foot on land. A delegation approached Lieutenant Cheek,
demanding they be let on shore. He declined. They threatened to riot.
Captain Paynter was sent for, and when the steam tug bearing him over
from the *Donegal* pulled alongside, a swarm of defiant rebels slid down
the tug's mooring hawsers and stormed aboard.

Paynter, evidently a sympathetic man, managed to calm the unruly
mob by assuring them that he was doing all he could to free them, but
until word came from the Crown law offices they would have to wait.
Two dozen musket-toting marines helped convince the unruly sailors
of his logic.

The Crown law offices issued their decision late the next morning.
It was proper for the British government to deliver up to the American
government "the ship in question, with her tackle, apparel, etc., and all
captured chronometers or other property capable of being identified as
prize of war." With respect to the officers and crew, the notice stated,
Mr. Adams had not demanded their surrender to the United States
government, and the only question suggested in his letter was whether
any of them ought to be proceeded against by the British government
for offenses "cognizable under British Law," i.e., piracy or violations of
the Foreign Enlistment Act.

"With regard to a charge of piracy, if the statements contained in
Captain Waddell's letter are true (that he had no knowledge that the
war was over and had desisted as soon as he learned it was) we hold that
there are no grounds for a charge of piracy. It is presumed that Her
Majesty's Government does not then possess any evidence to refute the
Captain's statements, or to show that piracy has in fact been
committed."

Further, the Foreign Enlistment Act applied only to natural-born British subjects, and the Crown denied any knowledge of British subjects among the crew. Therefore, "with respect to any persons who cannot immediately be proceeded against and detained under legal warrant upon any charge, the law offices are not aware of any grounds to prevent their going ashore and disposing of themselves as they see fit." In other words, unless any of the crew admitted to being British citizens, they were free to go.

Captain Paynter and Lieutenant Cheek immediately went to Waddell and asked if on his word of honor, he believed any of his crew were British citizens or had violated the Foreign Enlistment Act.

"I never asked," he replied. With the exception of the Hawaiians, Portuguese, and a few Swedes, he assumed all to be Americans. "I picked up and shipped them all on the high seas, so know nothing about it."

Paynter asked Lieutenant Whittle to muster the crew aft. The lieutenant produced a roll made out in pencil, and as each man's named was called, the individual stepped forward.

"Nationality?" asked Paynter.

"American."

The answer was the same every time.

"In no instance did any acknowledge himself a British citizen," wrote a gleeful Hunt (who could not have witnessed it, having already deserted the ship). "But several, who insisted that they had been born in some one of the Confederate states, had an unmistakably Scotch accent and probably opened their eyes for the first time on this world a good deal nearer the Clyde than the Mississippi!"

It is easy to imagine Captain Paynter rolling his eyes. In a follow-up letter to the Admiralty he wrote: "I trust I may be pardoned if as a British officer, accustomed during my whole period of service to the cleanly appearance of British men-of-wars' men, I could not pronounce on my own responsibility whether some of the dirty, drawling, ill-looking, gray-coated, big-bearded men who passed before me as the crew of the *Shenandoah* were British subjects or American citizens."* Nonetheless, he pronounced, "You are all free to go."

The crew greeted the news with three cheers. Within the hour, the last Confederate force was disbanded.

---

* Later, a young man named William Temple, who was a British subject born in Bengal, India, would testify that officers from the *Shenandoah* had circulated among the crew beforehand instructing the men what to say to Paynter. Temple had shipped aboard the *Sea King* as a steward when it left London and stayed on as an ordinary seaman. A malcontent, a good deal of the testimony Temple supplied was inaccurate. He also used a false name, enlisting as William John Jones.

Former Confederate naval officers at Learnington Spa, England, autumn 1865, following the return of CSS Shenandoah. *Those present include (seated) former Assistant Surgeon Edwin Gilliam Booth, and (standing, left to right): former Acting Master Irvine S. Bulloch; former Passed Assistant Surgeon Bennett W. Green; former First Lieutenant William H. Murdaugh; and former Passed Assistant Surgeon Charles E. Lining.*

(U.S. NAVAL HISTORICAL CENTER PHOTOGRAPH.)

Epilogue

A GENERAL AMNESTY GRANTED to all Confederate forces after the collapse of the South specifically exempted the officers of the *Shenandoah*. It would be years before many of them could go home. Quartermaster Lewis Peter Wiggins, the Russian émigré who had frostbitten his feet after escaping a Yankee prison and walking all the way to Boston, was one of the first, making his way back to Georgia the following year. When his wife answered his knock, the shock was so great she lost her power of speech; she had thought him dead for two years.

Lieutenant Grimball went into exile in Paraguay. Dabney Scales and Assistant Surgeon McNulty went to London. Tom Manning went to London too. The good-natured but bumbling Lieutenant Chew and Cornelius Hunt sailed for Paris, where Hunt settled down to wrote his memoir. Whittle and Mason joined forces with Smith-Lee and Brown in Argentina. The quartet prospected for a while before starting a small farm near Rosario. A few years later, as the animosity of the Federal government began to fade, Brown and Mason felt safe enough to return to Virginia. Eventually, Mason settled in Baltimore, where he became a lawyer, got married, and fathered four children. Whittle and Smith-Lee returned sometime later, after which Whittle too got married and settled down to a career as a succesful banker. Assistant Surgeon McNulty started a medical practice in Boston.

After seeing to the disposition of his crew, Waddell rented a small house near Liverpool, then sent for his wife and spent the next five years living the life of a retired sea captain. By 1875 he and Ann had slipped back to Annapolis, where Waddell once again took up the work of a mariner, sailing as master of the gleaming four-thousand-ton Pacific Mail Line steamer *City of San Francisco.* Two years later he was still in command of that vessel when it hit an uncharted rock off the coast of Mexico. In the best tradition of the sea, Captain Waddell was the last to leave the sinking ship and was credited with saving the lives of all 420 passengers on board by his cool handling of the situation. He died an old man, in his own bed, on March 15, 1886.

Almost all of the Southerners aboard the *Shenandoah* lived to be old. Not so for some of their Yankee victims. Ebenezer Nye, the crafty downeaster who escaped the raider in a small open boat and sailed through two hundred miles of ice to warn the rest of the fleet of its presence, kept right on whaling until 1880, when a dismasted ship drifted ashore on the Arctic coast of the Chukchi Sea. Aboard were four emaciated, freeze-dried corpses and Ebenezer's spectacles.

On the British side, once retired from his duties with Her Majesty's government, Lord Russell developed a keen interest in meteorology. A politician to the end, he spent his last days tinkering with a new device called an anemometer, calculating—literally—which way the wind was going to blow.

As for the *Shenandoah,* shortly after being abandoned to the British the old ship was turned over to the Americans. When the U.S. navy refused to touch it, Charles Francis Adams and Consul Thomas Dudley were forced to hire a Yankee merchant captain to deliver the ex-raider to New York. The Yankee failed. With only fifty sailors on board, he managed to get no farther than a day or two out of Liverpool before the winter weather so feared by the *Shenandoah*'s officers pounced, in the form of a raging storm that reduced her sails to tatters and so thoroughly frightened the hired master that he returned to Liverpool, where the weather-beaten ship was sold to the sultan of Zanzibar.

"His Sable Majesty," as James Dunwoody Bulloch called the sultan, planned to convert the *Shenandoah* into his personal yacht, but cost overruns ended the project before it could be completed. Renamed the *Majidi,* the once-proud raider was reduced to carrying freight around the Indian Ocean. In 1879 she tore her bottom out on a reef in the Mozambique Channel and sank. Only her German captain and four East Indian crewmen survived. But the effects of her voyage as a raider lingered on.

After the end of the Civil War, Charles Francis Adams had continued to press Great Britain for damages incurred at the hands of English-built raiders like the *Shenandoah*—claims Britain denied. Diplomats batted the matter back and forth for a couple of years, until both sides seemed inclined to let it drop from a combination of exhaustion, intransigence, and pressure from capitalists on both sides who wanted to forget about the war and get back to business. It was a dying matter, that is, until April 13, 1869, when Charles Sumner, a powerful senator from Massachusetts and chairman of the Senate Committee on Foreign Relations, rose to address the Senate with a burst of thundering oratory.

Prior to the war, Sumner—a big, strapping man with a handsome face and a gift for dynamic speeches—had been a great fan of the British, primarily for their efforts to eradicate slavery around the world, which he too bitterly opposed. So virulent was his hatred of slavery that he had once been brutally attacked by a congressman from South Carolina, who beat him senseless with a brass-headed cane in retribution for a blistering diatribe against the practice Sumner delivered on the Senate floor. Stung by what he saw as the great hypocrisy of

Britain's covert support of the Confederacy, and by extension the "foulest of crimes," Sumner rose to his feet and thundered, gesticulating wildly, that the Confederate raiders were "British in every respect except their commanders" and that "no candid person who studies this eventful period can doubt that the rebellion was encouraged by support from England; that it was strengthened by the concession of belligerent rights on the oceans; that it was fed to the end by British supplies; that it was quickened and renewed by every report from the British pirates, flaming anew with every burning ship. Nor can it be doubted that without British intervention the rebellion would have sooner succumbed under the well-directed efforts of the National government."

In other words, the English, by aiding and abetting Confederate efforts to disrupt American shipping, had both encouraged and prolonged the war. Sumner argued that the responsibility for all of the death, destruction, and material losses incurred after the Battle of Gettysburg lay at their feet—a full half of the most vicious and costliest war the world had ever seen.

"The rebellion was suppressed at a cost of more than four thousand million dollars," Sumner railed. "If through British intervention the war was doubled in duration, or in any way extended, as cannot be doubted, then England is justly responsible for the additional expenditure to which our country was doomed." The tab amounted to two billion dollars. Sumner intoned that "England has done to the United States an injury difficult to measure. Considering when it was done, and in what complicity, it is most unaccountable: At a great Epoch in history . . . when civilization was fighting in a last battle with slavery, England gave her name, her influence, and her material resources to the wicked cause and flung a sword into the scale with slavery."

It was a charge—and a sum—that inflamed the American public against Britain. In Massachusetts, Charles Francis Adams, now home and retired from his task as a diplomat, sighed that the "effect of this proceeding is to raise the scale of our demands for reparations so very high that there is no chance of negotiation." In London, Consul

Dudley reported a general sentiment among the English that a war with America was now almost inevitable.

Luckily, cooler heads prevailed. Still weary from four years of war, politicians under the sway of President Ulysses S. Grant, who understood that America needed large infusions of British capital to fund an explosion of postwar growth, proposed a uniquely American solution: Let's sue 'em!

And Britain, confronted with the alternative of an armed conflict with a nation whose military machine now far outstripped its own in both size and technology, agreed. By the terms of the Treaty of Washington, for the first time in history, two powerful nations were to settle a dispute in international court, through arbitration before a tribunal made up of representatives from several nations.

On December 15, 1871, a panel consisting of Charles Francis Adams as the American representative; Sir Alexander Cockburn, Britain's chief justice; Baron d'Itajuba of Brazil; and Count Frederic de Sclopis of Italy convened under an ex-president of the Swiss Confederation, Jacques Staempfli, in a parqueted and chandeliered room off an inner courtyard of Geneva's Hotel de Ville. For ten months lawyers from the United States and Britain railed, propounded, argued, and maneuvered through the question of whether Britain had incurred liability for the damage caused by the Confederate raiders, in a suit that became known as the Alabama claims for the most famous of the raiders. In the arguments against the *Shenandoah*, most damning was evidence that Britain had indeed violated its own Neutrality Act by allowing Waddell to enlist British subjects while in Melbourne; Staempfli stated flatly, "The authorities in Melbourne showed themselves in several respects negligent in the maintenance of their sovereignty as a neutral country in the case of the *Shenandoah*." On September 14, 1872, by a majority of three to two, the tribunal decided that Great Britain was responsible "for all the acts committed by the vessel after her departure from Melbourne" and handed its verdict down. Britain was to pay $15.5 million in damages, chiseled down from

Charles Sumner's proposed $2 billion. The award was to be paid in gold within one year. The tribunal's decision became the foundation of an entire body of international civil law that remains in effect to this day.

Britain lost the lawsuit, but in the end it could be argued that the British were the real winners of the Civil War: in 1860 two-thirds of the commerce of New York had been carried by American ships; by 1863, under the influence of rising insurance rates brought on by the presence of the Confederate raiders, three-fourths was being carried by foreign bottoms. By the time the *Shenandoah* lowered its flag in Liverpool, 715 American vessels had been transferred to the British flag to escape capture or bankruptcy, and another 250 had been sunk or burned. For $15.5 million, Britain gained dominance of the world's oceangoing commerce for the next eighty years, until World War II, when the depredations of German U-boats against English shipping would again give America the upper hand.

Saluting Gun. One of an identical pair from the Confederate cruiser
Shenandoah. *The original artifact is at the U.S. Naval Academy Museum,*
Annapolis, Maryland.

(U.S. NAVAL HISTORICAL CENTER PHOTOGRAPH.)

ACKNOWLEDGMENTS

W HEN AN AMATEUR sets out to recount an event from the past, he travels on the backs of many strangers—historians, mostly, but also a number of ordinary people, nonacademics like himself. As I followed the *Shenandoah* around the world from England to Australia, and on up through the Aleutian Islands into the distant reaches of the Arctic, it was the latter who most often eased my way. Always, I carried for company the books of such fine writers as John Bockstoce, whose years of research and experience in the Arctic make *Whales, Ice, and Men* perhaps the most informative and interesting work on the history of Arctic whaling extant, or Murray Morgan, whose work on the *Shenandoah* and the Aleutians is so rife with humor and wry insight that I often wished I could have sat in on some of his classes at Tacoma Community College before he passed away. James Tertius deKay, Jay Winik, Nathaniel Philbrick, and the Australian writer Cyril Pearl often jostled for space in my backpack, to be consumed over long nights in tents and hotel rooms around the world, and I am grateful for the work they and others did that allowed me to better understand what life was like for the men who beat their lives out on the decks of sailing ships or chasing whales during the Civil War. But a particular appreciation is owed to that remarkably generous subspecies of Homo sapiens, the librarians—those patient, easygoing people who always seem willing to go the extra mile to retrieve some obsucre nugget of information from the depthless mines they inhabit. Of these, Gladi Kulp and her co-workers at the Alaska State Historical Library deserve the Sweethearts of the Year award, and without John and Ruth Coski of the Eleanor S. Brockenbrough Library at the Museum of the Confederacy in Richmond, Virginia, this book could never have been written. Jim Simard certainly earned a beer or two for the help offered from his post at the University of Alaska Southeast, as did Professor Kurt Dunbar of Bellingham, Washington, for his ability to render complex bits of history clear and simple.

To Barry Crompton, at the *Age* newspaper in Melbourne, Australia, I doff my hat. His work cataloging and organizing material related to the *Shenandoah*'s stay in Australia is nothing short of superb, as was the hospitality I received from Dr. Stephen Gapps and the rest of the New York Sixty-second when they took me into their tents and let me join them in marching through the blazing heat of the outback during a reenactment of a Civil War skirmish.

Such hospitality, though a hallmark of my travels in the Southern Hemisphere, was also plentiful in the North, particularly above the Arctic Circle, in Barrow, Alaska, where Pat Riley's company made my stay much more than pleasant. And at the Hotel de Ville in Geneva, Switzerland, an unnamed docent in a brilliant red coat and wire-rimmed glasses led me across a cool stone courtyard and through a huge varnished door into the chandeliered room where the *Shenandoah*'s journey played out during the arbitration of the Alabama claims, and on through the labyrinthine archives of a dozen Swiss governmental departments in search of the records of that trial. In short, everywhere I went, people treated me like family.

And speaking of family, Sally Spangler was generous in providing information on her ancestor, Lieutenant Whittle, as was Kim Bixby, who shared her own fascinating research into her ancestor, Sergeant Canning, without hesitation. Among my own family, I owe a debt of gratutude to my brother, Lee Schooler, for making it possible for me to travel way-the-hell-and-gone out into the Aleutian Islands and survive, and to my sister, Luan Schooler-Wilson, for her willingness to plow through draft after draft of this book.

To all of the above, and to any others I may have neglected, my heartfelt thanks.

Lynn Schooler
Juneau, Alaska
August 30, 2004

SELECT BIBLIOGRAPHY

Bockstoce, John R. *Whales, Ice, and Men.* Seattle: University of Washington Press, 1995. First published by New Bedford Whaling Museum, 1986.

Bulloch, James Dunwoody. *The Secret Service of the Confederate States in Europe.* New York: Putnam & Sons, 1884.

Crompton, Barry. "The American Civil War Reported in Australia" and "The *Shenandoah* in Melbourne." Compilation of Australian newspaper articles circa 1864–65, for the American Civil War Round Table of Australia, Inc.

———. *Melbourne and the American Civil War.* Melbourne, Australia: Archer Memorial Library, 1994.

DeArmond, Robert N. "War's End in Bering Sea." *Alaska Sportsman,* July 1937.

deKay, James Tertius. *The Rebel Raiders.* New York: Ballantine Books, 2002.

Grimball, John. "Career of the *Shenandoah:* A Graphic Account of the Cruise of the Great Commerce Destroyer, from the Time of Her Fitting Out Near Funchal Madeira, October 1864, to Her Surrender to the British at Liverpool, November 1865." *Charleston (SC) Sunday News,* February 3, 1895.

Hill, Jim Dan. *Sea Dogs of the Sixties.* Minneapolis: University of Minnesota Press, 1935.

Hunt, Cornelius E. *The* Shenandoah, *or The Last Confederate Cruiser.* London: S. Low, Son, & Co., 1867.

Johnson, President Andrew. "Message from the President of the United States in Answer to a Resolution of the House of Representatives of the 8th Instant, Relative to the Reported Surrender of the Rebel Pirate *Shenandoah.*" (With accompanying correspondence of Adams, Russell, Clarendon, Waddell, Seward, Hunter Dudley, Moran, et al. January 26, 1866. Smith College Library.

Jones, Robert F. "Rebel Without a War." In *With My Face to the Enemy,* edited by Robert Crowley. New York: Putnam, 2001, 499–510.

Kiersey, Nicholas. "The Diplomats and Diplomacy of the American Civil War." University of Limerick, Ireland.

Lining, Charles E. Private Journals, Lecture Notes, and Military Records. Eleanor S. Brockenbrough Library, the Museum of the Confederacy, Richmond, Va.

Log of the CSS *Shenandoah*. Eleanor S. Brockenbrough Library, the Museum of the Confederacy, Richmond, Va.

Mason, John T. Private Journals and Letters. Eleanor S. Brockenbrough Library, the Museum of the Confederacy, Richmond, Va.

McNulty, F. J. "The CSS *Shenandoah* Cruise by One of Her Officers: Her Exploits in the Pacific Ocean, After the Struggle of 1861–5 Had Closed." *Atlanta Constitution*, November 1893. Reprinted in Southern Historical Society Papers, vol. 21, 165.

Metcalf, E. W. "Facts Relating to the Geneva Award and Legislation Thereon, As Stated to the H.R. Judiciary Committee, December 12, 1877." Washington, D.C.: GPO, 1877.

Morgan, Murray. *Dixie Raider: The Saga of the C.S.S.* Shenandoah. New York: E. P. Dutton, 1948.

Official Records of the Union and Confederate Navies in the War of Rebellion (ORN). (July 31, 1894). Reissued by Guild Press, Zionsville, Indiana, 1999.

Pearl, Cyril. Rebel Down Under. Melbourne, Australia: William Heinemann, 1970.

Philbrick, Nathaniel. *In the Heart of the Sea*. New York: Viking Press, 2000.

Robe, Cecil Francis. "The Cruise of the C.S.S. *Shenandoah.*" Master's thesis, University of Washington, 1929.

Smith, Page. *Trial by Fire*. Vol. 5. New York: McGraw-Hill, 1982.

Waddell, James I. *C.S.S.* Shenandoah: *The Memoirs of Lieutenant Commanding James I. Waddell*. Edited by James D. Horan. Annapolis, Md.: Naval Institute Press, 1960.

Whittle, Capt. W. C. "Tribute to John T. Mason and the *Shenandoah.*" *Confederate Veteran*, 2, no. 10 (October 1904).

Whittle, Lieutenant William C., Jr. "The Cruise of the *Shenandoah;* the Stirring Story of Her Circumnavigation of the Globe and Many Conquests on the High Seas." *Southern Historical Society Papers*, 35 (December–January 1907), 235–258

Winik, Jay. *April 1865—the Month That Saved America*. New York: HarperCollins, 2001.